Charles Lowe
Self-Fulfilling Science

Epistemic Studies

Philosophy of Science, Cognition and Mind

Edited by
Michael Esfeld, Stephan Hartmann, Albert Newen

Editorial Advisory Board:
Katalin Balog, Claus Beisbart, Craig Callender, Tim Crane, Katja Crone,
Ophelia Deroy, Mauro Dorato, Alison Fernandes, Jens Harbecke,
Vera Hoffmann-Kolss, Max Kistler, Beate Krickel, Anna Marmodoro, Alyssa Ney,
Hans Rott, Wolfgang Spohn, Gottfried Vosgerau

Volume 48

Charles Lowe
Self-Fulfilling Science

DE GRUYTER

ISBN 978-3-11-127474-4
e-ISBN (PDF) 978-3-11-074640-2
e-ISBN (EPUB) 978-3-11-074653-2
ISSN 2512-5168

Library of Congress Control Number: 2021936856

Bibliographic information published by the Deutsche Nationalbibliothek
The Deutsche Nationalbibliothek lists this publication in the Deutsche Nationalbibliografie;
detailed bibliographic data are available on the Internet at http://dnb.dnb.de.

© 2023 Walter de Gruyter GmbH, Berlin/Boston
This volume is text- and page-identical with the hardback published in 2021.
Printing and binding: CPI books GmbH, Leck

www.degruyter.com

Contents

Acknowledgements —— IX

1 Science: Camera or engine? —— 1
   1.1 Introducing self-fulfilling science —— 1
      1.1.1 The new oracle —— 1
      1.1.2 Science as self-correcting —— 3
      1.1.3 Science as self-fulfilling —— 5
   1.2 Questions of conceptualization, prevalence, and significance —— 8
   1.3 Alternative approaches —— 11
      1.3.1 Social constructionism —— 11
      1.3.2 Looping effects —— 13
      1.3.3 Performativity —— 18
   1.4 Outlook —— 22

2 The self-fulfillment of *homo economicus* —— 25
   2.1 Economic man: born or made? —— 25
      2.1.1 Outlining a paradigmatic case —— 25
      2.1.2 Polanyi and the 'economic fallacy' —— 26
   2.2 The empirical evidence —— 28
      2.2.1 Induced self-interest via direct economic training —— 28
      2.2.2 Three pathways to self-fulfillment —— 34
          2.2.2.1 Social norms —— 34
          2.2.2.2 Institutional design —— 35
          2.2.2.3 Language —— 39
      2.2.3 Summary —— 41
   2.3 The claim(s) —— 42
      2.3.1 Sample claims —— 42
      2.3.2 Who is *homo economicus*? —— 44
      2.3.3 What is self-fulfillment? —— 47
      2.3.4 Questions of conceptualization —— 49

3 Conceptualizing self-fulfilling science —— 52
   3.1 From prophecy to reality – or illusion? —— 52
      3.1.1 Merton's self-fulfilling prophecy —— 52
      3.1.2 Illusory self-confirmation —— 54
      3.1.3 Content contingency —— 55

3.2 Reflexive prediction —— 56
    3.2.1 Buck's acting-on-beliefs account —— 57
    3.2.2 Romanos' standard account —— 59
    3.2.3 Kopec's probabilistic account —— 61
    3.2.4 Scientific self-fulfillment as reflexive prediction? —— 64
        3.2.4.1 Truth as a criterion? —— 64
        3.2.4.2 Which (types of) entity? —— 66
3.3 Performativity —— 70
    3.3.1 'Barnesian' performativity —— 71
    3.3.2 Scientific self-fulfillment as performativity? —— 72
3.4 A new conceptualization —— 75
    3.4.1 'Aspects of science' as scientific representations —— 76
    3.4.2 'Practical use' as content-responsive action —— 81
    3.4.3 'More like' as increased conformation —— 88
    3.4.4 Applying the concept —— 91

4 Assessing prevalence —— 96
4.1 An *a priori* boundary —— 96
    4.1.1 Uniqueness to human affairs —— 97
    4.1.2 A faulty inference —— 100
    4.1.3 Criterion of malleability —— 103
4.2 Two strategies of assessment —— 104
    4.2.1 Meta-theories —— 105
    4.2.2 Mechanisms and mid-range theories —— 109
4.3 Applying the strategies —— 113
    4.3.1 Examples —— 113
    4.3.2 Challenges —— 118

5 Challenges of performativity —— 121
5.1 Assessing significance —— 122
    5.1.1 The purview of philosophy of science —— 122
    5.1.2 Self-fulfillment vs. 'realism'? —— 125
5.2 Epistemic success and evaluation in science —— 130
    5.2.1 Epistemic success —— 130
    5.2.2 Epistemic evaluation —— 133
5.3 Self-fulfillment vs. epistemic evaluation? —— 138
    5.3.1 Performatives and epistemically evaluable content —— 140
    5.3.2 Meta-theories and hypothetical content —— 147

6 The epistemic significance of self-fulfillment — 154
    6.1 Illusory self-confirmation and underdetermination — 155
        6.1.1   Specious validity — 155
        6.1.2   *Homo economicus* and human nature — 158
        6.1.3   Underdetermination — 161
        6.1.4   Fortifying transient underdetermination — 164
    6.2 Genuine self-fulfillment and epistemic evaluation — 170
        6.2.1   Self-fulfillment as self-improvement? — 170
        6.2.2   The return of self-correction — 172

7 An engine, *and* a camera — 175
    7.1 Summary — 175
    7.2 Multiple possible futures — 176

References — 179

Index of Names — 188

Index of Subjects — 191

Acknowledgements

This book is a revised version of a doctoral dissertation submitted and defended in 2019 at the Institute of Philosophy at Osnabrück University. I thank the university and its many staff members who have supported my work and well-being since coming to Osnabrück.

The members of my thesis committee, Susanne Boshammer, Nikola Kompa, Uwe Meyer, Wolfgang Ludwig Schneider, and Torsten Wilholt, made my defense an engaging, pleasurable, and memorable experience, and for this I express my sincere gratitude. Torsten Wilholt's probing questions and remarks as a thesis referee pushed me to clarify a number of arguments from the original manuscript, and the resulting book is much better for it. Special thanks are in order to my doctoral supervisor, Nikola Kompa, who, besides providing me with a steady supply of insightful and helpful comments and critiques during the process of refining the raw ideas and arguments that ultimately made their way into the book, always went out of her way to provide whatever sort of (context-sensitive) support I needed most during any particular phase of research and writing.

Philosophy, as we like to tell incoming students, is not a spectator sport, nor is it best practiced alone. I have benefited greatly from engaging discussions with many friends, colleagues, and acquaintances over the last years. Even more importantly, each has contributed in their own vital way to creating and maintaining an exceptionally warm, friendly, and spirited working (and socializing!) environment in and around the university: Benjamin Angerer, Lasse Bergmann, Frieder Bögner, Susanne Boshammer, Armin Egger, André Grahle, Gregor Hörzer, Attila Karakuş, Nikola Kompa, Christian Lavagno, Imke von Maur, Uwe Meyer, Asena Paskaleva-Yankova, Andrea Robitzsch, Nikola Ruck, Georgios Sagriotis, Sebastian Schmoranzer, Stefan Schneider, Marion Schultz, Kathrin Schuster, Achim Stephan, Jennifer Wagner, Sven Walter, and Jannik Zeiser.

Parts of this work were presented, discussed, criticized, and ultimately improved in various conferences, classes, and colloquia. Four groups in particular merit special mention for their helpful contributions: the extremely supportive community of researchers surrounding the European Network for the Philosophy of the Social Sciences (ENPOSS), the eager participants of an undergraduate seminar on "Philosophical Aspects of Self-Fulfilling Prophecy" that took place at Osnabrück University in the Winter semester of 2018-19, the consistently sharp-witted members of the Münster-Bielefeld-Osnabrück (MüBiOs) philosophy colloquium, and especially the dear colleagues that make up the weekly colloquium at my home institute, where some of the best qualities of philosophy are regularly on display: rigor without pedantry, critique without scorn, and a conspicuously enthusiastic pooling of creative and intellectual energies with the collective aim of achieving greater understanding.

Finally, I would like to thank my family (on both sides of the Atlantic) for all the love and support they have unfailingly shown me over the years. I regret that my grandparents Richard and 'Meme', who taught and supported me perhaps more than anyone else, did not live to see this project completed. Sandra, Lisbeth, and Emil Richard Lowe light up my life, and for that they deserve the greatest thanks of all.

1 Science: Camera or engine?

1.1 Introducing self-fulfilling science

1.1.1 The new oracle

Storytellers and their audiences have long been fascinated by the idea that premonitions of future events may not be simply borne out but may themselves beget the future they portend. Perhaps the most ancient and famous example in Western society is the tragedy of Oedipus. The king of Thebes, informed by the oracle of Delphi that he shall be killed by his own offspring, leaves his infant son on a mountainside to die. The boy, Oedipus, is raised in a neighboring country, his true parentage kept a secret. Oedipus flees his new home after being told by the oracle that he shall commit patricide, but while traveling meets and kills a man who is, unbeknownst to both, his father, the king of Thebes. Thus, the prophecies of the oracle come to be fulfilled precisely because of the actions undertaken by both father and son in an attempt to avoid their prognosticated fate.

Not all such stories end in tragedy. In the Arabian Nights, a poor man sets out for Cairo full of hope after dreaming he will discover a fortune there. Alas, upon arriving, he is robbed and jailed. When asked by the jailor why he has come to the city, the man relates his dream, upon which the jailor mocks him for acting so foolishly on the basis of a mere premonition. The jailor tells the man that he himself has often had a similar dream concerning the whereabouts of a buried treasure, but is too wise to act upon it. In a final twist, however, the poor man recognizes the location described in the other's dream as none other than his own courtyard, and upon returning home unearths the treasure. "Thus," as Sir Richard Francis Burton's classic translation of the story concludes, "Allah gave him abundant fortune, and a marvelous coincidence occurred."

We might be tempted to see such stories as making a point about the inevitability of one's fate. Maybe Oedipus would have come to kill his father even without the oracle's prophecy, albeit, perhaps, in a different manner. This is certainly a weighty thought, but what appears to me to make this such an effective trope is rather the irony and 'marvelous coincidence' inherent in the idea that had the protagonists not been exposed to the prophecy, or had they chosen not to act upon it, then the prophesized event would never have come about. Whether the result is tragedy or fortune, the key notion in both of the above stories, as in many similar ones from various times and cultures, is that the protagonists' belief that some future event would come to pass was, in fact, a crucial factor in the causal chain leading to that event's occurrence.

To put it lightly, for most of us today, oracles and dreams no longer possess the same degree of epistemic authority they once seemed to have concerning the future. This doesn't mean we've abandoned the idea of using knowledge about the likely course of future events to guide our actions in an attempt to avoid tragedy and achieve fortune. Where we once turned to oracles and dreams, we now consult scientific theories and predictions. Whether concerning the future of our health, economic growth, or just about any other domain concerning matters of fact, including the fate of the universe itself, science is now widely considered to be the best epistemic authority we have.

If the implied comparison between the oracle of Delphi and, say, Albert Einstein seems too far-fetched, one need only consult the writings of the early Enlightenment defenders of science to sense the atmosphere that reigned during the infancy of modern science. Their explicit adoption of religious rhetoric, for example, of the famous New Testament verse "And ye shall know the truth, and the truth shall make you free," and the explicit wish to establish a "scientific priesthood" seems to make clear the degree of epistemic authority to be attributed to scientists (cf. Kitcher 2001, 147). But hasn't this attitude gone out of style? Consider the following impassioned plea, made by the extremely popular and influential science communicator, astrophysicist Neil deGrasse Tyson, in a video created in support of the recent 'March For Science' rallies held as a sign of solidarity with scientists and dedication to a scientific worldview:

> [I]n this, the 21st century, when it comes time to make decisions about science, it seems to me people have lost the ability to judge what is true and what is not, what is reliable, what is not reliable, what should you believe, what should you not believe. And when you have people who don't know much about science, standing in denial of it and rising to power, that is a recipe for the complete dismantling of our informed democracy. [...] One of the great things about science is that it is an entire exercise in finding what is true. [...] Out of this [exercise] arises a new, emergent truth. It does it better than anything else we have ever come up with as human beings. This is science. It's not something to toy with. It's not something to say 'I choose not to believe $E=MC^2$.' – you don't have that option. When you have an established, emergent scientific truth, it is true whether or not you believe in it. And the sooner you understand that, the faster we can get on with the political conversations about how to solve the problems that face us. (Tyson 2017)

According to those sometimes called 'the scientific faithful,' the truth itself may not be enough to set us free, but it forms a necessary foundation of any potentially successful attempt to do so, and the legitimate arbiter in establishing the relevant truths is to be science itself. Of course, the very need for a 'March For Science' shows that this authority is neither absolute nor undisputed. However, it is largely uncontroversial that, for many if not most in Western society, science continues to enjoy a special status as the genuine arbiter of truth about the natural world we inhabit and our opportunities for acting upon it in an attempt to shape our own fate.

1.1.2 Science as self-correcting

The large degree of epistemic authority enjoyed by science means that its theoretical outputs come to shape our beliefs in significant ways. However, it is also generally understood that science is fallible. Thus, its authority can lead us and has, at times, led us down the wrong path by encouraging us to believe what were later shown to be falsities. The faithful are quick to point out, however, that although science is not unique among potential sources of knowledge in being fallible, it is special in possessing a unique set of mechanisms that serves as a counterbalance to the permanent uncertainty of its claims and its frequent false starts. Although science promises no certain truths, they say, it does guarantee a relentless, if plodding and meandering, march toward a better understanding of the world.

On the view in question, scientific theories purport to tell us about some part of the world. They generally do not meet the mark on the first try or perhaps ever entirely. However, by way of principled application of various scientific methods and adoption of a suitably scientific attitude, they are altered over time so as to gradually become better suited to their task. Science, as it is often said, is *self-correcting* (cf. Losee 2004, 98–102). One familiar means of self-correction might be called 'theory replacement': some theory T is introduced in an attempt to accurately represent, explain, or generate predictions about some facet of the world f, but is shown to be deficient in some way, and is eventually supplanted by a new or rival theory U, which either accurately represents and/or explains f or at least comes closer to doing so than T. Self-correction may also occur by means of 'theory modification': a theory T_1 targets some facet of the world f, initially misses the mark, but is gradually transformed via scientific practice to a new version of the theory, T_2, which either accurately represents and/or explains f or at least comes closer to doing so than T_1. Further research may lead from T_1 to T_2, from T_2 to T_3, and so on, perhaps *ad infinitum*. Despite the coarseness of such a lay theory of scientific progress, many scientists and philosophers of science commonly invoke processes such as these to account (at least partially) for the special epistemic success of science.[1]

---

[1] The oft-assumed self-correcting nature of science has also been challenged on both theoretical and empirical grounds. Many recent attempts to explain self-correction are (partially) grounded

The history of scientific attempts to explain the origin and global distribution of large-scale geological and (paleo)biological phenomena – the continents, mountain ranges, fossils, plant and animal species – arguably exemplifies both types of self-correction identified above. Oreskes (2003) relates the relevant details in her historical account of Plate Tectonics. In the late 19th century, Austrian geologist Edward Suess put forth a version of what has come to be called Contraction Theory. Working from the then commonly held assumption that the earth has been continually cooling and, thus, contracting since its initial formation, Suess suggested we think of the earth like a drying apple. Just as the apple's peel wrinkles, shrivels, and sometimes tears as it loses moisture and shrinks, the placement and characteristics of the continents were postulated to result from the 'wrinkling' of the earth's crust as it cools and contracts. This and other versions of Contraction Theory were eventually discredited by the discovery of radiogenic heat, which undermined the fundamental assumption of the earth's continual cooling.

In the 1920's, German meteorologist Alfred Wegener proposed an alternative explanation for the distribution of the continents. According to his Continental Drift Theory, not only continental distribution, but also other phenomena such as the origins of mountains, volcanoes, and earthquakes are explained by the fact that the continents drift around the earth's surface, sometimes breaking apart and sometimes colliding. The theory was considered suggestive but ultimately defective for a number of reasons until it was eventually subsumed under the more general theory of Plate Tectonics in the 1960s, which described the mechanisms responsible for continental drift alongside many other paleo-

---

in something akin to Popper's (1963) notion of critical rationalism, according to which scientific progress consists in the gradual rejection and replacement of conjectured hypotheses over time through critical assessment by peers. The theoretical difficulties surrounding Popper's falsificationist views are well-known (cf. Lakatos and Musgrave 1970 for a set of classic papers contrasting Popper's views on scientific progress with Kuhn's). But this picture of science also faces significant empirical challenges. To take just two recent examples: Cofnas (2016) examines the recent history of intelligence research to suggest that moral and political commitments have prevented many scientists from abandoning hypotheses seemingly disconfirmed by empirical evidence; Ioannidis (2012) traces the consequences of the so-called 'replication crisis' both for the credibility of science and its ability to self-correct. Although attempted replication arguably plays a central role in the process of rational criticism suggested by Popper, it is seemingly discouraged by many of the institutional realities of current scientific practice.

Of course, there are also other notions of scientific progress than that implied by an emphasis on self-correction. Other kinds of development that contribute to progress might include the asking of new questions, employment of novel concepts and methods, or even abandonment of certain lines of inquiry, such as alchemy or witchcraft. Losee (2004) presents a helpful overview of theories of scientific progress.

geographical and paleobiological observations. By the 1970s, Plate Tectonics was viewed as the undisputed unifying theory of the modern earth sciences and has since been subject to ongoing refinement and modification.

From our current standpoint, Plate Tectonics is unquestionably better suited to represent, explain, and generate predictions about the facets of the world it concerns than Contraction Theory was – earth science has, over time, 'self-corrected' as a result of theory replacement and modification. Where exactly we draw the line between replacement and modification of course depends upon our understanding of what theories are and how to properly individuate them. I won't delve into such details here, as my goal is simply to point out that whether we are dealing with theory replacement, theory modification, or some related notion I haven't considered here, the key notion of science as self-correcting is that our theories become more accurate and successful over time because we work to bring them more in line with the part of the world they are meant to represent and/or explain. Such ideas will come as no surprise to most.

More likely to be overlooked, however, is an implicit assumption that often accompanies the notion of self-correction: that the facet of the world we seek to better understand remains more or less unchanged during the process of theoretical refinement. Whether improvement is to be achieved by moving from T_1 to T_2, from T to U, or in some other, more complicated fashion, f is assumed to remain a constant and, for the most part, unchanging touchstone for the development and assessment of our theories. While Suess and Wegener proposed wildly differing accounts of the geological phenomena they sought to understand, neither would likely have seriously considered the possibility that the objects of study themselves had changed significantly during the course of their investigations.

1.1.3 Science as self-fulfilling

In the case of large-scale and long-term phenomena of planetary scope, ignoring the possibility of significant change on the part of objects of study during the course of inquiry might be seen as plain common sense. However, the world does change. Furthermore, when it comes to many more local and short-term phenomena, humans are arguably one of the single greatest agents of change. Even on the global scale, our impact is significant; so much so that scientists are currently considering whether our planet should be described as having entered a new geological epoch within the last century – the 'Anthropocene' (Waters et al. 2016). Science, we have said, comes to shape our beliefs and thereby our actions through its status as an epistemic authority. This fact, together with an appreciation for the ability of our actions to change the world, should alert us to the possibility of a process complementary in nature to that of scientific self-correction.

If science, through our actions, changes the world, then scientific theories may, in principle, come to more adequately represent and/or explain some facet of the world not because the science has been brought more in line with the world, but because the world has been brought more in line with the science. Using the crude terms already introduced: theory T is introduced targeting some facet of the world f, initially misses the mark, but over time becomes more accurate because, through T's influence, the world is transformed by human action such that f comes to exhibit the features ascribed to it by T.[2] Drawing on now familiar terminology first introduced by sociologist Robert K. Merton (1948), we might say that, in such cases, science is not self-correcting, but *self-fulfilling*[3]. Working out an adequate conceptualization of self-fulfilling science is one of the primary goals of this work; but, for now, let us employ the following preliminary characterization:

Science[4] is self-fulfilling when it owes its (apparent) epistemic success to the fact that it causes the world to come more into line with its postulates.

---

[2] Such a development is, in principle, compatible with (simultaneous) self-correction: T purports to represent f, f^* actually obtains, T is modified to become T^{**}, which represents f^{**}, and, in the process, f^* also becomes f^{**}. Something similar to this is discussed at the end of chapter six.

[3] Many different terms have been suggested to describe such phenomena. My adoption of the terminology of 'self-fulfillment' is explained in chapter three.

[4] I do not attempt to provide a general definition of 'science' in this book. The framework developed is meant to be compatible with various broad conceptions. However, one significant qualification is necessary: the notion of scientific self-fulfillment developed here presupposes that, whatever else science may be, it is also, to some significant extent, a genuinely epistemic and representational enterprise. This means that science and scientific representations are properly subject to evaluations of success concerning the kind and degree of knowledge they afford us about some empirical domain, and that the success in question depends to some significant extent upon some kind of 'fit' between representational content and states of affairs in the world.

This restriction is compatible with many different perspectives on science, including those that view it primarily in terms of a complex social practice or institution, so long as these permit that the results or products of science are properly subject to the type of evaluation outlined above. It is not compatible, on the other hand, with views that reject any genuinely epistemic dimension of science, such as those that treat it as being *merely* a matter of power relations, or with views that recognize an epistemic dimension, but deny that criteria of epistemic success have anything to do with representation.

Clearly, for theories like Plate Tectonics, there is no actual prospect of self-fulfillment. For one thing, the phenomena it is meant to account for are largely occurrences that took place long before humans inhabited the planet, and thus before postulation of the theory itself. Furthermore, it may seem that the natural processes it invokes are things that human action could have little impact upon. The (apparent) epistemic success of Plate Tectonics is clearly not due to any influence the theory itself has had upon the world. It may even seem obvious that, for these or related reasons, most scientific theories cannot possibly be self-fulfilling. Indeed, when the topic has at times cropped up in various literatures, it is often claimed that the natural sciences, at least, are entirely free of such strange phenomena.

The social sciences, however, are another matter. Beginning with British logician John Venn (1888), social scientists, and economists in particular, have occasionally reflected on the effect their theorizing may have upon objects of study. One common worry has been that public predictions of economic trends may prove *self-defeating*, rather than self-fulfilling. A prominent economist's prediction of an unusually high price for some commodity in the near future might lead producers to increase production, thus flooding the market and, ultimately, driving prices far below those predicted (cf. Grunberg 1986 and Mackinnon 2006 for overviews of this work). In such cases, the prediction has missed the mark, but neither in the same manner nor, we may feel, with the same consequences as with 'straightforwardly' incorrect predictions in the normal course of science. If we can reasonably speak of epistemic failure here, it is due to the change the prediction itself has affected in the world.

Later, following the work of Merton, sociologists and psychologists became intensely interested in the possibility that their theories or predictions may display (effects resembling) *self-fulfillment*. Sociological theories of crime or deviance long sought to lay bare the structural and societal causes of (what were then taken to be) social ills. In the 1960s, however, some theorists began to posit that labeling individuals as potential deviants might actually encourage and trigger deviant behavior. Psychologists investigated how theories of intelligence or expectations of student performance might lead to similar effects in educational settings (cf. Henshel 1978 and Jussim 2012 for overviews). In such cases, observed facts interpreted as attesting to the epistemic success of the theories, models, or predictions in question were revealed (it is claimed) to have been brought about by application of the science itself.

Finally, for a while at least, it seemed as though reflection upon such issues might also be poised to become a canonical, if minor, issue for consideration in mainstream philosophy of science. At least two of the dominant figures of the field in the 20th century took such phenomena to deserve serious scrutiny. Karl

Popper (1957, 13), in *The Poverty of Historicism*, considers whether "the Oedipus effect," or "the influence of the prediction on the predicted event (or, more generally, [...] the influence of an item of information upon the situation to which the information refers)" might endanger the possibility of objective or precise scientific prediction about the social realm. Ernest Nagel (1961, 470), in *The Structure of Science*, claims that "the frequent occurrence of suicidal and self-fulfilling predictions concerning human affairs is undeniable," adding that "no theory adequate to the subject matter of the social sciences can ignore the fact that actions undertaken in the light of knowledge about some patterns of social behavior can often change those patterns." In addition to these somewhat isolated considerations, a brief, yet spirited debate was also carried out in the 1960s and '70s concerning so-called *reflexive predictions*, which, for the most part, differ from the phenomena discussed by Popper and Nagel in name only (Grünbaum 1956; Buck 1963; Romanos 1973; Vetterling 1976).

1.2 Questions of conceptualization, prevalence, and significance

Despite this postwar burst of interest and humankind's general interest in the kind of wonderful tales described at the outset, philosophers of science have been largely silent on the topic of self-fulfillment since the 1970s. This may appear surprising given the emphatic claims made by such luminaries as Popper and Nagel. What might account for this apparent decline of interest? Several reasons may be identified.

First, it may be doubted that self-fulfilling science is possible at all. For reasons hinted at above and which will become clearer in the coming chapters, I take this to be clearly refutable. A much more plausible position, however, is that although self-fulfillment may be possible in principle, this possibility is of negligible significance in the real world. This may be either because it doesn't *actually* exist or is exceedingly rare, or because the effects of scientific self-fulfillment are entirely negligible in comparison to those of self-correction or other mechanisms of scientific progress. Let us call inquiry about the actual existence, frequency, and efficacy of scientific self-fulfillment *questions of prevalence*. Those who deny the prevalence of scientific self-fulfillment are unlikely to accord the issue much significance, and understandably so. Even granting in-principle possibility, if most science shares some of the features that ruled out Plate Tectonics as a serious candidate for self-fulfillment, then it may seem the topic is best reserved for writers of science fiction rather than philosophy of science.

Another reason for the apparent dearth of interest may be the belief that even if self-fulfillment exists, is frequent, and is efficacious, it is nevertheless of relatively little significance for either the practice of science or our understanding thereof. Perhaps this is really nothing more than a 'marvelous coincidence' to be noted or mused over, but is not deserving of more serious consideration. Alternatively, it may be a candidate for serious consideration, just not from the perspective of philosophy of science. It might fall outside the discipline's purview, or there could be simply little of interest to note about the phenomenon from this perspective. Let us call inquiry about the possible implications of self-fulfillment for scientific practice and/or our philosophical understanding thereof *questions of significance*.[5]

Finally, one further contributing factor to the phenomenon's current neglect is arguably the manner in which it and other closely related phenomena *have* at times been discussed. Earlier philosophical considerations of scientific self-fulfillment and reflexive predictions seem to have spiritual successors in several distinct, yet broadly related, fields of current inquiry. Among the most important are certain strains of social constructionism, debates surrounding Ian Hacking's (1995) work on so-called 'looping effects,' and what is known as the 'performativity approach' in the sociology of economics. It sometimes appears as if these nascent research programs have carried on the old torch, albeit while deploying new terminology and perspectives, and that those with questions of significance need only to look to them for illumination. As I argue in the following section, however, much of the scholarship from these (admittedly internally heterogeneous) fields either concerns phenomena that merely bear resemblance to scientific self-fulfillment, focuses on issues of comparatively little concern to philosophers of science, or tends to either overestimate or underestimate the philosophical significance of scientific self-fulfillment without much in the way of justification. As we will see, these tendencies are at least partly due to the manner in which the phenomenon in question itself has often been described. Let us call inquiry about how to adequately define scientific self-fulfillment and other closely related phenomena *questions of conceptualization*.

While philosophical interest in such issues has apparently waned in recent years, one specific self-fulfillment claim has grown quite influential among so-

---

[5] Unless otherwise noted, by 'significant' (or 'significance') I mean simply (the property of being) 'important' or 'worthy of serious consideration'. Furthermore, my primary concern is worthiness of serious consideration *from the perspective of (mainstream analytic) philosophy of science*. This, of course, does not rule out the phenomenon's possible significance for other branches of philosophy or non-philosophical approaches. To be clear, this use of the term has nothing to do with statistical significance.

cial scientists. This is the claim that economic theory in general, and (neo-)classical microeconomic accounts of so-called *homo economicus* in particular, have actually exhibited significant self-fulfillment effects through their impact on our expectations, institutions, and behavior. Broadly, it is proposed that the (apparent) epistemic success of predictions and explanations of human behavior (in certain domains) in terms of self-interest is at least partially due to the influence that microeconomic theory itself has come to exert on individuals and society.

This provocative notion, though prominently discussed among social scientists, has yet to receive significant attention from philosophers of science. However, such claims are highly pertinent to the three types of question just outlined. For one, they have been prompted by and have themselves prompted a good deal of empirical research that seems to lend support to the claim that scientific self-fulfillment actually exists and may, at least in certain domains, be both prevalent and efficacious. Furthermore, the presentation of these data and their interpretation in terms of self-fulfillment are often accompanied by claims concerning the phenomenon's significance for our scientific practice or understanding thereof. Some of these relate quite clearly to established topics of discussion in philosophy of science, whereas others suggest the possibility of new avenues of philosophical research. Finally, despite the often-dramatic sounding claims put forward concerning the purportedly self-fulfilling science of *homo economicus* and its significance, the key concept of scientific self-fulfillment employed in this literature is typically underspecified or actively misleading.

The primary goal of this book is to (re-)examine the questions of conceptualization, prevalence, and significance surrounding self-fulfilling science. In particular, I use the recent discussion among social scientists concerning the purported self-fulfillment of *homo economicus* as both springboard and touchstone for development of a new framework for considering the phenomenon from the perspective of philosophy of science.

Before moving on, let us consider what I've called the 'spiritual successors' to earlier discussions of scientific self-fulfillment in greater detail. This discussion serves several functions. First, it motivates the development of a novel account by showing that the phenomena discussed by these seeming alternatives are often, despite initial appearances, not precisely the phenomenon under consideration here. Second, by laying bare certain problematic assumptions or positions taken up by these alternative approaches, it alerts us to various pitfalls the novel account should avoid. And finally, it brings into sharper relief the goals, assumptions, concerns, and approach of my project and clarifies how they differ from those of others with which it could be mistaken.

1.3 Alternative approaches

According to the preliminary characterization of self-fulfilling science presented above, science is self-fulfilling when it owes its (apparent) epistemic success to the fact that it causes the world to come more into line with its postulates, often as mediated by the effect of its authoritative pronouncements on our beliefs and actions. At least three recent alternative research programs at times seem to examine phenomena of this sort: social constructionism, looping effects, and performativity.

1.3.1 Social constructionism

'Social constructionism'[6] is a term used to describe a famously disparate set of (sometimes conflicting) theses or approaches, found across many disciplines, that share a concern for the way in which different types of entities are brought about, molded, or otherwise 'constructed' by a variety of factors that might be reasonably bundled together under the heading of '(the) social'. Typically, the point of focusing on 'the social' is to point out its relative (yet oft-neglected) importance when compared to an alternative bundle of non-social factors often labeled 'natural', 'biological', or something similar. And the point of this, more often than not, is to argue that the constructed entity is somehow under human control to a greater degree than usually imagined (cf. Hacking 1999; Mallon 2019). This broad characterization is perhaps only slightly more helpful for understanding what kind of work actually goes on under the auspices of 'social construction' than simply repeating the term itself. However, it is enough to clarify one sense in which scientific self-fulfillment could be of interest to constructionists.

On the self-correcting view of science, objects of study are typically assumed to exist independently of, and be largely unaffected by, our attempts to understand them.[7] In the natural sciences, in particular, the factors responsible for the existence or make-up of these entities are taken to be 'natural', 'biological', etc. as opposed to 'social'. According to our preliminary characterization of self-fulfillment, however, science could conceivably contribute to its own success by

---

6 'Constructivism' and a host of other roughly cognate terms are also common, sometimes with differing meanings, sometimes without. Such terminological quandaries need not concern us here.
7 The intense excitement raised by the prospect that this may not always be so, for example in the famous case of the 'observer effect' in quantum physics, only attests to the fact that such an influence is usually assumed to be absent or negligible.

bringing about or influencing the facets of the world it targets. To the extent that science can be considered a 'social' factor, such influences likely fall within the purview of constructionist scholarship.

Certain constructionist approaches are content to explore how scientific practice or pronouncements act as social determinates of objects usually thought to be entirely 'natural,' while leaving traditional views of science as a genuinely successful epistemic endeavor largely undisturbed. This is especially true of what Mallon (2019) calls "naturalistic approaches to social construction," which tend to begin inquiry with the presupposition that science is a "central and successful (if sometimes fallible) source of knowledge about the world." The precise manner in which individual views and approaches are committed to such a 'naturalistic' view is difficult to spell out given the term's disparity of use. However, as Mallon explains, perhaps the central reason for adopting this label is to call attention to the fact that such approaches differ markedly from other constructionist programs that are *not* content to leave our general picture of science intact.

In fact, the term 'social constructionism' is often associated with thoroughgoing anti-realist and relativist critiques of science's claims to epistemic authority. Such critiques were (perceived to be) common during the so-called 'science wars' of the 1990s, a set of disputes between 'postmodernists' and 'realists' that with hindsight seem to have produced substantially more heat than light. To the extent that constructionists of this ilk might show interest in scientific self-fulfillment, it would likely be in order to stress that the '(apparent) epistemic success' of science referred to in our preliminary characterization should be read as '*merely* apparent'. The basis for such claims is often not that objects of study are causally influenced by scientific practice, as suggested above, but rather that such lofty things as *facts, truth, reality,* or *knowledge* are themselves socially constructed (cf. e.g. Gergen 2015). What exactly this is supposed to mean differs from author to author and is often simply unclear. However, in many cases, the point of such claims seems to be to call the very notion of science as a genuinely (successful) epistemic endeavor into question (cf. Kukla 2000).

There is nothing wrong with this sort of investigation per se, nor can the concerns raised by this tradition be simply dismissed by reference to the specter of self-defeating relativism, as Boghossian (2001) and others have supposed. However, in attempting to understand the significance of self-fulfillment for philosophy of science or scientific practice more generally, it will not do to start our journey by following in the footsteps of those who have often proven overeager to abandon the path of science as we know it altogether. As noted above, there are certainly strains of 'constructionist' scholarship that do not push us in this direction. All I wish to make clear is that the themes of science skepticism often associated with constructionism are not of immediate concern for the account I will develop. Indeed, one primary concern of this work is to explore the degree to which scientific self-fulfillment is *compatible* with our usual views of science as a successful epistemic endeavor. This is not to deny the possibility of tension between self-fulfillment and our usual convictions at the outset, but only to insist that it must be argued for rather than assumed.

1.3.2 Looping effects

Ian Hacking has done more than most to illuminate the often shadowy realm of constructionist claims about science. His 1999 book, *The Social Construction of What?*, became a touchstone for those who would attempt to disentangle, if not outright cleave, the Gordian Knot of the science wars. Although Hacking himself is famously disinclined to attach the label to his own work, purveyors of naturalistic approaches to social construction have seen him as something like a founding father. In fact, much of Hacking's work can be seen as an attempt to develop a more nuanced account of constructionist claims in reaction to tendencies toward oversimplification, overgeneralization, and overhasty condemnation of our usual views on science.

Of particular interest are a series of studies undertaken since the 1980s, in which Hacking (1986; 1995; 2007, 293) has sought to illustrate how "the human sciences" – which include "many social sciences, psychology, psychiatry, and a good deal of clinical medicine" – contribute to what he calls "making up people" and the "looping effect". To see how these notions relate to scientific self-fulfillment, consider Hacking's description of a paradigmatic example:

> I should briefly mention my first example of making up people and the looping effect, multiple personality. It is written up in *Rewriting the Soul*. It seemed misleadingly easy. Around 1970 there arose a few sensational paradigm cases of strange behaviour similar to phenomena discussed a century earlier and largely forgotten. A few psychiatrists began to diagnose multiple personality. It was rather sensational. More and more unhappy people started manifesting these symptoms. At first they had the symptoms they were expected to have. But then they became more and more bizarre. First a person had two or three personalities. Within a decade the mean number was seventeen. This fed back into the diagnoses, and entered the standard set of symptoms. It became part of the therapy to elicit more and more alters. The psychiatrists cast around for causes, and created a primitive, easily understood pseudo-Freudian aetiology of early sexual abuse, coupled with repressed memories. Knowing this was the cause, the patients obligingly retrieved the memories. More than that: this became a way to be a person. (Hacking 2007, 296)

As the passage suggests, the basic idea behind *making up people* is that scientific classifications and interventions may contribute to the possibility, existence, or character of 'kinds of people' or 'ways to be a person.' What exactly this means is complicated. For our purposes, it is enough to note that sometimes, the existence of these kinds of people and the behaviors manifested as a function of enacting a particular way to be a person are, in turn, interpreted as empirical support for the theories that brought them about in the first place.

Hacking's detailed case work on making up people is both fascinating and compelling, and has garnered significant attention from philosophers and social scientists alike. Furthermore, to the extent that the classifications he studies owe their (apparent) epistemic success to their ability to shape kinds of people in their image, they fit our preliminary characterization of self-fulfilling science. Indeed, commentators have read Hacking's notion of 'looping effects' as referring to such phenomena, and it is no stretch to imagine that the popularity of his approach has led researchers that might otherwise express their ideas in terms of 'self-fulfillment' to instead do so in terms of 'looping'. Despite initial appearances, however, looping effects differ from scientific self-fulfillment in important ways. Furthermore, the goals, assumptions, and concerns of Hacking's general project differ significantly from my own. Outlining a few of the most salient differences will help underscore the approach adopted in this book.

First, note that, despite the intuitive connection between self-fulfillment and the forces at work in Hacking's multiple personality case, this is not the only mechanism of change described in the passage above. Rather, the movement is two-way: scientific classifications both instigate change in the world (in this case, the behavior of classified patients) and are themselves changed in an attempt to bring them into line with this (changed) world. This two-way movement is a primary characteristic of *looping effects:*

> There is a looping or feedback effect involving the introduction of classifications of people. New sorting and theorizing induces changes in self-conception and in behaviour of the people classified. Those changes demand revisions of the classification and theories, the causal connections, and the expectations. Kinds are modified, revised classifications are formed, and the classified change again, loop upon loop. (Hacking 1995, 370)

At first glance, it might appear as if the two-way movement of Hacking's loops corresponds to the processes I identified earlier as self-correction and self-fulfillment. On the one hand, the 'theory' of multiple personality is put forward in an attempt to describe and explain a class of novel, unusual behaviors, and is gradually refined so as to better capture the phenomenon in question as more data comes in. On the other hand, patients came to exhibit types of behavior expected of them based on their diagnoses, thus contributing to the degree of fit between theory and world and, thereby, to the former's (apparent) epistemic success.

If self-correction and self-fulfillment were the only processes at work in Hacking's example, we should expect to see a kind of stability or equilibrium as the result. Roughly speaking, if both theory and world are modified so as to enhance the fit between the two, then the theory should soon come to accurately describe the behavior in question. But, in fact, things are decidedly more complicated in Hacking's picture. Although certain behavioral reactions to classification seem to accord with the preliminary characterization of self-fulfilling science, others shift in a manner that leads them to *escape* our attempts at description.

The number of 'alters' typically observable in those diagnosed, for example, is presented as continually outstripping theoretical expectations. When the theory postulated two or three alters, many patients began manifesting even more, leaving psychiatrists and psychologists to play catch-up. Though this point is often glossed over by observers of his work, Hacking (1995, 370) is emphatic that while classification *may* lead to behavior being "confirmed in its stereotype," it is also possible that "quite the opposite may happen." At times, there may even be a conscious effort among "kinds of people who are medicalised, normalised, and administered" to "try to take back control from the experts and the institutions" (2007, 311). In light of the complexity of changes brought about by classification and theorizing, it may seem that, in the case described, it is the picture of an erratic spiral rather than a stable loop that more aptly suggests itself.

This, in fact, is precisely one of Hacking's (2007) central claims: the kinds of people the human sciences seek to describe are, as he later comes to characterize them, "moving targets." In some circumstances, such movements can result in scientific self-fulfillment, but on the whole, Hacking persistently stresses the instability and unpredictability of reactions to classification. Just as often, volatile reactions to the realization that one has been labelled with an undesirable trait are likely to lead to (apparent) epistemic failure rather than success. More commonly, the movements in question are presented by Hacking as conforming clearly to neither of these processes.

As looping may result in scientific self-fulfillment, its opposite, or neither, the scope of Hacking's project and the phenomena he investigates are revealed to be much broader than what concerns us here. One could suggest that, given our more circumscribed interest, we might simply restrict focus to those cases of looping that include or encompass scientific self-fulfillment. However, there is also an important sense in which the scope of Hacking's investigations is exceedingly 'local': for his emphasis on the complexity and historical uniqueness of each case examined causes him to take a very dim view of the prospect of developing a *general* account of looping effects and making up people at all. Although his willingness to engage in generalizations has increased marginally in the 20 years separating his earliest and latest work, he remains, on the whole, steadfastly dedicated to a conviction outlined in his very first programmatic paper on the topic: "I do not believe there is a general story to be told about making up people. Each category has its own history" (Hacking 1986, 111).

In fact, Hacking is a self-proclaimed "philosopher of the particular case" (Madsen, Servan, and Øyen 2013), and this fact brings to light a set of interests and assumptions that differ substantially from those that inform this book. First, he assumes that (useful or interesting) generalizations are unlikely to be found, whereas this book asks how far we might go in developing a(n interesting) general account of self-fulfilling science (and later considers evidence suggesting that not all 'looping effects' are as erratic and unpredictable as Hacking often supposes). Thus, to the extent that this study could be shoehorned into the framework of looping, it would have to be understood not only as addressing just a subset of the phenomena investigated by Hacking but as doing so by adopting guiding assumptions at odds with his own. The most damaging aspect of such a move might be to discourage critical exchange. Hacking's historically detailed case-centered work is extremely valuable precisely for the insights it provides into the complexity of 'particular cases' of looping. Such generalizing and particularist approaches should be considered complementary, if not outright rivals, and fruitful critical exchange between them should not be discouraged by attempting to assimilate one to the other or downplay their differences.

Another significant difference is that when Hacking's work *does* highlight scientific self-fulfillment it often restricts focus to one specific 'mechanism' by which the phenomenon might come about, namely changes in behavior evoked by conscious reactions to scientific classification on the part of classified individuals. In his earlier work, Hacking distinguishes between entities that can and cannot become aware of their own classifications to motivate a strict ontological distinction between natural kinds and so-called 'human kinds' and argue that looping is possible only with regards to the latter.[8] This closely resembles a common claim concerning self-fulfilling science, namely that, if it indeed exists at all, it does so only in the context of the social sciences. However, this widespread and longstanding assumption, I argue, is false. As we will see, this is due in no small part to the fact that scientific self-fulfillment may come about through a

---

[8] Hacking eventually comes to reconceptualize this distinction as one between 'interactive' and 'noninteractive' kinds and, later still, to reject any kind of strict distinction between natural kinds and some alternative. A similar issue is examined in chapter four.

variety of different mechanisms, not all of which suppose widespread understanding, familiarity, or even awareness of the science in question.

A final, and perhaps, the most crucial difference between Hacking's approach and my own relates to the broader interests and motivations that underlie our projects. Compared to the great effort put into elucidating particular cases of looping and making up people, Hacking devotes surprisingly little attention to what consequences might be drawn from their existence. At least, this is the case in his primary works on the subject. When diving into Hacking's more 'peripheral' comments – those found in interviews, prize acceptance speeches, methodological asides, and the like – one gets the strong impression that his primary motivation is to explore the effect that scientific classification has on expanding human possibilities for action. His central question is how science might create new 'ways to be a person' rather than what looping may mean for our understanding of science. Thus, Hacking, despite being a distinguished philosopher of science himself, has surprisingly little to say about looping from the perspective of philosophy of science.

Hacking once seemed keen on exploring the *ontological* consequences of looping, some of which may be relevant to debates concerning scientific realism. However, he has long had a professed aversion to the topic of realism, and, in any case, later retreated from most of the stronger ontological claims of his earlier work on the topic.[9]

---

[9] The full story is more complicated. From the outset, Hacking sees his work on making up people as supporting a position he terms 'dynamic nominalism'. Often, the manner in which he discusses this idea suggests it has ramifications for scientific realism (cf. Hacking 1986, 106–108). In later work, he continues to champion dynamic nominalism, but explicitly divorces the position from any further claims concerning either the reality of the phenomena he discusses or realism more generally. This comes out most clearly when he asks us to consider two kinds of claims one might infer from his work on multiple personality:
(A) There were no multiple personalities in 1955; there were many in 1985.
(B) In 1955 this was not a way to be a person, people did not experience themselves in this way, they did not interact with their friends, their families, their employers, their counsellors, in this way; but in 1985 this was a way to be a person, to experience oneself, to live in society. (Hacking 2007, 299)
Although Hacking once defended A-type statements, he later views them as being unhelpful at best, and dedicates himself exclusively to ontologically less controversial B-type statements:
The first statement, A, leads immediately to heated but pointless debates about the reality of multiple personality, on which I have spilt too much ink and to which I shall never again return. But open-minded opponents could peacefully agree to B. When I speak of making up people, it is B that I have in mind, and it is through B that the looping effect occurs. (Hacking 2007, 299)

His consideration of the possible ramifications for broadly *epistemic* issues is, in a sense, even more limited. The clearest relevant statement can be found in his most recent major paper on looping effects. After characterizing several general methods typically employed in the human sciences, such as quantification, normalization, establishment of correlation, etc., Hacking (2007, 305) states that while often viewed as "engines of discovery" that "are thought of as finding out the facts," these methods "are also engines for making up people." Despite this striking claim, however, Hacking almost immediately discounts the notion that these differing pictures of science could stand in opposition. The successes of the various engines of discovery have, he says, been "astonishing," and the fact that they have sometimes led to looping and making up people is no reason, he supposes, to question this success (Hacking 2007, 306). The following statement all but exhausts Hacking's (2007, 312) comments on the issue: "I observe that we tend to think of [the engines of discovery] as directed at fixed targets. I suggest that the engines modify the targets. This in no way queries their objectivity."

Our preliminary characterization made parenthetical reference to the *apparent* epistemic success of self-fulfilling science. One major goal of this work to explore whether or not this skeptical qualification is indeed warranted. Whereas some constructionists have appeared overeager to proclaim the end of science as we know it, Hacking seems all but nonchalant in his dismissal of the idea that any serious tension could exist between the images of science as an engine of discovery or an engine of change. From the perspective adopted in this work, both conclusions appear overhasty and in need of further scrutiny.

1.3.3 Performativity

The suggestion that microeconomic theories of *homo economicus* could exhibit self-fulfillment has, at times, been discussed in terms of social construction (cf. Mackinnon 2006) and looping effects (cf. Kuorikoski and Pöyhönen 2012). In recent years, however, such claims have become more prominently associated with the notion of *performativity* as discussed in the sociology of economics and science studies.

'Performativity' describes a thesis or approach to studying the manner in which (economic) theory purportedly 'shapes,' 'constitutes,' 'enacts,' or 'performs' (economic) reality. The term itself is derived explicitly from J. L. Austin's work on linguistic performatives, utterances that 'do something' rather than simply describe or report something about the world. According to Austin, utterances such as 'I apologize for...' or 'I promise that...' do not simply state or describe some preexisting state of affairs but are rather constitutive of the act of apologizing or promising when properly performed in the appropriate context. By analogy, economic theories, models, and assumptions are sometimes said to be performative in the sense that they do not simply describe a preexisting economic reality, but are rather themselves part of (what brings about) that reality. Performativity scholars engage in detailed historical and empirical analysis of developments in economic theory and reality with an eye to how the former might bring about the latter.

The most celebrated single piece of performativist scholarship is Donald MacKenzie and Yuval Millo's (2003) study of the effect of the Black-Scholes-Merton equations of stock option pricing on financial markets. Put simply, a stock option is a kind of contract that guarantees one the right to buy or sell some asset at an agreed upon price on or up to some future date. Such 'options' can themselves be traded much in the same way more familiar stocks are. However, until fairly recently, there was relatively little interest in trading these or other similar stock 'derivatives' on the market. According to MacKenzie (2006a, 119–142), this was due in no small part to the fact that there was no reliable method available with which their value could be ascertained or estimated. This all changed, however, following the introduction of a set of equations and a more general theory of option pricing by economists Fischer Black, Myron Scholes, and Robert C. Merton[10] in 1973.

In conjunction with other factors, the Black-Scholes-Merton theory of option pricing helped spur on dramatic growth of the derivatives market throughout the 1970s and '80s. This influence is typically attributed to the fact that the equations upon which the theory was based were computationally (though not theoretically) fairly simple, could be and were implemented into new technologies and strategies used both to estimate and set option prices, and, crucially, seemed to enjoy an unprecedented degree of empirical support. Ross (1987, 332), writing for the *New Palgrave Dictionary of Economics*, expresses what seems to have been a common sentiment at the time: "When judged by its ability to explain the empirical data, option pricing theory is the most successful theory not only in finance, but in all of economics."

According to MacKenzie and Millo, however, the (apparent) empirical success of the theory was not due primarily to its ability to correctly describe, explain, or predict preexisting pricing structures or regularities. Rather, it was a result of the impact that the theory itself had upon traders' behavior – enabling

---

[10] Not to be confused with his father, sociologist Robert K. Merton, who introduced the notion of the self-fulfilling prophecy.

them to successfully generate profits by employing strategies of 'arbitrage' and 'spreading,' the details of which are not pertinent here. And, in fact, they point to evidence indicating that a high degree of empirical success came only relatively late after the theory's introduction and grew over time as the theory grew in influence. MacKenzie (2006a, 165–166), in his highly influential book-length case study, concludes that:

> At first the correspondence between the Black-Scholes-Merton model and patterns of prices on the Chicago Board Options Exchange was fairly poor. Soon, however, it began to improve. [...] The model may have been helped to pass its central econometric test 'with remarkable fidelity' (Rubinstein 1994, p. 772) by the market activities of those who used it. [...] The Black-Scholes-Merton model was used in the practice of arbitrage–especially, but not exclusively, in 'spreading'–and the effects of that arbitrage seem to have been to move patterns of prices toward the postulates of the model.

Clearly, MacKenzie sees himself as studying and identifying a phenomenon very close to the one characterized above as scientific self-fulfillment. As we will come to see, performativity scholars' historically and sociologically informed empirical approach, exemplified in the work of MacKenzie and Millo, presents a great boon to those who would reflect more carefully on questions of prevalence. Many social constructionists overemphasize the role of language, conceptualization, and explicit beliefs in bringing about the phenomena they discuss. Hacking too, by his own admission, tends to place excessive focus on the effect of classification on the self-conceptualization of those classified in explaining their behavior. Performativity scholars, on the other hand, have explored the complicated and non-obvious manner in which theorizing may become incorporated in things like technological innovations, institutional designs, and management trends, sometimes leading to significant changes in behavior even when those whose behavior is affected are entirely unaware of the science in question. Becoming responsive to such potential mechanisms of scientific self-fulfillment is a first step toward a subtler evaluation of the phenomenon's possible prevalence.

Unfortunately, the boon provided by performativity scholarship concerning questions of prevalence is counterbalanced by the confusion it sometimes sows concerning questions of conceptualization and significance. Discussion of these issues makes up a significant part of this book, and thus I will not enter into a deeper discussion here. To indicate what is to come, however, we need only to reflect briefly upon a statement by MacKenzie concerning his celebrated case study:

> The empirical success of the Black-Scholes-Merton model was a historically contingent process in which the model itself played a constitutive role. To say that is in no way to diminish the brilliant achievement of Black, Scholes, and Merton; it would be a curious prejudice to see a theory that changed the world (as their theory did) as inferior to one that merely reported on it. Rather, it is to assert that the model was a theoretical innovation, not simply an empirical observation; that the model's relation to the market was not always passive, but sometimes active; that its role was not always descriptive, but sometimes performative, even in the strongest, Barnesian sense. An engine, not a camera. (MacKenzie 2006a, 259)

There are two metaphors that inform passages such as these, not uncommon in the performativist literature, in important, yet perhaps misleading ways. The first is that of 'performativity' itself. As mentioned above, these scholars see their work as deriving from Austin's notion of linguistic performatives, words and locutions that 'do things' rather than merely describe them. Of course, it is no surprise that words 'do things' in just any sense of the phrase – we are moved to tears by the words of great poets, and even the word of a child sends her parents into a flurry of activity. But in these cases, it is through the causal effect that they exert on readers' or hearers' thoughts, beliefs, and expectations that our words 'do things'. This is not the case, however, for linguistic performatives as originally conceived by Austin – saying 'I promise' does not bring about a promise merely in virtue of the changes it causes in hearers' expectations. Rather, it is *in* uttering 'I promise' that we perform the act of promising and, we might go on to say, bring about a promise. Often, this relation between performative statements and states of affairs they help bring about is described in terms of *constitution*, rather than causation.

It is no fluke that MacKenzie writes that the Black-Scholes-Merton model 'played a *constitutive* role' in bringing about its own success. The language of performativity has at times, I will argue, encouraged both performativity scholars and readers of their work to conceive of the effects they describe in terms of constitution rather than causation. However, in many cases, and in the case of *homo economicus* almost assuredly, the effects under consideration are primarily causal in nature. Thus, performativists' preferred conceptualization often seems to be at odds with the phenomena they investigate. Even more damaging, however, is the fact that this conceptual ambiguity has led to some confusion concerning the potential significance of such phenomena for our usual understanding of science.

One of the most worrying of such confusions is suggested by the other metaphor employed in MacKenzie's passage. He, like Hacking, hits upon the image of an engine to describe the kinds of changes science might bring about in its objects of study. In fact, the final sentence quoted above makes up half of the title of his highly influential book: *An Engine, Not a Camera*. This is an explicit allusion to the manner in which Nobel prize-winning economist Milton Friedman (1953, 35) once characterized his field: as "an 'engine' to analyze [the world], not a photographic reproduction of it." Friedman's notion of economics as an engine of analysis should remind us of Hacking's engines of discovery. However, MacKenzie's (2006a, 12) use is meant to suggest something further: "Financial economics, I argue, did more than analyze markets; it altered them. It was an 'engine' in a sense not intended by Friedman: an active force transforming its environment, not a camera passively recording it."

What exactly the explicit distinction between science as an 'engine of transformation' or a 'passive camera' is meant to express is difficult to pin down in MacKenzie's writings. However, at times, the emphasis with which he presents the apparent tension between the two – an engine, *not* a camera – seems indicative of a belief that there is a significant tension between recognition of the performative nature of (economic) science and continued use of our usual notions of scientific accuracy and success. The Black-Scholes-Merton theory was a 'brilliant achievement,' but it is suggested that this evaluation depends more upon the theory's ability to 'change the world' rather than to, we might say, get things right. As I argue in later chapters, there are at least two ways of cashing out what some have seen as the performativists' prime intended lesson: performativity renders our usual epistemic notions of scientific success and evaluation either entirely inapplicable or, at the very least, generally ill-advised. Both claims, I will argue, are as worrisome as they are misguided.

1.4 Outlook

Earlier philosophers of science concluded that self-fulfilling reflexive predictions posed no significant threat to scientific methodology and thus lacked philosophical significance entirely. Certain constructionist approaches to science, on the other hand, have interpreted evidence of such phenomena as justifying skepticism concerning science's usually taken-for-granted claim to epistemic authority. Hacking comes down somewhere in the middle, recognizing the significance of science's role of as engine of change while denying that this undermines its epistemic ambitions. Finally, performativity scholars such as MacKenzie display ambivalence regarding whether or not there is an outright conflict between the images of science as an engine or a camera, while perhaps more clearly encouraging us to conceive of scientific success in terms of its ability to shape the world rather than generate knowledge about it.

Although none of these perspectives refer exclusively to the phenomenon I have termed self-fulfilling science, all have investigated what might be called *self-fulfilling prophecy-like phenomena*, those that bear some intuitive resemblance to this earlier sociological concept. The tendency to overstate or underestimate either the prevalence or significance of such phenomena has at times hindered or discouraged attempts to advance discussion of scientific self-fulfillment much beyond the same realm of 'marvelous coincidence' on display in our oldest literary myths. In the following chapters, I develop a framework with which we can move beyond mystification or superficial treatments by approaching the topic as a fully natural, yet not mundane, phenomenon deserving of sober and serious analysis. This means, on the one hand, taking seriously the notion that self-fulfillment could have significant repercussions for scientific practice and our understanding thereof, and undertaking to make clear what these could be. On the other hand, it means acknowledging self-fulfillment is undoubtedly limited in its pervasiveness and that any bold claims about its significance for our usual conception of science in general must be argued for rather than presupposed. Why should we assume that science cannot be at once both an engine, *and* a camera?

In this chapter, I introduced the notion of scientific self-fulfillment by way of an intuitive contrast with the widespread view that science owes its epistemic success to its self-correcting nature. According to a preliminary characterization, science is self-fulfilling when it owes its (apparent) epistemic success to the fact that it causes the world to come more into line with its postulates. I then offered a brief overview of earlier attempts by philosophers of science to gauge the significance of self-fulfilling predictions for their field, as well as the recent history of attempts to understand other seemingly related phenomena. The coming chapters make frequent reference to these earlier and alternative approaches in an attempt to (re-)evaluate the questions of conceptualization, prevalence, and significance that must be addressed in order to better understand how, if at all, a theory of scientific self-fulfillment should affect our usual understanding of science and its epistemic success.

In chapter two, I present some of the most prominent claims and evidence put forth in recent years in favor of the thesis that economic theories of *homo economicus* are self-fulfilling, and show how the conceptualization of self-fulfillment they employ is often underdeveloped or problematic. Chapter three sets out to develop a more adequate conceptualization. After examining two candidate notions in the literature and finding them wanting, I develop a novel account that both makes sense of the claims outlined in chapter two and may serve as a more general notion of scientific self-fulfillment. With this concept in hand, chapter four turns to examine several general strategies that might be employed

– and mistakes to be avoided – in addressing questions of prevalence. Chapter five critically examines the claim that self-fulfillment renders science entirely unamenable to the forms of epistemic evaluation traditionally thought to be central to successful science. After denying any significant tension at this general level of analysis, chapter six then turns to examine several ways in which credible claims of scientific self-fulfillment might indeed affect our practice of theory evaluation and development. Finally, chapter seven summarizes the book's arguments and briefly considers the provocative suggestion that the possibility of self-fulfillment should lead us to largely abandon the projects of describing, explaining, and predicting in favor of an approach that equates scientific success with the ability to engineer a more desirable future.

2 The self-fulfillment of *homo economicus*

2.1 Economic man: born or made?

2.1.1 Outlining a paradigmatic case

In the previous chapter, I suggested several reasons for treating recent claims concerning the purported self-fulfillment of economic theories of *homo economicus* as both springboard and touchstone for inquiry into questions of conceptualization, prevalence, and significance. Once again, briefly: first, they are prompted by and have themselves prompted empirical research thought to lend support to the claim that scientific self-fulfillment actually exists and may, in certain domains, be both *prevalent* and non-negligible. Second, discussion of these data is often accompanied by claims about the *significance* of self-fulfillment more generally, some of which apparently fall within the purview of philosophy of science. Finally, despite the strength of these claims, the *conceptualization* of the central notion of scientific self-fulfillment ungirding them is often lacking in important ways.

The centrality of this work is also recognized by one of the few recent papers on scientific self-fulfillment published in a mainstream philosophy of science journal, Bergenholtz and Busch (2016). Indeed, the authors designate "the notion of the self-interested homo economicus" as "the archetypical example of self-fulfillment," and offer a philosophical assessment of a high-profile disagreement between two sets of social scientists concerning the significance of their opposing claims on the matter (Bergenholtz and Busch 2016, 29). We will return to these issues in the coming chapters. First, however, it is necessary to outline the state of the debate of such claims recently carried out by social scientists.

In this chapter, I introduce certain prominent claims concerning the self-fulfillment of *homo economicus*, present several strands of evidence put forward in support thereof, and examine the manner in which they typically conceptualize self-fulfillment. I conclude by briefly arguing that the intuitive notion of self-fulfillment often employed is both underdeveloped and problematic. This sets the stage for the following chapter, in which a more adequate account is developed.

Note that the following does not aspire to present a comprehensive review of the relevant literature but is rather circumscribed in several important ways. First, discussion is limited to only a few examples from a few key lines of research often cited in support of the claims in question. Second, critical engagement with the details of the studies cited is, for the most part, kept to a minimum. Were this chapter meant to provide answers to questions of prevalence, this would be a defect. However, the goal here is more modest, namely to exhibit the type of empirical research some social scientists have *interpreted* as strongly suggesting the existence and/or prevalence of scientific self-fulfillment. Finally, I am not for the most part concerned here with the precise meaning of the term 'homo economicus,' the history of its use, or different concepts to which it might be applied (cf. Persky 1995 for an overview). Rather, as will become clear, I use the term as a useful piece of shorthand for characterizing a cluster of related notions. Many of the scientists whose work is discussed in this chapter employ the term, at least in passing, to refer to such notions. Others do not. What I wish to draw attention to is the shared phenomena they seem to have in mind.

2.1.2 Polanyi and the 'economic fallacy'

As recounted in Brissett (2019, 2–3), the claim that economic theory influences its objects of study enjoys a pedigree stretching back at least to the writings of Karl Marx. Marx (1844 [1988], 93) wrote of Adam Smith's labor-based political economy that it must be considered not only as a product of the forces of modern industry but also "as a force which has quickened and glorified the energy and development of modern *industry* and made it a power in the realm of *consciousness*."

This general insight was taken up and further developed by Karl Polanyi, one of the founding figures of economic sociology. In *The Livelihood of Man*, Polanyi postulates an 'economistic transformation' of human society, self-conception, and possibilities for action grounded, in large part, by what he calls the *economic fallacy:*

> [T]he error was in equating the human economy in general with its market form [...]. The fallacy itself is patent: the physical aspect of man's needs is part of the human condition; no society can exist that does not possess some kind of substantive economy. The supply–demand–price mechanism, on the other hand (which we popularly call the market), is a comparatively modern institution of specific structure, which is easy neither to establish nor to keep going. To narrow the sphere of the genus *economic* specifically to market phenomena is to eliminate the greatest part of man's history from the scene. (Polanyi 1977, 6)

Polanyi sees the widespread adoption of this fallacious equivocation and the new economic realities of the Industrial Revolution as conspiring to render certain types of individual economic behavior virtually necessary for survival. In turn, "such an enforced utilitarian practice fatefully warped Western man's understanding of himself and his society":

> As regards *man*, we were made to accept the view that his motives can be described as either 'material' or 'ideal' and that the incentives on which everyday life is organized necessarily spring, from the material motives. It is easy to see that under such conditions the human world must indeed appear to be determined by material motives. If, for example, you single out whatever motive you please and organize production in such a manner as to make that motive the individual's incentive *to produce*, you will have induced a picture of man as altogether absorbed by that motive. [...] The motive selected will represent 'real' man. (Polanyi 1977, 11)

Furthermore,

> As regards *society*, the kindred doctrine was propounded that its institutions were 'determined' by the economic system. The market mechanism thereby created the delusion of economic determinism as a general law for all human society. Under a market economy, of course, this law holds good. (Polanyi 1977, 12)

Polanyi (1977, 12) concludes that, given the new predominance of the market mentality and the entirely contingent, yet undeniably real 'economistic transformation' of societal institutions that accompanied it, "it was almost impossible to avoid the erroneous conclusion that, as 'economic' man was 'real' man, so the economic system was 'really' society."

Polanyi's method for investigating the rise of 'economic man' – *homo economicus* – is thoroughly historical. In the cited passages, however, we may recognize the seeds of two subsequent lines of empirical research claimed as evidence that economic man is not so much 'born' as 'created'. The first investigates how individuals' personal familiarity with economic theory affects their willingness to engage in various types of 'self-interested' behaviors. The second considers how economic assumptions come to be embedded in institutional designs, normative expectations, and linguistic practices, and what effects this has on both individual and collective economic behavior. Although the researchers in question have only sometimes interpreted their studies in terms of self-fulfillment, their results have been cited by others to argue that "economic theories [are] self-fulfilling at the market (or institutional) level and also at the individual level" (Mastilak et al. 2018, 115). In the following sections, I review some of the literature typically cited in support of such claims before turning to examine the nature of the claims themselves.

2.2 The empirical evidence

2.2.1 Induced self-interest via direct economic training

Empirical investigation of individual-level effects of economic theorizing is often presented as an unexpected offshoot of research by experimental psychologists Marwell and Ames (1981), who initially set out to test 'the free rider hypothesis' as a predictor of behavior in collective action situations.[11] At the time, the hypothesis had become "one of the most widely accepted propositions in the literature on the provision of public goods by groups" despite the fact that most arguments put forward in its favor were based on anecdotal evidence or theoretical speculation (Marwell and Ames 1981, 295). Thus, in a series of experiments, Marwell and Ames measured participants' willingness to contribute their own resources to the provision of a public good against the prediction, derived from a strong version of the free rider hypothesis, that absolutely no resources would be contributed. Their conclusions concerning the strong hypothesis are clear:

> [O]ver and over again, in replication after replication, regardless of changes in a score of situational variables or subject characteristics, the strong version of the free rider hypothesis is contradicted by the evidence. People voluntarily contribute substantial portions of their resources—usually an average of between 40 and 60 percent—to the provision of a public good. (Marwell and Ames 1981, 307)

One specific variation in subject characteristics, however, produced a surprising result: economics graduate students were much more likely to free ride than any other group tested, contributing on average only about 20% of their resources. Furthermore, these students' responses to a post-experiment questionnaire about the importance of fairness differed substantially from their peers', with the former being only half as likely to indicate any concern for fairness and much more likely to see little to no contribution at all as being 'fair'.

Although only tangentially related to the hypothesis they set out to test, Marwell and Ames (1981, 309, emphasis added) speculated as to possible explanations for the observed behavioral differences:

> Perhaps these results make sense. Economists may be *selected* for their work by virtue of their preoccupation with the 'rational' allocation of money and goods. Or they may *start behaving* according to the general tenets of the theories they study.

---

[11] Kirchgässner (2005) discusses several earlier treatments, but most reviewers of the literature begin with Marwell and Ames (1981).

These unexpected findings inspired further investigations by social scientists of various stripes intent on assessing how the behavior of those with economics training may or may not differ from that of their peers. The studies in question differ significantly along multiple dimensions, including: methods employed (e. g. real-world observational data, survey data, game theoretic experiments); makeup of the groups compared (e. g. economics majors vs. non-economics majors, economics professors vs. professors of other disciplines, those with formal training in microeconomics vs. those without); types of behavior or judgment measured ([un]willingness to e. g.: contribute to charity, cooperate in prisoner's dilemma or ultimatum games, engage in price gouging, accept bribes, voluntarily return lost money, maximize profits at the cost of worker welfare); and manner in which the behavioral differences under consideration are conceptualized (in terms of e. g.: cooperativeness, honesty, ethicality, corruption, generosity, greediness, fairness, pro-sociality, selfishness, self-interestedness).[12] Despite their differences, however, these studies are often presented by their authors as tackling the shared question of "Are economists different, and if so, why?" (Carter and Irons 1991), and are perhaps most often summarized in terms of 'self-interest'.

Although the findings of the individual studies are not directly comparable given the differences in specific aims and methods just mentioned, most are presented as supporting one of three conclusions. First, there may be *no effect:* despite initial appearances, there is in fact no real, significant difference in behavior and/or judgment between economists and non-economists. Second, even if significant differences do exist, these could be primarily attributable to a *selection effect:* those more naturally predisposed to the behaviors lumped together under the heading of 'self-interested' are more likely to study economics than others. Or, third, differences could be due to what is alternatively called either a 'learning' or 'indoctrination' effect: the tendency to engage in self-interested behavior is induced by or at least significantly strengthened by undergoing economic training.[13] For the sake of rhetorical neutrality, I follow Cipriani et al. (2009, 456) in referring to the latter as a *treatment effect*.

---

12 These dimensions may be observed in, among others, the following studies: Marwell and Ames (1981), Carter and Irons (1991), Frank et al. (1993; 1996), Yezer et al. (1996), Laband and Beil (1999), Frank and Schulze (2000), Frey and Meier (2003), Cipriani et al. (2009), Rubinstein (2009), and Bauman and Rose (2011).

13 Some studies (cf. Yezer et al. 1996) are interpreted to support a fourth possible conclusion: namely that those with economic training are in fact *less* likely to engage in such behaviors than peers. However, such results are far less common than the others and will not be considered here.

Research on this topic is ongoing, and the evidence in favor of any one of the three options is far from conclusive. However, this has not stopped some from citing claims of a treatment effect as evidence of the self-fulfillment of economic theorizing about *homo economicus*. Given my aim of exhibiting research social scientists have called upon to argue *in favor* of self-fulfillment claims, I will not further consider studies supporting either the 'no effect' or 'selection effect' hypotheses, but instead relate the details of one frequently cited paper favoring the 'treatment' hypothesis.

In a seminal paper, Frank, Gilovich, and Regan (1993) pose the provocative question: "Does Studying Economics Inhibit Cooperation?" The paper's two halves are meant to rule out, respectively, the no-effect and selection effect hypotheses. The first cites Marwell and Ames' unexpected findings as well as an ultimatum game experiment by Carter and Irons (1991) as indication of a possible behavioral difference between economics students and their peers. Noting that this evidence is suggestive but not conclusive, Frank et al. present survey-based and experimental data of their own.

Survey data was generated using questionnaires concerning individuals' contributions to charity, which were mailed to 1245 randomly selected college professors distributed among 23 disciplines. Economists made up 75 of the 576 respondents included in the study. Frank et al. (1993, 162) found that the proportion of "pure free riders" – those who reported donating nothing whatsoever – was highest among economists, at 9.3 percent, compared to that of most other disciplinary groups, which ranged from 2.9 to 4.3 percent. They also found that economists were "among the least generous" in terms of the median amount donated to "large charities" relative to estimated salary (Frank et al. 1993, 162). Behavior was "little different" between the groups along a number of other dimensions: economists were slightly less willing to take "costly administrative action" to prosecute students suspected of cheating, were slightly above average in the number of hours spent engaging in "volunteer activities," and were slightly below average in their frequency of voting in presidential elections (Frank et al. 1993, 162–163). Unfortunately, the authors include no discussion of statistical significance concerning any of the measured dimensions, nor do they include further details concerning the questionnaire itself or what constitutes a 'large charity,' 'little difference,' 'costly administrative action,' or 'volunteer activities' in the context of the survey.

Thankfully, Frank et al. expend considerably more effort detailing their experimental data, which compares the behavior of economics majors and non-majors in a prisoner's dilemma game. Participants were given an extensive briefing detailing the rules and payoff schemes of the game before being divided into groups of three. Each individual would play the game exactly once with each of their two group members. Subjects were informed that they would be playing for real money and that complete confidentiality would be maintained so that their responses would remain unknown to the other group members. Then they were given the opportunity to interact with one another before being taken to separate rooms to fill out a form indicating whether they would like to cooperate with or defect from each of the other players.

The circumstances of pre-game interaction differed in three conditions. In the *unlimited* condition, players were told they were allowed to make promises to one another not to defect, but that the confidential and non-repeating nature of the game rendered such promises unenforceable. In the *intermediate* condition, players interacted for 30 minutes but were not permitted to make any promises concerning their responses. The *limited* condition differed from this only in reducing interaction time to 10 minutes. Other independent variables included participant sex and class standing (freshman to senior). The dependent variable under investigation was subjects' choice of strategy: cooperate or defect.[14]

The authors found that in the unlimited condition, when subjects were allowed to make promises concerning their strategies, the rate of defection differed only marginally between economics majors and non-majors. Members of both groups were more likely to defect in the intermediate and limited conditions, but economics majors were much more likely to do so than non-majors. Pooling these latter conditions, Frank et al. (1993, 166) report that "the defection rate was 71.8 percent for economics majors and just 47.3 percent for nonmajors, levels that differ significantly at the .01 level." Part of this difference, they admit, is reasonably attributable to well-known sex differences concerning cooperation in prisoner's dilemmas. However, even controlling for this factor by assuming (based on evidence available at the time) that the probability of males defecting is nearly 0.24 higher than for females, it appears that, across all conditions, "the probability of an economics major defecting is almost 0.17 higher than the corresponding probability for a nonmajor" (Frank et al. 1993, 166).

In light of the earlier studies cited as well as their own survey and experimental data, Frank et al. (1993, 170) think a compelling case can be made for "a large difference in the extent to which economists and non-economists behave self-interestedly." They admit, however, that the data also provide evidence

---

14 The sample used for statistical analysis is restricted by the authors to those participants who either cooperated with or defected from both of their partners, excluding those that cooperated in one case and defected in the other. This is necessary, state Frank et al. (1993, 164), because the fact that each subject played the game twice renders the individual responses not statistically independent, which in turn makes "the most direct test of statistical significance, the chi-square test, [...] inappropriate for the sample as a whole."

of economists acting in more "communitarian" manners under certain conditions, such as in the unlimited condition of their prisoner's dilemma experiment or regarding the number of hours devoted to volunteer work reported in the survey data. They are also keenly aware that the differences they report could possibly be accounted for by a selection effect. Thus, in the second half of the paper, they present evidence that formal training in economics in fact plays a causal role in making economists behave less cooperatively.

Their attack on the selection effect hypothesis begins by pointing out a further interesting result of the aforementioned prisoner's dilemma experiment. Overall, it was found that defection rates decreased significantly as students progressed through school; the probability of defection seems to decrease each year by almost 0.07. However, Frank et al. found that rates in the no-promises conditions did not fall to the same degree for both groups – whereas rates for non-majors dropped from 53.7 percent for underclassmen to 40.2 percent for upperclassmen, rates for economics majors remained largely unchanged, dropping from 73.7 to 70.0 percent. The authors acknowledge that this does not prove causation, but see it as being at least compatible with and suggestive of the hypothesis of a treatment effect.

Frank et al. (1993, 168–170) then set out to investigate the specific type of training carried out in economics courses and how it might affect student behavior with another survey study. The survey was completed by two groups of students attending introductory microeconomics courses and one control group attending an introductory astronomy course, once during the first week of class and once again during the final week. The students responded to two ethical dilemmas. In the first, the owner of a small business orders and receives ten computers but is mistakenly billed for only nine. Students were asked first to estimate the likelihood that the store owner would point out the mistake to their supplier, then to indicate the likelihood that they themselves would do so, were they the store owner in question. The second dilemma asked similar questions concerning a lost envelope containing $100 and labeled with the owner's name and address. First, they were asked to imagine that they had lost the envelope and to estimate the likelihood that a stranger would return it to them, then to estimate the likelihood that they would return the money to a stranger, were the roles reversed. For each question, students were coded as being 'more honest' if the indicated likelihood rose between the initial and final weeks of class, as 'less honest' if it fell, and as 'no change' if it remained the same.

Crucially, the two introductory economics courses in question were taught by different instructors with different focuses. Instructor A was a "mainstream economist" who placed a "heavy emphasis on the prisoner's dilemma and related illustrations of how survival imperatives often militate against cooperation"

(Frank et al. 1993, 168). Instructor B, on the other hand, was a specialist in the economic development of Maoist China who "did not emphasize such material to the same degree, but did assign a mainstream introductory text" (Frank et al. 1993, 168). On the basis of these known differences in focus and material, it was hypothesized that any observed effects would be more pronounced in the responses of instructor A's students.

And, in fact, it was found that the proportion of 'less honest' responses grew the most for instructor A's students, while those in instructor B's class gave 'less honest' responses than the control group. Frank et al. (1993, 169) acknowledge the possibility of a selection effect in relation to the instructors – perhaps students predisposed to "more cynical" responses gravitated toward instructor's A courses on the basis of reputation. However, they argue that even if students in this class displayed higher levels of such responses at the outset, their responses nevertheless showed the highest degree of shift toward 'less honest' during the course of the semester. Unfortunately, the authors once again omit any discussion of statistical significance or even very basic information such as the number of subjects in the study as a whole or in each class.

Frank et al. are typical among investigators of the effects of economic instruction in *not* conceptualizing their results in terms of scientific self-fulfillment. However, they do employ another type of framing that helps open the path toward eventual interpretation along these lines. Already in the opening lines of their seminal paper, the authors very clearly display the kind of rhetorical shift suggested above between claims about subtle, *specific* differences in *specific* types of behavior among *specific* groups, to a more *general* claim of significant differences between economists and non-economists expressed in terms of self-interest. Though the studies they cite differ significantly with regards to methods, makeup of the groups compared, types of behavior or judgment measured, and manner in which the differences in question are characterized, Frank et al. (1993, 159) see themselves as investigating "whether exposure to the self-interest model commonly used in economics alters the extent to which people behave in self-interested ways."

Ultimately, the authors adopt a strikingly confident position regarding this question. In a later response to criticism by Yezer et al. (1996), Frank et al. sum up their view that, despite the ambiguity, inconclusiveness, and shortcomings of the data,

> three important points remain clear. First, all parties concede that economics training encourages the view that people are motivated primarily by self-interest. Second, there is clear evidence that this view leads people to expect others to defect in social dilemmas (Marwell and Ames, 1981). Third, there is also clear evidence that when people expect their partners

to defect in social dilemmas, they are overwhelmingly likely to defect themselves (Frank, Gilovich and Regan, 1993, p. 167). The logical implications of these three points appear to place a heavy burden of proof on those who insist that economics training does not inhibit cooperation. (Frank et al. 1996, 192)

2.2.2 Three pathways to self-fulfillment

Organization and management scholars Ferraro, Pfeffer, and Sutton (2005) have been some of the most vocal proponents of the view that social scientific theories, and those of microeconomics in particular, may be self-fulfilling. The claims of their 2005 paper, "Economics Language and Assumptions: How Theories Can Become Self-fulfilling," are of particular interest to our inquiry for several reasons. First, their boldly stated account of self-fulfillment in economic theories of *homo economicus* has been highly influential. Their paper has been cited well over 1000 times across a number of social scientific disciplines. This includes positive citation by other influential authors addressing scientific self-fulfillment and closely related topics, such as performativity scholars (e. g. MacKenzie 2006a; Callon 2007) and those favoring Hacking's notion of looping effects (e.g. Kuorikoski and Pöyhönen 2012). Second, critical discussion surrounding their claims brings up multiple issues that appear to bear on well-established or emerging debates within philosophy of science. Finally, and of more immediate concern, their account is often celebrated for going beyond general statements about scientific self-fulfillment by identifying and 'operationalizing' three specific pathways or mechanisms whereby it might come about.

For these reasons, much of the following discussion in both this and subsequent chapters will focus on the claims of Ferraro et al. and, later, their critics. For now, I continue to consider the empirical evidence cited in favor of self-fulfillment claims by summarizing the three mechanisms they identify: *social norms, institutional design,* and *language*.[15]

2.2.2.1 Social norms
Ferraro et al. see the work of Marwell and Ames, Frank et al., and others claiming that familiarity with economic theory affects individuals' behavior as sug-

---

[15] Although these are presented as three distinct mechanisms, it is clear that they are conceived of by Ferraro et al. as often acting in tandem. I largely ignore the complex interactions that may occur between the three in the following discussion.

gesting how economic theories can become self-fulfilling by helping establish *social norms:*

> There is, then, a large and growing body of literature that suggests that economists and economics students act differently from others. Why?
> Miller (1999) proposes that studying economics, with its assumptions about the norm of self-interest, helps people learn what is appropriate behavior, and they respond accordingly. [...] This explanation suggests that many of the experimental results of the tendency of economics students and economists to defect more, cooperate less, and, in general, behave more in accordance with the dictates of self-interest may be mediated by belief in the norm of self-interest and its prevalence. No tests of mediation in any of these studies are reported, but the argument and empirical implication are straightforward: one effect of economics training is to strengthen beliefs in the pervasiveness, appropriateness, and desirability of self-interested behavior, which, in turn, should lead to exhibiting more self-interested behavior. (Ferraro et al. 2005, 8)

However, increased explicit awareness of economic assumptions through formal economic training is considered only one particular manner in which the establishment of social norms may lead to self-fulfillment. Those whose behavior is the descriptive or explanatory target of some theory may also be influenced despite being unaware of its postulates. For example, managers who study economic theories in business school might allow (their understanding of) microeconomic assumptions to affect their managerial style and decisions. Even if managers themselves are not thereby led to exhibit self-interested behaviors, they may come to accept the 'norm of self-interest,' and thus to expect their subordinates to act accordingly, ultimately implementing strategies and policies based on this assumption. And this, in turn, may lead to the self-fulfillment of microeconomic theories through a further pathway: *institutional design.*

2.2.2.2 Institutional design

In a departure from those who focus only on the impacts of economic training, Ferraro et al. (2005, 12) also consider subtler, less direct paths of influence, noting that:

> A theory can become true to the extent that people, acting on its ideas and underlying assumptions, introduce practices, routines, and organizational arrangements that create conditions favoring the predictions made in the theory.

The case of the Black-Scholes-Merton formula and its embedding into technological and strategic possibilities for effective action on the options market presented in the previous chapter is perhaps the clearest example of such an effect.

Wide adoption of this option pricing theory led to the establishment of institutional conditions in which certain types of trading behavior – 'arbitrage' and 'spreading' – became highly profitable. "And," as MacKenzie (2006a, 156) argued, "the effects of that arbitrage seem to have been to move patterns of prices toward the postulates of the model." Building on this, the observation that "modern microeconomic theory has been used to design auctions, organize markets, [and] guide privatization efforts" more generally suggests, argue Ferraro et al. (2005, 11), that similar effects might be expected in various economic and societal domains (cf. also McMillan 2003; Roth 2002).

If the Black-Scholes-Merton model represents a particularly clear case of self-fulfillment of *economic* theory via institutional design, other evidence cited in this context is more readily understood as concerning the self-fulfillment of *homo economicus* in particular. Alongside the microeconomic assumption that workers' behavior is motivated primarily by self-interest, managers might also learn that extrinsic incentives, such as monetary compensation, are the most effective means of encouraging desirable behavior. However, one strand of research suggests that use of extrinsic rewards as incentives may lead originally present intrinsic motivations for some behavior to be replaced or 'crowded out'. Thus, the assumption that extrinsic rewards are necessary to encourage desired behaviors because humans are by and large motivated by rational self-interest might contribute to bringing about states of affairs in which this assumption is (apparently) largely accurate.

One of the first suggestions that extrinsic rewards or motivations may displace preexisting intrinsic ones comes from Richard Titmuss (1970), whose book *The Gift Relationship* makes the claim that introducing cash rewards for blood donations unexpectedly led to decreased willingness among citizens to donate. Titmuss had little evidence to back up his initial claim; however, the phenomenon he suggested has since become an important topic of study within social psychology, where it is known under a variety of terms, including *the hidden cost of reward*, the *overjustification hypothesis*, the *corruption effect*, or, perhaps most commonly, the *motivation crowding-out effect*, which I employ henceforth (cf. Frey and Jegen 2001 for a broader overview).

In one oft-cited, classic investigation, Lepper et al. (1973) performed a field study in which preschool children who showed significant intrinsic interest in a drawing activity were subjected to various conditions that introduced extrinsic rewards for participation. Intrinsic motivation was measured over several days by surreptitiously observing the amount of time children spent drawing in a setting in which they could freely choose between this and other activities. Two weeks later, children who displayed a high level of motivation during baseline observations were individually invited to join an experimenter in the 'surprise room,' where they were either asked and agreed to perform the same drawing activity in order to 'win' a personalized certificate with a gold seal and ribbon called a 'Good Player Award' (*expected-award condition*), unexpectedly provided with the same reward after finishing the activity (*unexpected-award condition*), or neither expected nor received any reward (*no-award condition*). One to two weeks later, another round of surreptitious observations was carried out. It was found that children in the expected-award condition spent significantly less time drawing during these later free-play sessions than those in the other two conditions. Lepper et al. (1973, 136) interpret their results as showing that it is possible to produce a motivation crowding-out effect under specific circumstances, but explicitly warn against hasty overgeneralization from this experiment to the conclusion that "contracting to engage in an activity for an extrinsic reward will always, or even usually, result in a decrement in intrinsic interest in the activity."

Early studies by social scientists like Titmuss and psychologists like Lepper et al., explain Frey and Jegen (2001), initially gave rise to two largely independent lines of research into motivation crowding. Although the former posited unexpected, policy-relevant phenomena like the apparent negative effect of introducing monetary compensation on the willingness to donate blood, they were often at a loss to explain how this could be, given that it seemingly contradicts the usual fundamental economic assumption that monetary incentives positively influence motivation. On the other hand, psychologists were unsure how robust the suggestive results of their highly specific and somewhat artificial experiments might be in other contexts, as evidenced by Lepper et al.'s explicit warning against hasty overgeneralization.

Frey and Jegen (2001) examine subsequent attempts to integrate crowding-out theory into economics more directly, both by identifying specific psychological mechanisms that might explain such economically counterintuitive effects and reviewing the relevant empirical literature. The two psychological mechanisms most commonly invoked to explain replacement of previously extant intrinsic motivations by extrinsic ones are either a "change in preferences" or a "change in the perceived nature of the performed task, in the task-environment or in the actor's self-perception" (Frey and Jegen 2001, 592). Regarding the latter, it is suggested that the psychological conditions under which crowding-out appears are usually those in which external interventions are perceived as being 'controlling'. This leads to feelings of impaired self-determination (i.e. 'external circumstances force me to behave in a specific manner, regardless of my internal motivation to do or not do so') and self-esteem (i.e. 'any intrinsic motivation I may have is neither recognized, appreciated, nor encouraged'), upon which "individuals react by reducing their intrinsic motivation in the activity controlled"

(Frey and Jegen 2001, 595). Following discussion of the possible theoretical underpinnings of motivation crowding-out, they cite a range of laboratory, field experiment and econometrics studies as "strong empirical evidence" for the existence and relevance of crowding-out in a variety of economic and societal domains, including:

> children's learning behaviour; patients' readiness to take prescribed medication; monetary and symbolic rewards for undertaking various laboratory tasks; the tendency to reciprocate in the laboratory setting, reflecting work conditions in a firm; the amount of trust exhibited in a laboratory situation of incomplete contracts; the reaction of managers to various forms of supervision by their superiors; the readiness to offer voluntary work; the observation of time schedules in daycare centres; the on-time flight performance in the airline industry; the readiness to accept nuclear waste repositories (and other locally unwanted sites); and the amount of civic virtue exhibited, in particular with respect to fulfilling one's tax obligations (tax morale). (Frey and Jegen 2001, 606)

Despite concluding that motivation crowding-out is 'empirically relevant' in economic domains, Frey and Jegen do not consider whether economic theory itself could contribute to crowding-out or thereby result in self-fulfillment. However, others have drawn explicitly on such work linking motivation crowding-out and economics to support claims that institutional design can cause self-fulfillment of economic theory. Kuorikoski and Pöyhönen (2012, 196) offer a particularly clear-cut account:

> The guiding principle [of the economics-based tradition of institutional design] is to conceptualize people as rational agents competently pursuing their interests and then to formulate incentives in a way that would steer these rational agents to act in accordance with some socially beneficial outcome. Usually such incentives are monetary, and free-riding as well as principal-agent problems (e.g., moral hazard) are controlled by means of sanctions and bonus schemes.
>
> This kind of incentive-based social engineering may have adverse long-term consequences. [...] Conceptualizing the consequences of decision alternatives in terms of expected gains and costs diminishes the intrinsic motivational force of such things as civil virtues, expressive rationality, and the intrinsic value of the possible actions. When everything is given a price, obligations, commitments, rights, and the common good are classified as goods to be consumed within the limits of the budget constraint.
>
> Explicit incentives that render the intended manipulation transparent to the agent constitute another mechanism leading to the crowding out of intrinsic virtues. This diminishes the agent's sense of autonomy and also usually leads to more cynical, calculative behavior. The conceptualization of people as rational economic agents can be a powerful self-fulfilling prophecy.

Ferraro et al. also refer to a number of studies they see as providing at least indirect evidence of such an effect. The promulgation of economics assumptions by compensation consulting companies has led to the widespread use of 'merit-based' pay in organizations, which assigns salaries based on individual performance level (cf. Kay 1998; Wood 1996). Not only do such pay schemes lead to reduced job satisfaction and disrupt social relationships in the workplace, claim Ferraro et al. (2005, 20), but rather the effect such assumptions have on institutional design means that:

> there are feedback processes that cause an emphasis on pay and extrinsic incentives to create attitudes and behavior that make emphasizing pay essential for motivating and directing behavior. That is because emphasizing pay actually makes pay more important to employees.

Thus, it is claimed, such practices, which were developed and adopted on the belief that extrinsic rewards such as financial gain are essential in motivating behavior, actually tend to create an atmosphere in which this is more likely to be the case.

2.2.2.3 Language

In addition to affecting managerial practices and institutional design, Ferraro et al. also posit that economic theory may influence language in a manner that leads to self-fulfillment. Their reasoning here builds on the assumption of some degree of linguistic relativism: broadly, the notion that language is not only used to communicate the independent products of non-linguistic thought, but rather itself shapes, structures, and constrains cognition. To this end, they cite Lakoff and Johnson's (1980) cognitive-linguistic 'conceptual metaphor theory' as well as Berger and Luckmann's (1966) sociological classic on the 'social construction of reality'. Given this background, it is probably more fitting to refer to this third pathway to scientific self-fulfillment in terms of *conceptual frameworks*, rather than (just) language.

Particular focus is placed on the role of language in establishing behavioral norms:

> The argument is simple. Language evokes certain associations, certain motives, and certain norms. Acting on the basis of that language in ways consistent with those norms and assumptions, we do things that, in turn, will produce behavior on the part of others consistent with our linguistic frame. Language produces a social reality that reinforces and validates the terminology we use. (Ferraro et al. 2005, 16)

Liberman et al. (2004) present the concrete working of this mechanism in broadly economic contexts by investigating the impact of different naming conventions and situational labels on players' behavior in a prisoner's dilemma game. Dormitory resident advisors at an American university were asked to nominate subjects for a 'study on negotiation' from the pool of student advisees with whom they were well acquainted. Specifically, they were asked to nominate those students they considered most likely to either cooperate or defect in the first round of the game and to indicate the likelihood of cooperation or defection for each. Finally, they were to reassess this likelihood were the game to be introduced to players as either the 'Wall Street Game' or the 'Community Game'. Subjects were actually recruited only if estimated at least 85% likely to cooperate or 85% likely to defect regardless of which game-naming convention was employed. Participants were given detailed instructions on the nature of the game and the payout matrix involved. During the instructions, the game was referred to twice as either the 'Wall Street Game' or the 'Community Game'. In all other respects, the games played were identical. Subjects played seven rounds and were informed of their partners' decisions after each.

Surprisingly, results showed that the nomination status of participants as most likely to either cooperate or defect displayed almost no predictive power at all concerning their actual game behavior, either in the first round or overall. Conversely, the name of the game seems to have exerted a very strong effect on participants' choices:

> When playing the Community Game, 67% of the most likely to cooperate nominees and 75% of the most likely to defect nominees cooperated on the first round. When playing the Wall Street Game, 33% of participants with each nomination status cooperated [...]. Choices over the entire seven rounds presented essentially the same picture. [...] More detailed inspection of the responses of individual dyads over the seven rounds revealed that in the Community Game, mutual cooperation occurred on 43 of 84 possible occasions, whereas mutual defection occurred on 16 occasions. By contrast, in the Wall Street Game, mutual cooperation occurred on only 11 of 84 possible occasions, whereas mutual defection occurred on 42 occasions. (Liberman et al. 2004, 1177)

Such evidence is cited in concert with studies (and general observations) attesting both to the dominating success of economic thought and language in society (cf. Dumont 1977) and the effect that adoption thereof might have on the cognitive framing of more everyday situations and phenomena. McCloskey, for example, invokes Lakoff and Johnson's conceptual metaphors to examine the "metaphors economists live by" and consider how economists and non-economists alike might be brought to engage in more typically 'economic' forms of cognition by (implicitly) employing market metaphors:

> When economists look at, say, childcare, they think of markets. "Childcare"—which to other people looks like a piece of social control or a set of buildings or a problem for new parents—looks to economists like a certificate on the New York stock exchange. By the choice of metaphor the economists are driven to identify a demand curve, a supply curve, and a price. If they are of the mainstream, neoclassical kind, they will see "rational" behavior in such a market; if they are Marxist or institutionalist or Austrian economists, they will see other things, but in any case through a market metaphor. (McCloskey 1995, 215)

Ferraro et al. (2005) bring the conversation back to organizational settings, drawing on the above sources to suggest that the common images of a company or business as a 'community' or 'family' prevalent in the United States preceding World War II have been displaced by a 'market' metaphor through which employees come to be viewed primarily as just another commodity to be manipulated so as to maximize profitability. The upshot, they think, is as clear as it is predictable: "just as companies feel no particular social obligation or moral tie to their employees, employees, now told to look out for themselves, do precisely that" (Ferraro et al. 2005, 19). And, to the extent that various types of self-interested behavior that might constitute 'looking out for oneself' in such a setting are thereby rendered necessary for success (or survival), it seems the adoption of economic language and conceptual frameworks concerning *homo economicus* are another path by which self-fulfillment may occur.

2.2.3 Summary

The previous sections present what I take to be a fair and representative, though in no way comprehensive, overview of several strands of empirical evidence commonly put forward in favor of claims of the self-fulfillment of microeconomic theories of *homo economicus*. Though it is not my primary intent to engage in critical assessment of this literature, it seems safe to conclude that a good deal of suggestive, though certainly inconclusive evidence exists for some non-negligible link between adoptions of microeconomic theorizing and a set of distinctive behaviors and/or motivations in a variety of groups of people and settings.

As was the case concerning the purported effect of formal economic training on trainees, the studies cited as evidence of less direct pathways of influence vary along a wide variety of dimensions, including methods, group makeup, types of behavior measured, and the precise manner in which the behaviors are characterized. Nonetheless, many authors, even those critical of self-fulfillment claims (cf. Felin and Foss 2009a), seem content to view this literature as bearing on the broader question of whether or not economic theorizing leads to, encourages, or otherwise induces (higher degrees of) self-interested motivations or behaviors. In order to simplify the remaining discussion, I will refer to such effects as *induced self-interest*.

We have now seen a representative selection of evidence and, along the way, have already come across several suggestions of economic self-fulfillment. It remains to be seen, however, how exactly such claims are to be understood. The remainder of this chapter presents more explicit examples of self-fulfillment claims before going on to argue that their exact meaning as employed in the literature is often unclear.

2.3 The claim(s)

2.3.1 Sample claims

Bergenholtz and Busch (2016, 29), who have advanced one of the only recent examinations of claims of scientific self-fulfillment from a distinctively philosophy of science perspective, state that "the archetypical example of self-fulfillment relates to the notion of the self-interested *homo economicus*." They, like many others, cite Ferraro et al. (2005) as a central source of such claims. Interestingly enough, however, the latter authors do not in fact explicitly employ the term 'homo economicus' or its English cognate in formulating their central claims, which instead make reference to the self-fulfillment of "social science theories", "economic theory", or "fundamental ideas of economics" (Ferraro et al. 2005, 8). I will return to their conception in a moment; for now, however, let us gather a few other influential claims.

The work of business and management theorist Sumantra Ghoshal is often cited alongside Ferraro et al. as including particularly straightforward claims of the purported self-fulfillment of *homo economicus*. Ghoshal and Moran (1996, 14) argue that business firms' implementation of Oliver Williamson's version of "transaction cost economics," which seeks to explain not only cases of buying and selling, but also a wide variety of more day-to-day interactions on the assumption of self-interested "opportunism," might itself lead to a "self-fulfilling prophecy whereby opportunistic behavior will increase with sanctions and incentives imposed to curtail it, thus creating the need for even stronger and more elaborate sanctions and incentives."

Building on this, Ghoshal (2005) ascribes much of the blame for the rise of high-profile corporate scandals in the United States to business schools and their promotion of problematic management practices. "Mainstream economics," he writes, "has, in the main, always worked on the assumption of *Homo Economi-*

cus – a model of people as rational self-interest maximizers" (Ghoshal 2005, 82). In his view, the dominance of this assumption has led business scholars to develop a methodology they take to be 'scientific,' but which actually minimizes "any role for human intentionality or choice," and to generally adopt a "gloomy vision [...] about both individuals and institutions." Such views, in turn, have encouraged scandalous behavior because "unlike theories in the physical sciences, theories in the social sciences tend to be self-fulfilling" (Ghoshal 2005, 77).

Michel Callon, chief progenitor of current performativity scholarship, has also often been read as claiming something about the self-fulfillment of *homo economicus* (cf. Santos and Rodrigues 2009). Callon (1998) views attempts by sociologists and other critics to either flesh out or denounce what they see as an impoverished economic model of human motivation, rationality, and behavior as largely unhelpful and/or misguided. "In both cases," he writes, "we formulate the same critique: *homo economicus* is pure fiction" (Callon 1998, 51). The position of the performativity scholar, however, is to maintain the contrary and investigate the conditions under which this could come to be:

> Yes, *homo economicus* really does exist. Of course, he exists in the form of many species and his lineage is multiple and ramified. But if he exists he is obviously not [sic] be found in a natural state–this expression has little meaning. He is formatted, framed and equipped with prostheses which help him in his calculations and which are, for the most part, produced by economics. (Callon 1998, 51)

Kuorikoski and Pöyhönen (2012, 196), although interested more generally in mechanisms of various kinds of looping effects, turn also to the topic of economic man and self-fulfillment as a paradigmatic example of looping by motivation crowding-out:

> The conception of man as a rational economic actor may thus be a self-fulfilling prophecy due to the feedback mechanism of the crowding out of intrinsic motivations. Crowding out is the socio-psychological mechanism that sustains the cluster of properties characteristic of the newly created *homo economica*.

Finally, it was previously noted that most of the empirical researchers cited by Ferraro et al. do not themselves explicitly interpret their results in terms of self-fulfillment. With the growing influence of such claims, however, this seems to be changing. To give just one of a number of recent examples, Mastilak et al. (2018, 114) present the results of experiments on the effect of exposure to agency theory on business students' ethical behavior as supporting the notion that "agency theory can act as a self-fulfilling prophecy." These experiments closely resemble the earlier studies cited by Ferraro et al., Ghoshal, and others in support of their claims, and it seems that the success of these accounts may now be leading others to interpret their results as bearing on the broader question of scientific self-fulfillment.

This is but a smattering of claims concerning the purported self-fulfillment of economic theories of *homo economicus,* albeit one that includes some of the most widely cited and influential examples.[16] However, despite frequent reference to 'economic man,' 'self-interest(edness),' and 'self-fulfillment,' the exact nature of the claims in question is often rendered ambiguous because their proponents fail to specify or identify either the exact (content of) the economic theories, models, or assumptions in question or the relevant notion of self-fulfillment.

2.3.2 Who is *homo economicus?*

Not everyone who posits the self-fulfillment of what I've been calling 'economic theories of *homo economicus*' in fact use the term 'homo economicus'. As already mentioned, Bergenholtz and Busch present Ferraro et al. (2005) as a primary source of such claims despite the fact that the latter authors do not so much as mention the term. What matters, however, is not whether this specific term is employed in making such claims, but rather what specific economic theories, models, assumptions, etc. are interpreted as being 'self-fulfilling' in light of the evidence summarized above. However, pinning down the nature of economic man, or rather, the theories, models, or assumptions associated with such ideas, proves rather difficult.

Although Ferraro et al.'s (2005, 11) central claim concerns the self-fulfillment of "social science theories" more generally, they place special emphasis on the "fundamental ideas of economics that enjoy increasing dominance in social science discourse." Citing Amartya Sen, who in turn cites F. Y. Edgeworth (1881), an important figure in the development of neoclassical economics, they identify the most fundamental assumption of all as that of *self-interest:*

> Edgeworth asserted that "the first principle of Economics is that every agent is actuated only by self-interest." This view of man has been a persistent one in economic models,

---

16 Of course, there are also critics of such claims. Of particular note for the coming chapters are Felin and Foss (2009a; 2009b), who forcefully criticize Ferraro et al.'s account. I abstain here from presenting an overview of negative or counter-claims, given my primary aim in this chapter of examining how the positive case for self-fulfillment has been constructed.

and the nature of economic theory seems to have been much influenced by this basic premise. (Sen 1977, 317)

Ferraro et al. view self-interest as the foundation of other fundamental assumptions of mainstream economics, making its influence directly responsible for the three pathways of economic self-fulfillment they identify. In the case of motivation crowding-out and institutional design, for example, they note that "if people pursue their own interests, it follows that incentives will be essential for obtaining desired behavior from people, which is why economic researchers place so much emphasis on extrinsic incentives" (2005, 11). Given the frequent reference by Ferraro et al. and many other authors cited above to the centrality of 'self-interest,' it seems clear that whatever scientific theory is ultimately at stake in these self-fulfillment claims, it revolves centrally around the notion of self-interest in humans.

But how exactly are we to understand the central claim concerning self-interest at stake? Much ink has been spilled on the question of how economics' central assumptions are to be understood, and it would go far beyond the scope of this chapter to examine this issue directly. Instead, I merely point out two sets of distinctions which may give rise to quite different understandings of the claims made above but that are often ignored or glossed over by central proponents of self-fulfillment.

The first distinction concerns the scope of the assumption in question. According to Edgeworth, the fundamental assumption of economics is that 'every agent is actuated only by self-interest.' But, if read in a literal sense to mean something like '*every* action by *every* agent is motivated *only* by self-interest,' then this seems to be a highly counterintuitive, if not clearly false, notion. More to the point, we might wonder if it is the sort of thing that could ever be 'self-fulfilling' in the first place.

Indeed, not only has the validity of such assumptions been increasingly called into question in light of recent evidence from behavioral economics (e.g. Caporael et al. 1989; Henrich et al. 2005), but the unrealistic nature of the assumption is recognized even by Edgeworth (1881, 104) himself, who writes that "the concrete nineteenth century man is for the most part an impure egoist, a mixed utilitarian." This might cause us to question 'how much' self-interest must be induced before claims of economic self-fulfillment are justified. Should we understand the theories in question to include an assumption of (near) universal scope, or is something more local and limited to be taken as the relevant measuring rod? Perhaps surprisingly, proponents of self-fulfillment claims seldom consider such questions explicitly.

The second distinction concerns what 'entity' exactly the term 'self-interested' describes in the first place. Specifically, it is unclear whether self-fulfillment claims are premised on the inducement of either a) increased defection in prisoner's dilemmas and other such (seemingly) self-interested *behaviors* or b) a higher degree of self-interested *motivations* (that themselves perhaps explain the inducement of related behaviors) through the influence of economic theorizing.[17]

For example, on one hand, Ferraro et al. (2005, 8–9, emphasis added) write that:

> Social science theories can become self-fulfilling by shaping institutional designs and management practices, as well as social norms and expectations about behavior, thereby *creating the behavior they predict.* [...]
>
> Theories can also become self-fulfilling when, regardless of their initial ability to predict and explain behavior, they become accepted truths and norms that govern behavior. People act and speak as though the theory were true [...] thereby *making self-interest a more powerful predictor of behavior* simply because people believe that to behave otherwise is illegitimate.

These passages suggest that a theory should be considered self-fulfilling when it brings about behaviors that at least coincide with those expected or predicted by the theory or, in this case specifically, when it promotes a "tendency [...] to defect

---

[17] It should be noted that these are not the only contenders for the central subject of the microeconomic theories in question. Indeed, many scholars identify the central feature of *homo economicus* as relating neither to what agents do nor what they desire, but instead to "process-centered assumptions about the way in which those desires [...] issue in action," which ultimately "boil down to the assumption that people's actions serve their desires well, given their beliefs about such matters as the options available, the likely consequences of different options, and so on" (Pettit 1995, 309). Persky (1995) traces the original notion of economic man to John Stuart Mill (1836 [2008]), who argued on largely methodological grounds for conceiving of humans as having (only) four distinct interests: accumulation, leisure, luxury, and procreation. However, Persky (1995, 223) likewise argues that "we make a serious error if we read into this animal the modern identification of economic man with rationality itself," going on to note that "in much contemporary usage, the essence of economic man lies not in what he picks, but in his rational method for making choices."

Despite this, I focus primarily on behaviors and motivations in the following, both because these seem to better accord with what proponents of self-fulfillment claims have in mind, and because the distinction between these two options suffices to make the intended point, which is that clear identification of *some* specific theoretical content is required to make sense of any self-fulfillment claim. Some scholars do in fact show occasional sensitivity to such distinctions, as when Ghoshal and Moran (1996, 18) charge Williamson with failing to explicitly distinguish between "opportunism as an attitude (i.e., inclination or proclivity) and opportunism as a type of behavior or action." More often, however, distinctions of this sort are not drawn in the first place or are applied inconsistently.

more, cooperate less, and, in general, *behave more in accordance with the dictates of self-interest*" (Ferraro et al. 2005, 14, emphasis added).

On the other hand, however, Ferraro et al. (2005, 11) often present the fundamental assumption of economics as relating not primarily to behavior, but rather to self-interest as a "cardinal human motive" or the "pursuit of self-interest." Furthermore, their citing of Edgeworth, who writes of humans being 'actuated' (i.e. 'moved to action' or 'motivated') by self-interest, seems to suggest that they understand the underlying assumption of economics as relating more closely to motivations rather than (perhaps associated) behaviors. As we will see moving forward, it makes a very significant difference how exactly we conceive of *homo economicus* when considering the veracity of self-fulfillment claims.

2.3.3 What is self-fulfillment?

Just as not all of the above authors employ the term 'homo economicus,' neither do all formulate their claims primarily in terms of 'self-fulfillment'. Kuorikoski and Pöyhönen (2012) prefer Hacking's framework of 'looping'. Callon introduced the notion of 'performativity,' which has since been widely adopted and adapted in the social scientific literature. Others have expressed similar ideas in terms of 'reflexivity' (cf. Soros 2013), 'reflexive predictions' (cf. Kopec 2011), 'bootstrapped induction' (cf. Barnes 1983), and the Oedipus effect (cf. Popper 1957), among others.

Even when these other terms are employed, however, the authors in question almost always *also* refer to 'self-fulfillment' or the 'self-fulfilling prophecy' in framing their claims. In some cases, these alternative concepts are explicitly presented as being closely related to Merton's original notion of self-fulfilling prophecy or broader phenomena of which self-fulfilling prophecies are a specific type. At other times, the concepts in question are explicitly contrasted with the self-fulfilling prophecy, most notably in MacKenzie's (2006a) influential characterization of 'Barnesian performativity'.[18] At least the term, if not the concept, of 'self-fulfillment' has arguably played a central role in structuring much of the recent discussion surrounding the claims examined in this chapter. So how, then, do the authors in question understand 'self-fulfillment'?

---

18 The term "Barnesian" comes from the surname of sociologist Barry Barnes, whose work on the role of self-validating or 'bootstrapped' inference in the constitution of stable social institutions (cf. Barnes 1983) has served as inspiration to performativity researchers.

According to Merton's (1948, 195) original characterization, "the self-fulfilling prophecy is, in the beginning, a *false* definition of the situation evoking a new behavior which makes the originally false conception come *true*." There is much to unpack here, and I expend some effort toward doing so in the following chapter. For now, however, I highlight just one central feature of this characterization as it is often understood and briefly indicate how this might complicate an intuitive understanding of the claims under discussion. As commonly read, whatever else self-fulfillment amounts to on Merton's characterization, it at least seems to entail that the 'prophecy,' 'definition of the situation,' or 'conception' in question *becomes true* as a result of its dissemination.

Perhaps surprisingly, many of the authors cited above fail to give an explicit (or even working) definition of self-fulfillment or whichever alternative notion they use. For example, notwithstanding the centrality of the term 'self-fulfilling theory' for their claims, Ferraro et al. (2005) provide no explicit definition or characterization thereof. Although they do favorably cite Merton's characterization of self-fulfilling prophecies, this is presented merely as a starting point for their discussion; there is no indication it is intended to be understood as a definition. They also note that ideas such as theirs have been discussed under the heading of 'reflexive predictions' in philosophy of science and 'performativity' in science studies, but again offer no explicit characterization of either. Despite this, however, we often see these authors falling back on the intuitive notion of a theory's 'becoming true' as the seemingly relevant criterion for self-fulfillment, as seen in the following collection of statements:

> Transaction cost theory may *become self-fulfilling and therefore true* [...] (Ferraro et al. 2005, 9, emphasis added)

> [Economic] assumptions are diffused as normative rules of behavior, *rendering the theories true* through their effects on the behaviors they are purported to explain. (Ferraro et al. 2005, 10, emphasis added)

> In each of these ways, the assumptions and ideas of economics come to *create a world in which the ideas are true* because, through their effect on actions and decisions, they produce a world that corresponds to the assumptions and ideas themselves. (Ferraro et al. 2005, 12, emphasis added)

Nor are Ferraro et al. alone in connecting the notions of 'self-fulfillment,' 'becoming true,' and the effect of economic theorizing:

> As this self-fulfilling prophecy plays itself out, management perceptions that employees are opportunistic would become increasingly valid. (Ghoshal and Moran 1996, 27)

> Whether right or wrong to begin with, *the theory can become right* as managers—who are both its subjects and the consumers—adapt their behaviors to conform with the doctrine. (Ghoshal 2005, 77, emphasis added)

Bergenholtz and Busch also present the central claim in debates concerning the self-fulfillment of social science theories as stating that:

> not only will the behavior of individuals change to some degree due to the adoption of a scientific theory, but some underlying empirical regularities [...] will also change, which might *turn the theories from false to true*. (Bergenholtz and Busch 2016, 29, emphasis added)

2.3.4 Questions of conceptualization

Although the thesis of self-fulfillment of economic theories has grown popular among social scientists in recent years, a general lack of clarity concerning the central phenomenon of 'self-fulfillment' remains quite apparent. Philosophers are sometimes wont to demand more explicit definitions than scientists deem necessary to get on with their work. In general, both sides may have good reasons for their relative (lack of) concern; here, however, there is a substantial case to be made for taking a closer look. For, the purported existence of scientific self-fulfillment is claimed by proponents to have serious consequences for how we should go about developing, teaching, and implementing scientific theories. However, the intuitive understanding of 'self-fulfillment' suggested by Merton's original notion of self-fulfilling prophecies – revolving around 'becoming true' – in fact makes it difficult to see how such theories could be self-fulfilling in the first place or how the empirical evidence presented might bear on such claims. My argument for this claim is presented in the following chapter; for now, I close the current discussion by briefly gesturing toward the deeper waters ahead.

Given the basic notion of truth as correspondence with reality, it is unclear in what sense economic theories of *homo economicus* could *become* true on some of the readings proposed above. For example, if we are to understand the theory's scope as approaching universality – i.e. that *all* humans at *all* times are actuated *only* by self-interest – then it seems counterintuitive that any theory incorporating this notion (as part of its descriptive content)[19] could, in fact, be true. But it

---

19 There are some who argue that the 'assumption' of *homo economicus* is not, in fact, to be understood as part of the descriptive content of microeconomic theories, but rather as a purely methodological and/or normative constraint or strategy. There is a very difficult and nuanced discussion to be had here; however, we can largely ignore this, for it is clear that those involved

seems outright impossible that such a thing could *become* true. For, stating it bluntly: either all humans at all times have been, are, or will be actuated by self-interest or they have, are, or will not be – it is a point of simple logic that there is nothing economics (or anything else for that matter) could do to make this the case, were it not already so.

Even considering a claim of more limited scope, it remains unclear how inducement of self-interested *behaviors* should qualify economic theories as self-fulfilling on the very reasonable assumption that *homo economicus* relates at least to some significant degree to self-interested *motivations* (or ways of reasoning, etc.). For we can clearly imagine a case in which adoption of such theories brings about certain kinds of behavior without thereby significantly affecting the 'true' motivations of the actors involved.

Indeed, this was just the sort of story told by Polanyi. One consequence of the 'economic fallacy,' he thought, was inculcation of the belief that the "incentives on which everyday life is organized necessarily spring from the material," rather than "ideal", "motives" (Polanyi 1977, 12). However, according to his account, *this view is illusory.* It merely *appears* that we are dictated only by rational self-interest because the economistic transformation of societal institutions has created conditions under which actions *seeming* to reflect a dog-eat-dog attitude are necessary for survival. Under such conditions, Polanyi concludes, "it was almost impossible to avoid the *erroneous* conclusion that, as 'economic' man was 'real' man, so the economic system was 'really' society" (Polanyi 1977, 1 emphasis added).

Thus, on this common understanding of 'self-fulfillment,' it makes quite a difference if we think of the self-fulfillment of *homo economicus* as amounting to the bringing about of either certain types of behaviors or motivations. Unfortunately, the majority of authors cited in this chapter are silent on such questions. In the coming chapters, it will become clear that this lack of conceptual clarity generates ambiguity not only in the current case, but that this is just one example of a more general issue that goes back to Merton's original discussion of the self-fulfilling prophecy and has since come to infect much the work on similar phenomena that has followed.

In the following chapter, I examine several possible candidates for conceptualizing scientific self-fulfillment more precisely. I begin by outlining Merton's account of self-fulfilling prophecy and several problematic aspects thereof.

---

in debates concerning the self-fulfillment of such theories treat this assumption as making up part of the empirical content against which the epistemic success of the theories in question is to be gauged. The latter point is spelled out in more detail in chapter five.

I then turn to examine in more detail two of the more promising and influential candidate notions, *reflexive prediction* and *performativity.* I argue that both are, in fact, ill-suited both to account for the claims presented in this chapter as well as those of scientific self-fulfillment more generally. Ultimately, I go on to develop a novel answer to the question of conceptualization that draws and builds on the relative strengths of these alternatives.

3 Conceptualizing self-fulfilling science

The previous chapter introduced what has been called 'the archetypical example of self-fulfillment' of scientific theories, the purported self-fulfillment of microeconomic theories of *homo economicus*. After presenting several lines of empirical evidence put forward in favor of such claims, I turned to scrutinize the claims themselves. It was shown that many of the most influential and oft-cited proponents of self-fulfillment claims fail to make sufficiently clear either the concept of 'self-fulfillment' they employ or what conditions a theory must meet in order to be considered 'self-fulfilling'. The chapter closed by gesturing toward a problem to which this lack of clarity may give rise: on the intuitive understanding of self-fulfillment as involving *becoming true*, it is unclear, on some readings, how theories of *homo economicus* could ever be self-fulfilling and, on others, whether or not the evidence cited by proponents of such claims even bears directly on the question of economic self-fulfillment.

The aim of this chapter is to move us toward an explicit characterization of scientific self-fulfillment that might better capture the intended claims of the previous chapter and, ultimately, serve as a more general explication of the phenomenon. I begin by examining Merton's notion of the self-fulfilling prophecy in more detail and pointing out several seeming ambiguities in his account that have been overlooked by those drawing on his work or concept to frame claims of scientific self-fulfillment. Following this, I turn to critically examine two explicit concepts put forward in the literature to characterize such phenomena as they relate to science, namely *reflexive predictions* and *performativity*. Noting significant issues with each, I ultimately develop a novel account that builds on the strengths of each of these alternatives while attempting to avoid their weaknesses, and examine how it may be applied to understanding the claims of the previous chapter.

3.1 From prophecy to reality – or illusion?

3.1.1 Merton's self-fulfilling prophecy

Merton's (1948, 195) characterization of the self-fulfilling prophecy as "in the beginning, a *false* definition of the situation evoking a new behavior which makes the originally false conception come *true*" has been extremely influential since its introduction in his original 1948 paper. Even more widely known than his explicit characterization, however, is the intuitive example he cites to demonstrate it, the bank run: a false rumor is spread among the patrons of the Last National Bank that the bank is insolvent; those who believe the rumor rush to withdraw their money; this draining of the bank's assets lends further credence to the rumor, leading even more depositors to cash out; finally, the bank's debts exceed its assets and it succumbs to insolvency, thus making the original 'prophecy' (appear to be) vindicated after all.

Despite the prominence of Merton's characterization and intuitive example, however, his original paper displays some ambiguity concerning the nature of 'self-fulfillment' involved in self-fulfilling prophecies. This becomes apparent when contrasting the well-known bank run with another example usually overlooked despite being the primary subject of Merton's original paper. Self-fulfilling prophecies, Merton (1948, 196) argues, account for much of the "dynamics of ethnic and racial conflict" in the United States. To illustrate, he considers the case of forced segregation in trade unions at the beginning of the 20th century, which he attributes to widespread belief among majority whites that blacks were inherently prone to anti-union behavior such as strikebreaking. This belief led to black workers being shut out of the unions, which in turn caused many to in fact turn to strikebreaking for lack of other professional options, thus seemingly confirming the original belief that "'it just ain't in the nature of the nigra' to join co-operatively with his white fellows in trade unions" (Merton 1948, 209).

The cases of the bank run and racial segregation in unions suggest two different, competing notions of self-fulfillment.[20] In the former, a prophecy (or prediction[21]) counts as 'fulfilled' by virtue of the fact that the event or state of affairs it prognosticates actually occurs or obtains. It is '*self*-fulfilled' because it is the issuing of the prophecy itself that ultimately causes the occurrence of the predicted event. The content of the prediction in the classic example is understood to be something like 'bank X will become insolvent within the immediate future'; the prediction is considered 'fulfilled' if the bank in fact becomes insolvent, and is considered 'self-fulfilling' if the issuance of the prediction itself led to the behavior that caused the bank's insolvency to come about. Thus, self-fulfillment in such cases seems to entail something like the notion of 'becoming true' discussed in the previous chapter.

---

20 Later in this chapter I argue that they also imply a distinction between self-fulfilling *predictions* and other types of self-fulfilling *representations* that will be crucial for the account moving forward. Discussion of this issue will be postponed until several other considerations have been put in place; until then, I will not distinguish sharply between the two notions.
21 I use the terms 'prophecy' and 'prediction' interchangeably in connection with self-fulfillment claims.

3.1.2 Illusory self-confirmation

In the case of the union segregation, however, Merton seems to be suggesting something quite at odds with this usual understanding. If white workers' belief concerning black workers includes the imputation of a *natural* or *inherent* tendency on the part of the latter to engage in anti-union behaviors, then it is clear that Merton cannot take this belief to be 'fulfilled' in the sense of its being or becoming true. For it is precisely his point that the strikebreaking and other apparently anti-union behaviors carried out by black workers were not due to some natural tendency, but rather to the working of the 'prophecy' itself. In this case, the belief itself simply is (and remains) false, and the only reasonable thing we might mean by calling it 'self-fulfilling' is that the behaviors it evoked contributed to the *mistaken* impression of fulfillment in the above sense. A corresponding reformulation of Merton's characterization might read: 'a false definition of the situation evoking a new behavior which makes the originally false conception *seem* true despite its not being so'. Let us call this *illusory self-confirmation* to distinguish it from the phenomenon usually associated with Merton's account, which we might term *genuine self-fulfillment*. Moving forward, when I speak of 'self-fulfillment,' I mean *genuine* self-fulfillment unless otherwise noted, and it is this phenomenon which serves as the focal point for the characterization of scientific self-fulfillment to be developed.

Genuine self-fulfillment seems to imply a certain measure of epistemic success absent in cases of illusory self-confirmation. After all, the hypothetical bank in Merton's more familiar example does in fact become insolvent, and someone who believes the bank to be insolvent after the prediction has had its effect believes correctly. Contrast this with the illusorily self-confirming belief of blacks' inherent anti-union nature, which is merely made to *appear* true despite remaining false even after its effect has taken hold. However, it should also be noted that genuine self-fulfillment itself often includes its own type of epistemic failure or illusion. For, even if the resulting belief of the bank's insolvency in the aforementioned case is true, those unaware of the working of the self-fulfilling prophecy are likely to hold false beliefs about the causal factors that led to this outcome or other seemingly relevant facts pertaining to the situation. The most important point at this junction is to note that we are dealing here with two distinct phenomena and, it would seem, different types and degrees of epistemic failure that go hand in hand with each.

The distinction between genuine self-fulfillment and illusory self-confirmation will prove crucial in the pages to come for a number of reasons. First, it appears that proponents of the claims discussed in the previous chapter have often failed to notice the difference between these two phenomena, and have, following in Merton's footsteps, referred to both by way of the term 'self-fulfilling'. Second, having a clearer view of this distinction will help us more adequately consider what kind of evidence must be put forward in order to demonstrate something about the existence and prevalence of science that is genuinely self-fulfilling, and not merely illusorily self-confirming. Finally, this distinction will have serious repercussions for our understanding of the significance of scientific self-fulfillment for philosophy of science.

3.1.3 Content contingency

The distinction between these two phenomena should also alert us to the importance of specifying the content of a given prediction when claiming it to be self-fulfilling. If the relevant belief in the union workers' case were specified as including only the imputation of a given likelihood among black workers to engage in strikebreaking, without specifying that this likelihood is attributable to a natural or inherent tendency, then the prophecy in question may have turned out to be genuinely self-fulfilling after all.

Thus, it appears necessary to alter our judgment concerning whether a certain prediction is genuinely self-fulfilling, illusorily self-confirming, or neither depending on its precise content. Let us call this the feature of *content contingency*. Content contingency poses little problem in purely hypothetical cases, as we are more or less free to simply stipulate the content in question. However, things look quite different when considering the content of real-world (scientific) predictions, theories, or models, which are expressed in many different ways with varying degrees of vagueness, indexicality, context sensitivity, and the like. This is likely to give rise to ambiguity and, perhaps, serious disputes concerning the relevant content of purportedly self-fulfilling theories. Such issues were noted already in connection with *homo economicus* – which theories and which content are singled out by the claims of the previous chapter?

Despite the importance of the distinction between self-fulfillment and illusory self-confirmation and the accompanying feature of content contingency, it also seems that placing too much emphasis on the latter may cause us to fail to capture the spirit of claims concerning self-fulfilling prophecies or theories. For example, consider a variant of the usual bank run example in which the prediction in question explicitly reads 'bank X will become insolvent by 12:00 tomorrow,' and the resulting run causes the bank to become insolvent by 12:01. Strictly speaking, this should not count as a case of genuine self-fulfillment, if we take the becoming true of the prediction in question to be a necessary condition for its being self-fulfilling.

Even given one and the same chain of causal events, we may arrive at different judgments concerning the genuinely self-fulfilling or illusorily self-confirming nature of some prediction based solely on the content we impute. For example, we might decide to simply stipulate that the content of any prediction should be understood as implicitly including a qualifying clause that rules out any causal influence of the prediction itself, such as 'bank X will be insolvent by the end of next week (due to factors having nothing to do with the issuing of this prediction)'. On this interpretation, the prediction would not qualify as self-fulfilling even if the bank became insolvent due to the actions of customers who heard and acted upon it.

However, in both types of cases, we still rightfully feel that something significant and noteworthy has occurred, and that this judgment does not and should not depend too strongly upon whether we assign this or that content to the predictions involved. This feeling may be heightened when reflecting that outside of the hypothetical realm, in which content may simply be stipulated, there is likely no generally applicable procedure or mechanism whereby the 'real' content of some prediction or scientific theory may be ascertained. Although there may be cases in which all parties can agree to a specific imputed content, there are also liable to be many in which serious disputes arise. Recognition of these three facts – the fact of content contingency, the fact that there is likely no principled manner in which to clearly delineate the 'real' content of some prediction or theory, and the fact that we feel that something noteworthy has occurred when considering chains of events often interpreted in terms of self-fulfillment – despite consideration of the first two facts – constitute what I'll term the *problem of content contingency*.

This problem will rear its head again later in this and other chapters. Now, however, I move on to consider two alternatives to characterizing self-fulfillment as it pertains to science, both of which are cited by Ferraro et al. and others from the previous chapter and can be seen as building upon and/or reacting to Merton's account of self-fulfilling prophecy.

3.2 Reflexive prediction

Self-fulfilling prophecies are sometimes considered to be just one of a number of phenomena characterized by their so-called *reflexivity*. This use of the term has its origins in mathematics, where it denotes (among other things) mathematical relations that relate every element of some set to itself. Since the mid 20th century, however, the term has come to be used in various (especially social) scientific disciplines to refer to a number of causal, ontological, logical, or other relations in which something may be said to 'bend back' upon itself. Given the range of fields that have employed the term – including, at least, anthropology, economics, ethnography, linguistics, and, especially, various forms of sociology – it is unsurprising that both the 'something' and the notion of 'bending back' in question vary considerably (cf. Guala 2016c, 119–131).

This variance of usage suggests several ways in which an unqualified notion of reflexivity is too broad for our purposes. First, it is clear that induced self-interest is not the result of a logical or mathematical but rather a causal relation or process. Second, even if we restrict the notion to causal relations, it seems that the general notion of reflexivity, like that of the looping effect, is not inherently directional in nature. That is, while it might pick out causal effects of theories on the states of affairs they target, it does not specify that the outcome thereof will be such as to bring the world more in line with our picture of it. Finally, the sheer number and dissimilitude of various understandings of the general term are, I contend, a reason in and of itself to avoid its use. It may not be incorrect to claim that scientific self-fulfillment is or entails a kind of reflexivity; however, is not particularly enlightening.

This does not, however, rule out the possibility that a more specific notion of reflexivity, or of a more specific reflexive relation or process, may fit the bill. And indeed, the notion of *reflexive prediction*, suggested by Ferraro et al. as one possible understanding of self-fulfillment as it relates to scientific theories, initially seems to fair much better. Of the candidate notions discussed in this chapter, reflexive prediction has by far received the most attention in terms of developing an explicit and appropriate definition.

The following sections examine the suitability of reflexive prediction for cashing out claims about the self-fulfillment of *homo economicus*. I first review the main line of argument presented by philosophers of science concerning the appropriate definition of reflexive prediction, from Buck (1963), to Romanos (1973), to the recent revival of Kopec (2011). Following this, I argue that such attempts ultimately fail to fully capture what is at stake in the claims in question. Despite this, there are also insights to be gleaned from both the philosophical discussion concerning reflexive prediction itself and the precise manner in which such accounts seemingly fall short for our purposes. These insights inform the positive account developed at the end of the chapter.

3.2.1 Buck's acting-on-beliefs account

Noting a widespread belief that self-fulfilling and self-defeating predictions are pervasive in the social sciences, Buck (1963) sets out to answer three questions concerning so-called *reflexive predictions*, roughly understood as encompassing both self-fulfilling and self-defeating prophecies. First, how should reflexive predictions be precisely defined? Second, what kind of special methodological issues, if any, might such predictions raise for the social sciences? Finally, is the phenomenon restricted to the social sciences, or might it occur in the natural sciences as well? Only the first of these questions concerns us here; the others will be taken up in later chapters.

Buck initiates discussion of the proper definition of reflexive prediction by way of explicit reference to Merton's characterization of the self-fulfilling prophecy. Noting the difficulties that arise from attempting to read Merton's talk of 'originally false' predictions becoming true in a strictly temporal sense, Buck asserts that what is actually being contrasted in such claims must be understood as (the truth value of some prediction in) the situation that *actually* occurred, in which the prediction in question was disseminated, with (the truth value in) the situation that *would have* occurred had the prediction not been issued.[22] This is, essentially, a counterfactual reading of Merton's characterization.

Buck (1963, 360) then considers several features purportedly shared by "all the standard examples in the literature," by which he seems to mean bank runs, bandwagon effects, and economic forecasts. First, the causal effect of dissemination in these cases is "mediated by the formation of beliefs on the part of the various actors on the social scene, and by their behaving in a way which can be reasonably described as 'acting on' those beliefs" (Buck 1963, 360). Second, these mediating beliefs typically include a belief in the truth of the prediction itself. And finally, only those predictions the actual dissemination of which is somehow noteworthy are considered reflexive.

---

[22] Similar worries about Merton's account were expressed previously by Miller (1961) and Krishna (1971). Buck's suggestion of a counterfactual reading does not solve these issues so much as evade them. We might still ask, for example, what truth value, if any, a prediction that eventually turns out to be self-fulfilling has or had at the time of its dissemination. Buck (1963, 360) himself is skeptical that there may be "any clear meaning in the notion of a prediction, the very same prediction of the very same event, having at one time one truth-value, and at another time, the other," however it seems clear that this, as well as any other concrete view on the matter, depends greatly upon one's views on a number of further issues in metaphysics and the philosophy of language. His evasion of such issues is largely unproblematic in the cases he implicitly favors, namely those in which a claim is made concerning the self-fulfilling nature of a past prediction. Given that I ultimately favor a counterfactual reading, I do not further consider this issue.

These considerations move him to formulate what I term the *acting-on-beliefs account* of reflexive prediction, on which a prediction is reflexive if and only if:

(1) Its truth-value would have been different had its dissemination status been different,
(2) The dissemination status it actually had was causally necessary for the social actors involved to hold relevant and causally efficacious beliefs,
(3) The prediction was, or if disseminated, would have been believed and acted upon, and finally
(4) Something about the dissemination status or its causal consequences was abnormal, or at the very least unexpected by the predictor, by whoever calls it reflexive, or by those to whose attention its reflexive character is called. (Buck 1963, 361–362)

3.2.2 Romanos' standard account

Romanos (1973) criticizes Buck's proposed definition on a number of grounds, ultimately arguing against the appropriateness of all but the first clause. Buck justifies his second and third clauses on the basis that the 'standard examples' of reflexive predictions involve mediating beliefs that include belief in the truth of the prediction itself. However, Romanos correctly points out that by making these *necessary* conditions, Buck conceptually rules out the possibility of 'non-standard' examples in which some mechanism other than belief (in the prediction's truth) may be at work. This appears all the more problematic because the acting-on-beliefs requirement is later used by Buck in an apparently circular line of reasoning meant to deny that a purported (non-standard) counterexample to one of his claims in fact constitutes a case of reflexive prediction at all.[23] Finally, Romanos argues that Buck's fourth clause relates most directly to controversies surrounding the distinction between something's being '*a* cause' or '*the* cause' in general and is thus out of place and superfluous here.[24]

---

23 This line of argument is considered in the following chapter.
24 Buck's fourth clause and Romanos' rejection thereof are largely unimportant for our current purposes, but interesting nonetheless. To illustrate the elusive point of discussion, imagine a bank director makes a private, i.e. non-disseminated, prediction that their bank will *not* fail during the next week. Being in good financial standing, the bank indeed does not fail, and the prediction is thus fulfilled. Suppose, however, that *had* the prediction been disseminated, that customers would have found it extremely odd and upsetting given its apparently unprovoked nature, and because of this, initiated a panic resulting in the bank's failure. Without the addition of Buck's 'abnormality clause,' the original private prediction would be considered self-fulfilling, given that its eventual truth depended upon its actual dissemination status (namely, non-dissemination). Buck (1963, 361) asserts that it is "fatuous" to treat such predictions as reflexive,

Having pared down Buck's definition to its initial clause, Romanos then turns his sights on the central notion of a prediction's 'dissemination status.' On Buck's account, the dissemination status of a given prediction can take only one of two values: private or public. This presents two problems according to Romanos. First, the notion of public 'dissemination' carries a connotation most at home in the acting-on-belief conception of reflexive prediction he ultimately rejects.[25] Second, there are clearly many different, if not innumerable, specific manners in which a prediction may be made public, and not every form thereof is likely to have the same causal effects.

Romanos thus suggests replacing the notion of dissemination status with that of a prediction's *formulation/dissemination style* (F/D-style). This includes both the manner in which the content of the prediction is formulated or otherwise brought to expression (F-style) as well as the manner in which the prediction in a specific F-style is disseminated, reproduced, or otherwise 'transmitted' (D-style). For example, a prediction of bank failure may be formulated in Japanese or English, and may be transmitted in either language by way of a newspaper article, a television interview, or a whisper. F-styles, emphasizes Romanos (1973, 105), are not restricted to natural languages, but may also consist of "electric impulses, bodily movements, puffs of smoke, or anything else which may be interpreted as expressing a prediction." Clearly, different combinations of F-styles and D-styles are likely to give rise to very different causal effects, and thus it is not a prediction per se, but rather a *prediction in a given F/D-style*, that may or may not be reflexive.

---

offering the following analogy as argument: "One does not pick out just any old necessary condition for an event and call it a cause. The presence of oxygen is a necessary condition for the occurrence of fire, but it could properly be called the cause of some specific fire only in rather special circumstances," such as in a scientific apparatus where we would normally expect an absence of oxygen. Romanos finds this is unconvincing because Buck moves the goalposts within the two sentences cited above: one doesn't typically single out the presence of oxygen as *the* cause for some fire in a context where its presence is to be expected, but it is quite natural to grant it the status of being *a* cause. Romanos grants that there is a substantial issue up for discussion here, but sees this (properly, I think) as something to be sorted out by philosophical accounts of causality more generally rather than of reflexive predictions in particular.

25 As later pointed out by Vetterling (1976, 280), Romanos' rejection is not clearly justified by his charge of circularity. On the one hand, Buck could offer a non-circular answer to the question of why his cases are the 'standard' ones, such as simply noting that *these* are the kinds of cases most people consider to be paradigmatic. On the other hand, it could be argued that Romanos' decision to allow for 'non-standard' examples that do not meet the acting-on-beliefs condition itself constitutes a similarly problematic form of circular reasoning. We need not adjudicate this disagreement here; below I argue against both Buck's account and Romanos' counterproposal on the grounds that they are too narrow and broad for our purposes, respectively.

With these modifications in place, Romanos (1973, 106) suggests the following necessary and sufficient condition for a prediction's being reflexive, giving us what I term the *standard account* of reflexive prediction:

R_1 The formulation/dissemination style of the prediction must be a causal factor relative to the prediction's coming out true or false.

Despite their differing opinions on definitory matters, Buck and Romanos agree in one point: reflexive prediction does not pose a significant threat to the possibility of carrying out successful social science, nor is it a matter of much concern to philosophers of science more generally. With the exception of a short comment by Vetterling (1976), the philosophical discussion of reflexive prediction that began with Buck thus effectively ended with Romanos in 1973. Until recently, the few philosophers and social scientists who have explicitly invoked reflexive predictions have treated Romanos' definition as decisive, hence the appellation of 'standard account'. Recently, however, Kopec (2011) has attempted to revive philosophical debate surrounding reflexive prediction by arguing that the consensus definition is overly narrow and thus closes the door on a class of apparently relevant predictions.

3.2.3 Kopec's probabilistic account

Kopec (2011) begins by collapsing Romanos' dual notion of F/D-style into a simplified *mode of dissemination*. Part of his reasoning is that predictions are propositions that may be expressed in ways not readily amenable to talk of 'formulation'. For example, placing a new student into a group designed for poor performers may express the prediction that they will in fact perform poorly, despite the lack of any act directly approximating a linguistic formulation. Such manners of expression may even, Kopec contends, extend as far as the designing of an institution around a prediction. Kopec's reasoning here notwithstanding, Romanos' (1973, 105) insistence that F-styles may consist of "anything which may be interpreted as expressing a prediction" seems in fact to cover all such manners of expression. Thus, there seems to be little in the way of actual disagreement between the authors here.

After introducing this bit of terminology, Kopec examines the potentially ambiguous notion of a prediction's F/D-style or mode of dissemination being a 'causal factor relative to the prediction's coming out true or false'. This is most plausibly read, he argues, as stating that a prediction is reflexive if and only if its "mode of dissemination is sufficient to switch the truth-value of the prediction from what it would be if not disseminated" (Kopec 2011, 1252).[26] This brings him to his main point of contention: the suggested sufficiency condition rules out any prediction for which the actual outcome depends, even minimally, upon chance. To show this, Kopec presents a hypothetical case in which a bandwagon effect heavily influences the likelihood that a certain political candidate will be elected without completely determining the final result:

> Smith and Jones are running for president of the United States. After applying some theoretical machinery to an extensive amount of unpublished poll data, a well-respected analyst determines that Jones will win the election. Before our analyst decides to disseminate

---

[26] The argument for this reading is less than entirely convincing. Kopec (2011, 1251) reformulates Romanos' definition to read:

> *Revised Romanos's Reflexive Predictions.* A prediction is reflexive if and only if the mode of disseminating the prediction is a causal factor relative to the prediction's coming out true or false.

Surprisingly, in his revised definition, Kopec changes the exact wording of the original, which stated that the F/D-style of a prediction *must be* a causal factor, to now refer simply to the mode of dissemination's in fact *being* a causal factor. He then cites a later passage in Romanos (1973, 107) as an indication of the apparently intended reading:

> I would like to consider first a case of a self-fulfilling prediction. Let us suppose that we are scientists of some kind and we wish to test some theory (hypothesis) or other which we will refer to as T_1. From T_1 (together with, we may suppose, certain empirical assumptions) we derive a certain prediction, P, that an event, e_1 will occur. [...] Let us suppose that our prediction P has just one such F/D-style and that its *occurrence in this F/D-style* is an event which we will refer to as e_2. Now I suggest that P will turn out to be a self-fulfilling (reflexive) prediction just in case there is some other, well accepted or likely theory, T_2, such that according to T_2, given certain conditions C (which obtain), e_2 is sufficient to bring about the occurrence of e_1 (i.e. the event originally predicted by P).

Kopec accuses Romanos of confusing ontological with epistemological analysis here, namely what it is for a prediction to be self-fulfilling with what it is to know or believe that it is such. Urging us to ignore this apparent misstep, Kopec (2011, 1252) concludes on the basis of this passage that "Romanos clearly thinks that the relationship is one in which (if C obtains) e_2 is a sufficient condition for e_1 to obtain." However, there is a simpler explanation for Romanos' apparent lapse: namely, that his statements here are in fact not meant as a further explication of his definition, but rather are meant to give us some hint of what conditions need to be met in order to make a justified claim that some prediction is in fact self-fulfilling.

Admittedly, Romanos' true intentions in the quoted passage are less than crystalline, nor does he indicate what sense of modal force is suggested (if any) by his inclusion of the phrase 'must be' in the original definition. The exegetical work required to sort out Romanos' intended position and evaluate Kopec's critique clearly exceeds its expected utility for our purposes.

this prediction, the situation is as follows. The Americans who will vote in the election and who have decided for whom they will vote actually favor Smith by nine votes. There are only 10 undecided voters in the country, and each one plans to flip a coin: heads she will vote for Smith, tails she will vote for Jones. But if our analyst decides to disseminate the prediction over the television, a bandwagon effect (cf. Simon 1954) will cause 18 additional Americans to vote for Jones, even though they previously had no intention to vote at all. Neither the previously decided voters nor the coin flippers are affected by the news. Notice how disseminating this prediction in this way causes a difference. If the analyst says nothing, then the probability that Smith will win the election is greater than 99.9% since only one of the 10 coins would have to come up heads. But if she spreads her prediction that Jones will win the election over the airwaves, then the probability that Jones will win is greater than 99.9%. (Kopec 2011, 1252)

Although such cases "obviously have reflexive tendencies," writes Kopec (2011, 1253), they do not qualify as reflexive predictions on (his reading of) Romanos' definition:

> It is not the case that the mode of dissemination is sufficient for the election results to flip since there is still some chance (no matter how small it is) that the truth-value stays the same, even after the analyst goes on television.

Because the truth of predictions in the social sciences usually bears to some degree on chance, the standard account fails to classify even such intuitively plausible cases as reflexive. In response to this perceived failing, Kopec (2011, 1253) formulates what I term the *probabilistic account* of reflexive prediction, which introduces the notion of *weakly reflexive predictions:*

> A prediction is weakly reflexive if and only if the mode of dissemination is sufficient to change the probability of the predicted event occurring from what it would be if not disseminated.

On this account, the phenomena picked out by Romanos' standard account constitute *strongly reflexive predictions*, a special subset of weakly reflexive predictions characterized by the change in probability being such as to entirely guarantee a predicted event's coming about.

Kopec claims several advantages for his revised definition. First, it captures a broader range of intuitively relevant cases, e.g. those similar to the hypothetical case of the candidates Smith and Jones. Second, it allows us to distinguish between reflexive predictions of varying strength within this range. While both count as weakly reflexive, predictions that make the occurrence of a predicted event significantly more probable are stronger than those that make it only marginally so. Finally, by shifting focus to probability, Kopec claims that his account highlights certain methodological issues that escaped his predecessors. In particular, he argues, the existence of even weakly reflexive predictions might cause serious problems for those who employ Bayesian or likelihoodist confirmation-theoretic frameworks, as dissemination of such predictions can change the evidential import of observing their obtainment. This serves as a good example of how clarifying the key features of cases we intuitively view as self-fulfilling science is an essential step in evaluating their philosophical significance, a point we will return to in the coming chapters.

3.2.4 Scientific self-fulfillment as reflexive prediction?

How do the three accounts described above fair at cashing out claims about the self-fulfillment of *homo economicus*? There are at least two serious issues here. Perhaps the more obvious of the two arises from the apparent mismatch between the types of entities to which the term 'self-fulfilling' is attached. Ferraro et al., for example, are ostensibly concerned with self-fulfilling *theories*, whereas Buck, Romanos, and Kopec seek only to elucidate reflexive (and self-fulfilling) *predictions*. I return to this issue below. First, however, I consider the somewhat less obvious problem, which arises from the fact that, despite their differences, none of the above accounts differ significantly from their Mertonian origins by tying the notion of self-fulfillment closely to the actual or possible truth or becoming true of the prediction in question.

3.2.4.1 Truth as a criterion?
Accounts of reflexive prediction make a prediction's truth, or a change in its probability of becoming true, a necessary condition for its being self-fulfilling. However, this turns out to be too strong a condition, even in its weaker, probabilistic guise, to capture what seems to be at stake in claims concerning the self-fulfilling nature of *homo economicus*. In fact, all of the above definitions either fail to characterize some of the cited effects as self-fulfilling at all or recognize them only as an exceedingly weak form of self-fulfillment. This contrasts starkly with the view of many social scientists that induced self-interest is a particularly strong and clear, and thus paradigmatic, example of self-fulfilling science.

The crucial point can be illustrated by considering a simplified, hypothetical version of the type of experiment performed by Marwell and Ames, presented in the previous chapter, concerning participants' willingness to contribute resources to the provision of a public good. Imagine we are dealing with a single experiment and a one-shot prediction concerning the free-rider hypothesis. The strong hypothesis predicts that participants will contribute no portion (0%) of their resources to the provision of the public good. In our hypothetical setup, this prediction is communicated to only one subset of participants. Those informed of the prediction contribute on average only 20% of their resources, while the others contribute around 50%. Evidence that this discrepancy is most reasonably attributable to dissemination of the prediction rather than to some other factor is interpreted as suggesting the prediction was in some sense self-fulfilling. But in what sense?

Clearly, the prediction in this case is not self-fulfilling according to either the acting-on-beliefs or the standard account of reflexive prediction, given that both require the prediction in question to actually come out true. Because some portion of goods was contributed, the prediction of 0% total contributions comes out false. In Kopec's terms, such a prediction would not meet the requirements for being strongly reflexive. As already noted, he criticizes the definitions of his predecessors precisely for being too narrow to capture many apparently relevant cases. But does the prediction in this hypothetical case meet the requirements for being weakly reflexive? That is, is it plausible to claim that the prediction's dissemination makes it more likely to come out true than would otherwise have been the case?

If the predicted outcome of 0% total contributions were, strictly speaking, impossible for any reason, then we must answer no, because we could not then meaningfully speak of an increase in the probability of such an occurrence. This would be the case, for example, if there existed some yet unidentified psychological law that caused each participant to contribute at least a single resource. Of course, we have no reason to believe such a law actually exists, nor that anything else stands in the way of the in-principle possibility of the predicted occurrence. Indeed, taking the strong free rider hypothesis seriously seems to require taking this to be a possible, however unlikely, outcome. This being the case, it might be reasonably claimed that the reduction of contributions caused by dissemination in our example increased the probability of the predicted outcome and, thus, that the prediction was indeed weakly reflexive.

However, the degree to which probability is increased in such a case is marginal at best. Although we can't exclude the possibility in principle, we feel quite justified in assigning a vanishingly small probability to an outcome in which *all* participants, including those in the 'uninformed' condition, will fail to contribute *any* resources whatsoever. Such a result would fly in the face both of the actual results of Marwell and Ames' experiments and our experiences with human subjects more generally. Because the probability of the predicted outcome of 0% total contributions depends strongly on the probability that the uninformed group will contribute nothing, the fact that the latter is vanishingly small means the former is as well.

This is the case no matter how strongly dissemination might influence the behavior of the informed group. Even if the effect were so strong as to *guarantee* a complete lack of contributions from the informed group, the probability of the predicted event itself would still remain vanishingly small, we feel, even if marginally increased by dissemination. Because the probabilistic account measures the strength of reflexive predictions according to the degree of increased probability their dissemination causes, it treats such cases as exemplifying only an exceedingly weak form of self-fulfillment.[27]

This judgment conflicts with what seems a quite reasonable intuition, namely that a reduction of contributions by 30% caused by dissemination of the prediction in question represents an extremely significant 'reflexive' effect. Less speculatively, it plainly contradicts the statements of social scientists who view induced self-interest via 'learning' or 'indoctrination' effects, of which our hypothetical example may be considered simply a highly compressed version, as a particularly clear, strong, and thus a paradigmatic example of scientific self-fulfillment. Thus, although Kopec's account fairs better than Buck's or Romanos' by at least encompassing cases in which the predicted occurrence *could* come about, despite not actually doing so, it may ultimately fail to adequately gauge the *strength* of the effect in such cases. Perhaps even more problematically, it seems to be entirely inapplicable in cases pertaining to states of affairs that could not, strictly speaking, come about. The following section reveals why this amounts to a further serious hurdle.

3.2.4.2 Which (types of) entity?

The second problem we encounter when attempting to apply accounts of reflexive prediction to claims of scientific self-fulfillment more generally becomes apparent when we more carefully consider which entities, exactly, are supposedly self-fulfilling according to the authors cited in the previous chapter. As already noted, it is not immediately clear if an account of self-fulfilling *predictions* can be applied to Ferraro et al.'s claims, which ostensibly concern self-fulfilling *the-*

---

[27] We again feel the pressure of content contingency at this point: were the content of the prediction in question restricted to a claim concerning just the behavior of the 'informed' group, then the strength of reflexivity would be appropriately higher. Because this is a hypothetical example, we can simply stipulate that the prediction's content is to be read as written, i.e. pertaining to the behavior of the combined group. Again, however, such judgments may be more ambiguous in real-world cases.

ories. To do so, it would first need to be shown either that accounts of reflexive prediction can be extended to cover other kinds of entities or that other self-fulfillment claims can be reformulated in terms of the correct type of prediction. I argue neither option is plausible.

Consider what is required by the first option. Let us grant for the sake of argument that a case can be made in general for such an extension of reflexive prediction. Let us furthermore assume that some solution can be found for the problem raised in the previous section, such that the truth criterion for self-fulfillment is still on the table. Granting all this, in order to apply the notion of reflexive prediction, we still must be able to identify a specific entity of which it is appropriate to claim that the dissemination thereof is sufficient to bring about (strongly reflexive) or make more probable (weakly reflexive) its truth in a strict and literal sense. This, in turn, requires the entity in question to be both truth-apt and have a clearly delineable content.

However, this may not hold for the targets of the self-fulfillment claims considered in the previous chapter. Closer examination of Ferraro et al.'s (2005) claims, for example, reveals considerable ambiguity concerning the type of entity implicated in the first place. The title and abstract of their paper suggest an exclusive concern for social scientific *theories* that may become self-fulfilling by influencing institutional designs, social norms, and expectations. Yet in describing induced self-interest, they add that "the core economic *assumption* of self-interest is a *prediction* about how people will behave, but also serves as a norm that regulates behavior" (Ferraro et al.'s 2005, 14, emphasis added). It seems there are at least three kinds of entity Ferraro et al. might claim to be self-fulfilling in the case of induced self-interest: a theory, an assumption, or a prediction.

The authors' explicit statement that the core economic assumption of self-interest upon which they place so much emphasis is 'a prediction about how people will behave' leads us to briefly consider the second option mentioned above. Can Ferraro et al.'s claims be reasonably reformulated in terms of the type of predictions discussed by scholars of reflexive prediction? It seems not. If it is to act as a 'core economic assumption,' one that "forms the foundation for other fundamental premises in economics" (2005, 11), then this 'prediction' must be understood rather more in the sense of a general description of behavioral patterns and/or motivations that account for them. This does not square well with the type of one-shot prediction concerning particular future events exclusively discussed in the reflexive prediction literature. Nor, as we will see, do the other options they discuss.

Despite their apparent emphasis on theories, Ferraro et al. seldom make reference to any *specific* theory that is supposedly self-fulfilling, but instead most often refer generically to the self-fulfillment of 'economic theory'. Furthermore, it seems difficult to identify any single theory to which they may be referring, given that the effects they posit might plausibly arise due to the influence of multiple theories of differing (and possibly even conflicting) content. Most of the studies concerning the effect of direct economic training made no attempt to establish the precise content of trainees' economic education. And even if the studies in question were designed so as to ascertain the relevant course content, it remains unclear how the influence of familiarity with each particular theory upon trainees' behavior might be disentangled.

There are notable exceptions to this generalizing tendency, such as Ghoshal and Moran's (1996) study of Williamson's specific version of transaction cost theory and MacKenzie and Millo's (2003) account of option pricing theory. However, these exceptions may indeed be exceptional. MacKenzie (2006b, 51) himself notes that specific cases of 'strong performativity' may be difficult to "identify unequivocally," admitting that the celebrated case of option theory is "probably unusual" in there being "a single, stable, canonical form of the theory: the Black–Scholes–Merton model." However, even such cases are usually presented as evidence of the larger scale self-fulfillment of microeconomic theorizing more generally, and much of the evidence cited in favor of this hypothesis does not come even close to laying out such directly perceptible pathways from specific theories to specific causal effects.

Perhaps the clearest target of Ferraro et al.'s claims is the 'core economic assumption' of self-interest itself. There are, however, three issues here. First, as already mentioned, taking Edgeworth's universalistic formulation seriously and employing the 'becoming true' or 'becoming more likely' criterion for self-fulfillment means rendering claims of *homo economicus*' self-fulfillment wildly implausible if not outright paradoxical. Intuitively, either all actions at all times are motivated by self-interest or amount to self-interested behavior, or they are not. Even a single instance of non-self-interested behavior or motivation is enough to render such a claim false for all time, and nothing can be done to make it become true or even more likely to become true.[28]

---

[28] There is an interesting question looming here concerning whether such a descriptive component of scientific theories, models, assumptions, etc. should be understood more in terms of a proposition or something more like a sentence expressing a proposition. On common accounts, it makes little sense to speak of a change in the truth value of a proposition, though it is reasonable to do so in the case of sentences, given that they can be uttered or evaluated in different contexts or, on some accounts, may even come to express different propositions over time. Even if we adopt the latter reading here, however, the fact that a single contravening example is enough to make either the 'becoming true' or the 'becoming more likely' of the claim in ques-

Second, it is often argued that this 'assumption' itself should not be conceived of as being or entailing a precise descriptive claim in the first place. Rather, it is thought to work within the realm of economic theorizing as an explicit methodological idealization. This leads many to believe that it is a mistake to consider the assumption of self-interest as a properly truth-apt entity in the first place (cf. Friedman 1953; Musgrave 1981; Mäki 2000). Once again, such a picture seemingly cannot be reconciled with the notion of becoming true or more probable presupposed by accounts of reflexive prediction.

Third, it is simply unclear exactly what reading Ferraro et al. and many of the others cited in chapter two have in mind when making their claims. The most plausible rendering might be one on which the core assumption of self-interest is taken to be an empirical generalization of a much more moderate scope than considered above. If such a thing were to be identified, perhaps it could serve as the kind of entity required by accounts of reflexive prediction. However, as already noted, Ferraro et al. offer us neither any explicit formulation other than Edgeworth's, nor any further clues concerning a single, clearly delineable, truth-apt entity of which it might be claimed that its dissemination is sufficient to bring about or make more probable its truth. In particular, it remains unclear whether their primary claim is meant to focus on the inducement of self-interest *behaviors*, *motivations*, both, or something else entirely.

Given these issues, and in light of content contingency, it might seem that our only option at this point is to conclude that many of the claims examined in the previous chapter are potentially misleading, inflationary, or otherwise inadequate because they commonly fail to identify a specific theory, model, or other entity that is supposedly self-fulfilling. However, two considerations speak against this conclusion. First, as in the case of the hypothetical bank insolvency that came one minute too late to fulfill a prophecy, it seems that focusing too intently on the 'letter' of claims concerning the self-fulfillment of *homo economicus* might cause us to miss the 'spirit' thereof. Explicit and precise identification of the relevant theoretical content seems unnecessary to comprehend the sense of surprise, interest, and worry that might accompany the discovery that formal economic training encourages people to engage in significantly more self-interested behavior than they otherwise would, or that this might have significant implications for our understanding of the science of economics. Contesting such claims on the grounds that economic theories may not, in fact,

---

tion impossible makes accounts of reflexive prediction poor candidates for presenting an even remotely plausible rendering of the claims encountered in chapter two, if they are read as concerning universalistic claims.

be self-fulfilling because their content does not match *precisely* with the states of affairs their adoption brings about seems to somehow miss the point.

Second, even though proponents of self-fulfillment claims often cite Merton's terminology and characterization of self-fulfilling prophecies, we needn't conclude that the inability to reconcile their claims with the common understanding of this concept or its more developed descendent, reflexive prediction, means the claims themselves are defective. Rather, we might conclude that these are simply not the best concepts with which to interpret them. Of course, it would be possible to attempt yet another revised definition of reflexive prediction that does away with the features that proved problematic here. However, this would take us so far afield of the original account so as to make the connection between them entirely tenuous. Furthermore, notions such as strongly and weakly reflexive predictions pick out a set of interesting phenomena that may itself constitute a more specific type of the general phenomenon that interests us.

Below, I argue we can learn from the issues facing reflexive prediction in order to develop a novel, more flexible account of scientific self-fulfillment. The notion of content contingency and the distinction between genuine self-fulfillment and illusory self-confirmation will also remain important moving forward. In fact, despite the reservations outlined here, I opt to retain the terminology of *self-fulfillment* for the account to be developed, not only because it is the most easily recognizable way of signaling the broad ideas in question, but specifically in order to draw attention to this crucial distinction. Before moving on to this, however, I first consider another candidate notion that has been steadily growing in prominence in recent years.

3.3 Performativity

As laid out in chapter one, much recent work on the issues concerning us here, especially within the sociology of economics, has latched onto the language of 'performativity'. Despite the amount of well-received empirical work and the growing popularity of the approach, however, the central notion of *performativity* itself has remained relatively unclear and contested. Of those who have offered explicit characterizations, MacKenzie (2006a) has provided one of the clearest and most widely cited. For this reason, as well as for the fact that Ferraro et al. cite MacKenzie's work favorably, I focus on his account here. I argue that, although performativity initially seems to fair better than reflexive prediction for our purposes, its suitability as a general notion of scientific self-fulfillment is ultimately debatable at best.

3.3.1 'Barnesian' performativity

At the most general level, writes MacKenzie (2006a, 16), the *performativity thesis* states that "the academic discipline of economics does not always stand outside the economy, analyzing it as an external thing; sometimes it is an intrinsic part of economic processes." More specifically, he distinguishes three types of performativity:

> "Generic" performativity: An aspect of economics (a theory, model, concept, procedure, data set, etc.) is used by participants in economic processes, regulators, etc.
>
> "Effective" performativity: The practical use of an aspect of economics has an effect on economic processes.
>
> "Barnesian" performativity: Practical use of an aspect of economics makes economic processes more like their depiction by economics. (MacKenzie 2006a, 17)

It is only the third sense that interests us here. MacKenzie (2006a, 19–20) notes that one might read 'Barnesian' performativity as simply another term for Mertonian self-fulfilling prophecy, but offers several reasons for "preferring the terminology" he uses. Interestingly, his remarks here suggest that he sees Merton's term and his own mostly as reflecting two different stances or approaches to describing one and the same phenomenon, rather than as picking out two substantially different ones.[29] However, as stated, there is a substantial difference: whereas self-fulfilling prophecy involves the bringing about of a state of affairs that makes what would otherwise have been a false prediction true, Barnesian performativity requires merely that 'processes' become 'more like their depiction' via 'practical use' of an 'aspect' of the science in question.

In the last section, we saw the need for a more flexible notion than reflexive prediction, one that does not require us to make a claim concerning effects on the actual or probable truth of a single, clearly delineable theory, model, or assumption. Reflecting explicitly on the difference between self-fulfilling prophecies and Barnesian performativity just mentioned reveals that the latter provides a better fit for claims concerning induced self-interest, at least at first glance. If we are willing to characterize the behaviors witnessed in such cases as 'econom-

---

29 MacKenzie (2006a, 19–20) presents three specific reasons for "preferring the terminology" of Barnesian performativity: first, to stress that this is a strong form of the more general phenomenon of 'generic performativity'; second, to place emphasis on forms of "incorporation" of theory that go beyond their effects of beliefs and worldviews; and finally, to avoid the "connotation of pathology" suggested by Merton's occasional suggestions that *incorrect* or *arbitrary* beliefs are 'made true' through self-fulfilling prophecy.

ic processes,' and understand the three causal mechanisms described by Ferraro et al. as being implemented through 'practical use' of their 'depiction' by economic theory, understood in a fairly loose sense, then performativity seems to largely avoid the traits that rendered the concept of reflexive prediction problematic for our purposes. It may seem to be enough to say, in this case, that widespread practical use of economic depictions of self-interest in economic training, managerial practices, and so on, has, on the whole, made some actual economic behavioral patterns 'more like' the depictions themselves.

3.3.2 Scientific self-fulfillment as performativity?

Although Barnesian performativity seems intuitively to avoid the specific failings of reflexive prediction, there are other good reasons to rethink the recent growing trend of framing debates concerning scientific self-fulfillment and its possible philosophical significance primarily in such terms. If the performativity approach provides a notion that seems apt to understand such claims, it does so at the cost of also introducing a good deal of conceptual ambiguity and distracting theoretical baggage.

While we were looking for a looser notion, performativity as defined by MacKenzie is *too* loose. Without further spelling out of such key notions such as *depiction* and *making processes more like* their depictions, this characterization seems to be little more than a slightly rephrased repetition of the preliminary characterization of scientific self-fulfillment we began with: the notion that science somehow 'brings the world more in line' with itself.

Unfortunately, performativity researchers offer us little in the way of further explication of these central notions. This is perhaps understandable, given that their interests lie primarily in constructing detailed historical and sociological case studies of real-world cotemporaneous developments of (economic) theory and reality. For such purposes, it may be enough simply to provide evidence of an effect's having occurred, even if the exact nature of the effect itself remains somewhat obscure. However, such obscurity obviously calls the notion's suitability for a general account of scientific self-fulfillment into question.

More problematic is that such accounts are often not merely conceptually underdeveloped but even positively misleading concerning the real nature of the intended claims. Most fatal in this regard is a failure to clearly distinguish between broadly 'causal' and 'constitutive' readings. Mäki (2013) argues that by co-opting the language of performativity from Austin, MacKenzie and other performativity scholars imply that the posited relationship between economic theory and reality is a constitutive one. Just as uttering 'I promise to...' under the proper circumstances does not simply cause a promise to come about, but rather establishes its existence constitutively, a constitutive relationship in economics "would require that uttering or writing down an economic model for an audience (that understands the model and perceives the uttering as genuine and done in appropriate circumstances) establishes the model world as part of the real world" (Mäki 2013, 447). Because the connection between economic theory and reality envisioned by performativity scholars requires 'practical use' that goes far beyond simple uttering, Mäki argues, their claims should be understood to refer to causal rather than constitutive processes.

We should be somewhat weary of Mäki's easy linking of constitutive relations and the act of uttering in particular. Some scholars have indeed placed a premium on the role of language. Most prominently, Austin's student John Searle (1995, 32–34) famously holds that a whole slew of things, from "money, [...] elections, private property, wars, voting, promises, marriages, buying and selling, political offices, and so on," depend upon human institutions and collective intentional attitudes for their very existence, and that "a very large number" of these so-called 'institutional facts,' "though by no means all of them, can be created by explicit performative utterances." Later, Searle (2010, 11) significantly strengthens the role of language in his account, proclaiming that "all institutional facts, and therefore all status functions, are created by speech acts of a type that in 1975 I baptized as 'Declarations'." Other scholars, however, have increasingly called such an extreme focus on the role of language, conceptual practices, and intentional states into question. These authors emphasize the role of 'material' and other non-linguistic practices in the social (constitutive) construction of social roles, kinds of people, race, gender, and a host of other things (cf. Hacking 1999; Haslanger 2012; Mallon 2019 for relevant discussions). Thus, the mere fact that performativity scholars often focus on processes that are not exclusively or primarily linguistic in nature, for example the influence of economic theorizing on institutional design, should not be taken as ruling out the possibility that their claims refer to relations of constitutive construction.

Despite this caveat, however, Mäki's central point still stands. Once we have been made aware of the distinction between causal and constitutive effects or relations, it seems rather clear that the claims examined in chapter two are better understood in terms of the former.[30] A thematically relevant claim in terms of a

---

[30] In fact, scientific self-fulfillment as it is considered in this work usually entails that an object of scientific scrutiny is subject to a form of causal social construction termed *discursive construction* by Haslanger (2012, 88): "Something is discursively constructed just in case it is the way it is, to some substantial extent, because of what is attributed (and/or self-attributed) to it." Because of this, many of the philosophical issues raised in connection with causal and/or discur-

constitutive relation might be that some behaviors are 'self-interested' only in virtue of having been defined as such by economic theory, where 'defining' is understood as something closely related to the kind of performative speech act described by Austin or Searle. This would amount to a claim concerning the constitutive construction of *self-interestedness* that might make an interesting subject of consideration on its own terms. However, Ferraro et al. and their kin make no claims of this sort, nor is it at all obvious how the evidence they cite could be brought to bear on them. Rather, these authors argue that the adoption of economic theory brings about an increased incidence of self-interested behavior or motivation through various *causal* mechanisms. These mechanisms may often work through or even require language for their effectivity. But it is neither claimed nor, I think, particularly cogent, that 'uttering' or otherwise 'using' theories of *homo economicus* under the right circumstances constitutively brings about induced self-interest in a manner similar to the performative creation of promises or the ascription of 'being money' to slips of colored paper through collective intentionality.

Because of their failure to explicitly distinguish between causal and constitutive claims, accounts of performativity are sometimes associated with strong forms of scientific anti-realism about economics or the objects it depicts. This has tended to direct what little philosophical attention has been paid to the phenomenon of induced self-interest toward its possible significance to debates concerning scientific realism. Unfortunately, this narrow focus has resulted in the overshadowing of other legitimate, and possibly more fruitful, approaches to examining questions of significance.

As in the case of 'reflexivity,' 'performativity' is used by many different authors to mean many different things, and a theoretical account capable of clarifying and demystifying this notion and the phenomena it purportedly refers to has yet to emerge. In fact, given the lack of a clear theoretical framework, it may be wiser to view performativity as a research program held together by a shared set of historical and sociological interests and methodological strictures, rather than as an explicit account or thesis. And even if a general account of perform-

---

sive construction are likely relevant to cases of scientific self-fulfillment as well. In general, there has been a tendency among recent constructionist scholars to ignore or downplay the significance of causal forms of social construction in favor of constitutive forms (cf. Díaz-León 2013; 2018). However, this neglect has recently begun to be challenged for a number of reasons; among other things, it is argued that any case of constitutive construction in fact entails causal construction as well (cf. Marques 2017). Although the connection between scientific self-fulfillment and causal construction offers many interesting matters for consideration, further discussion thereof goes beyond the scope of this work.

ativity were to be developed that clears up the conceptual ambiguities and conflation, I claim that the connotations called up in association with the term tend to be so damaging to understanding the significance of scientific self-fulfillment that it should be largely abandoned for the description of cases such as the purported self-fulfillment of *homo economicus*. This argument is developed more thoroughly in chapter five.

3.4 A new conceptualization

Although each was ultimately argued to be ill-suited to our task, we can still learn something from the approaches discussed above. Reflexive prediction, building on Merton's account of self-fulfilling prophecies, makes explicit and highlights the counterfactual nature of claims concerning induced self-interest. In the cases that have interested social scientists, it seems that, had dissemination of a scientific prediction or theory not taken place, then some state of affairs standing in the right kind of relation to it would have failed to or been less likely to obtain. However, such accounts seem to have difficulty providing a suitable criterion with which to gauge the presence or strength of scientific self-fulfillment in the case of *homo economicus* because they presuppose such claims to concern a clearly delineable, truth-apt scientific entity that seems difficult to reconcile with the statements and evidence offered by Ferraro et al. and others.

Barnesian performativity, on the other hand, apparently avoids this issue by requiring only the 'making' of some part of reality to be 'more like' its 'depiction' by science through 'practical use' of some 'aspect' of that science. Intuitively, this description seems a better fit for the relevant claims; however, I have argued that this is achieved only at the cost of failing to further elucidate key terms and encouraging a misleading conception of the philosophical significance of such phenomena.

In the remainder of this chapter, I develop a novel account that builds on the respective strengths of these previous attempts by spelling out in more detail the nature of the various components hinted at in MacKenzie's formulation of Barnesian performativity without thereby leading us into the problems encountered above. I begin by elucidating the required understanding of the relevant notions of 'aspects of science,' 'practical use,' and 'more like,' respectively. Then, I show how the resulting characterization can be applied to make sense of Ferraro et al.'s and others' claims concerning induced self-interest and *homo economicus*.

3.4.1 'Aspects of science' as scientific representations

We have already considered what type(s) of entity might be implicated in the self-fulfillment claims surrounding *homo economicus*. Let us now examine the nature of entities to which self-fulfillment in the relevant sense may be properly ascribed more generally. On the surface, accounts of self-fulfilling prophecy and reflexive prediction are restricted to claims concerning *predictions*, roughly understood as statements describing future states of affairs. MacKenzie's (2016a, 17) account of Barnesian performativity, on the other hand, is apparently much more permissive, allowing that a relevant 'aspect' of science could be "a theory, model, concept, procedure, data set, etc." (It is unclear whether or not predictions might feature among the 'etc.' here.)

MacKenzie's approach seems intuitively more well-suited to capturing Ferraro et al.'s claims, which refer most saliently to theories, models, and assumptions. Moreover, it is no great stretch of the imagination to suppose that other 'aspects,' such as statements, diagrams, or even aphorisms are implicated in the mechanisms of induced self-interest they identify. Although this approach seems to expand our options for ascription of self-fulfillment, however, MacKenzie has little else to say about the nature of these 'aspects'. But we shouldn't be tempted to leave things at this level of generality as overcompensation for the perceived narrowness of reflexive prediction. What else can be said about the entities to which self-fulfillment might be reasonably ascribed?

Sociologists of science – both those interested in scientific self-fulfillment and others – are often ambivalent concerning science's status as a genuinely epistemic endeavor. One might be forgiven, therefore, for wondering if MacKenzie's choice of the terms 'aspects of economics' and 'depiction' amounts to a tacit strategic avoidance of more epistemically loaded terms such as 'representation' or 'reference'. We might be similarly tempted to move in this direction because certain plausible readings of self-fulfillment claims concerning *homo economicus* may require us to understand their targets as kinds of entities difficult to evaluate according to their (possible) truth: e.g. as non-truth-apt idealizations or conglomerates of varied and possibly mutually inconsistent theories, models, etc. that make up a more generalized 'economic theory'. However, an account of self-fulfillment that does away with or is ambivalent about the epistemic dimension of the entities in question will not do.

At the outset of the chapter, I laid out two possible understandings of the central notion at the heart of self-fulfilling prophecy-like phenomena – *genuine self-fulfillment* and *illusory self-confirmation*. It should be clear that either understanding presupposes that any entity claimed to be 'self-fulfilling' must be properly subject to evaluations concerning the 'fit' between the (content of the) entity in question and some state of affairs in the world. 'Fulfillment' in the sense of genuine self-fulfillment denotes a kind of success with regards to this fit; 'illusory confirmation' entails a (masked) lack thereof. Success of fit in predictions, understood as statements that describe future states of affairs, is often thought to be most properly evaluated using semantic notions such as truth. The same might be thought to hold for theories, which, according to what is variously called the 'classical,' 'received,' or 'syntactic' view in philosophy of science, are best understood as "sets of sentences in a given logical domain language" (Winther 2016). Unfortunately, we have already seen the issues that arise when attempting to cash out this notion of fit in terms of (probable) truth in the case of scientific self-fulfillment.

In recent years, however, many philosophers of science have become increasingly convinced of the importance of kinds of representation in science that do not amount to (linguistic) description (Suárez 2016). In particular, it is now often argued that *models*, rather than theories, are the primary representational units of science (Frigg and Nguyen 2016). This is interesting in light of the issues encountered above, given that models are also typically thought to exhibit features that render evaluations of successful content-world fit in terms of truth problematic. For example, models often include idealizing assumptions that are known to be false, and yet are nevertheless judged to be in some sense 'accurate' representations. Furthermore, even though models are given pride of place in recent accounts of scientific representation, there is also increasing recognition of the importance of other (linguistic or non-linguistic) forms of representation besides models and theories. Frigg and Nguyen (2016, 2) note that scientific representations are "a heterogeneous group comprising anything from thermometer readings and flow charts to verbal descriptions, photographs, X-ray pictures, digital imagery, equations, models, and theories."

There are a number of general problems that arise from the new literature on scientific representation, which are helpfully summarized by Frigg and Nguyen (2016). First is the question of how scientific representations are to be *defined*, which has typically been understood as the attempt to provide an answer to the question of "what fills in the blank in 'S is a scientific representation of T iff___', where 'S' stands for the object doing the representing and 'T' for 'target system', the aspect of the world the representation is about" (Frigg and Nguyen 2016, 4; cf. also Suárez 2016 for more on the relevant notions of 'sources' and 'targets'). Closely related to this is the question of whether or not *scientific* representations can be successfully demarcated from non-scientific or otherwise epistemic ones.

Although no single account enjoys wide consensus support, many accept that any successful theory of scientific representation must account for a number of specific features. First, the possibility of *misrepresentation* should be given. If some *S* fails to accurately represent *T*, then it should emerge as a misrepresentation rather than a non-representation. This condition holds even, it is sometimes argued, when target systems turn out not to exist, such as in the case of phlogiston (cf. Frigg and Nguyen 2016, 6). Second, the *directionality* of representation must be accounted for. Representations in general tend to be about their targets without the converse holding as well – a postcard of the Eiffel Tower represents the tower, but the tower does not represent the postcard (cf. Goodman 1976). Finally, and perhaps most crucially, a theory of scientific representation must provide us with some understanding of the possibility and success of *surrogative reasoning*, the process of manipulating, considering, and employing models and other representations in order to learn about and yield claims concerning their target systems (cf. Swoyer 1991).

Aside from these issues, taking seriously the idea that very different things (from brain scans, to ball-on-stick models, to mathematical equations) are genuine scientific representations (rather than e.g. merely heuristic devices for developing or supporting them) requires acknowledging that there are likely to be various (ontological) *kinds of entities* that may represent target systems in various *styles of representation* with differing *standards of accuracy* (cf. Frigg and Nguyen 2016, 8–9).

Despite the many complex issues yet to be worked out in this burgeoning literature, we can use the suggested general notion of *scientific representation* to orientate our thinking concerning the types of entity to which self-fulfillment might be ascribed. Apart from the independent reasons they provide for taking the role of representations other than theories seriously, such accounts also show us that evaluations of success concerning content-world fit needn't necessarily be cashed out in terms of truth. We'll examine the question of standards of accuracy in more detail below. Beyond this, however, there seems to be little need to further specify or qualify the kinds of entities that may feature in claims of scientific self-fulfillment beyond the considerations just presented. This is because the intuitive starting point for our inquiry was simply the usually ignored observation that some measure of science's (apparent) epistemic success could be the result of changes in the world caused by our theorizing about it. And all this presupposes is a general conception of epistemic success of science that is at least partially co-constituted by the right type of content-world relation, which recent accounts of scientific representation attempt to account for in the form of 'accuracy' that goes beyond semantic notions like truth.

Adopting this perspective still leaves considerable room for debate concerning whether any specific (type of) entity implicated in self-fulfillment claims in fact qualifies as a scientific representation. One might doubt that some of Mac-

Kenzie's 'aspects,' such as 'procedures,' may be sensibly judged on the relevant notion of accuracy. The same might apply, given certain answers to the questions outlined above, to the non-truth-apt idealizations and conglomerates of 'theory' that may be targets of self-fulfillment claims. But this needn't be understood as a problem for the development of an account of self-fulfillment capable of rendering such claims cogent; here we are merely elucidating the terms of the debate. If it happens that such 'non-standard' entities are implicated in these claims, and one rejects the idea that these types of entities fulfill the criteria outlined here, then one must conclude that the claims are misguided or express something about a phenomenon other than scientific self-fulfillment.

Before moving on, one further important qualification must yet be considered. We began this chapter with a consideration of self-fulfilling prophecies and reflexive predictions – but where do *predictions* figure in the new philosophical literature on scientific representation? Perhaps surprisingly, although we may intuitively consider predictions to be a specific type of scientific representation, they are not usually considered as such in the accounts introduced above. Instead, if they are mentioned at all,[31] they are typically presented as one type of conclusion that may be drawn concerning target systems through use of surrogative reasoning (cf. Swoyer 1991). This suggests that the relationship between scientific representations and predictions is conceived of in a similar manner to that between theories and predictions on more traditional views, in which the former are used in order to derive or otherwise produce the latter and, very often, in which observation of the predicted state of affairs is then taken as offering some measure of empirical support for the theory or model in question (cf. McMullin 1984, 48–51).

Even aside from the implicit support for such a distinction found in the literature, we have a very good reason for considering predictions separately from other types of representations. Distinguishing the two may aid us in clearly separating a number of otherwise potentially ambiguous claims concerning self-fulfillment. Recall that the two examples discussed in Merton's original paper – bank runs and union segregation – seemed to suggest two conflicting readings of 'self-fulfillment'. The hypothetical bank run is a case of what I've called genuine self-fulfillment, in which a prediction's dissemination leads to a state of affairs that renders it true. White unionists' conviction of black workers' anti-union dispositions, on the other hand, illustrates what I've termed illusory self-confirmation. Assuming the belief in question includes imputation of a *natural* tenden-

---

[31] Frigg and Nguyen's (2016) overview article in the *Stanford Encyclopedia of Philosophy*, for example, does not explicitly mention 'predictions' or 'predicting' at all.

cy to engage in strikebreaking and other such activities, Merton must be understood as arguing that the working of this belief brought about a state of affairs in which the original belief merely *appeared* true, despite actually being false.

Supplementing the distinction between genuine self-fulfillment and illusory self-confirmation by a further distinction between self-fulfilling *predictions* versus other types of self-fulfilling *representations* can help us present a more coherent picture of the latter case. A general belief that a certain group of people have a natural tendency to engage in certain types of behavior can be used to generate specific predictions concerning expected behavior in particular situations. Some of these predictions may be self-fulfilling. A prediction of imminent strikebreaking might lead to distrust, acrimonious exchanges, feelings of inevitability, and other effects that in fact precipitate the carrying out of such behaviors when they would otherwise not occur.

However, even if a representation generates self-fulfilling predictions, this does not entail that the representation itself is equally self-fulfilling. The mere fact that a genuinely self-fulfilling prediction of anti-union behavior may be generated via surrogative reasoning carried out on a 'model' of some group as possessing a natural tendency toward such behavior is not enough to make the latter genuinely self-fulfilling as well. In Merton's telling, as in real life, the original belief in question was, is, and remains straightforwardly false.[32] Indeed, the issuing of self-fulfilling predictions may be a powerful mechanism whereby representations generate or maintain their own illusory self-confirmation. Each particular case in which black workers engage in strikebreaking, though perhaps precipitated by a lack of alternative opportunities brought about by predictions made on the basis of the original (false) belief, might be construed as evidence of its truth. Explicitly distinguishing the belief from the predictions it may generate alleviates much of the ambiguity felt in our initial analysis. And this, in turn, gives us a much clearer understanding of Merton's (1948, 195–196) statements concerning the "reign of error" resulting from the "specious validity" of self-fulfilling prophecies in such cases:

> As a result of their failure to comprehend the operation of the self-fulfilling prophecy, many Americans of good will are (sometimes reluctantly) brought to retain enduring ethnic and racial prejudices. They experience these beliefs, not as prejudices, not as prejudgments, but

---

[32] Whether or not such a belief turns out to be self-fulfilling based on some standard of accuracy other than truth or falsity is, admittedly, less straightforward. In any case, this line of argument supports the notion that the strength of self-fulfillment observed in a prediction generated by some representation cannot be simply 'carried over' to the representation itself.

as irresistible products of their own observation. "The facts of the case" permit them no other conclusion.

As we will see, a quite similar story may be told concerning economic theorizing and *homo economicus*. These issues are taken up in more detail in chapter six.

3.4.2 'Practical use' as content-responsive action

If the entities that may be implicated in claims of self-fulfillment are understood in terms of scientific representations as outlined in the previous section, what might their 'practical use' amount to? Common to the perspectives discussed in this chapter is recognition of the fact that it is not scientific representations *themselves*, but rather the things that are done with them, we might say, that lead to the causal effects that interest us. For those who explicitly treat such representations as abstract entities, such as Kopec (2011, 1251), this is obvious, for abstract entities are usually understood to lack causal powers. But even for those who take a much more concrete view, understanding representations as being (constituted by) things such as certain mental states of scientists, computer models, textbook diagrams, and the like, it seems the effects we are concerned with are typically the results of causal chains that essentially include or rely upon scientific representations, without it being the case that the representations themselves perform the bulk of the causal work.

Despite apparent agreement on this point, the exact nature of the 'things done with representations' is not immediately clear. Consider the different associations awakened by reflexive prediction scholars' preferred language of 'formulation' and 'dissemination' compared to those suggested by MacKenzie's 'practical use'. The former stress the fact and manner of making the content of some scientific representation public, whereas the latter emphasizes some kind of action going beyond this, such as the incorporation of the content into technological devices. Both sets of associations seem to find their place among Ferraro et al.'s claims. The mechanism of self-fulfillment through *language* or conceptual schemes might most directly imply use of the relevant representation in the sense of formulation/dissemination. Self-fulfillment via *institutional design*, on the other hand, likely includes types of incorporation that go beyond making the content in question publicly available.

A bit of reflection reveals, however, that this distinction captures more a difference of focus than anything else. The identified effects of language would likely be far weaker, if not entirely absent, if they carried no further consequences of a more concrete nature. It is not simply because workers are *told* they are being conceptualized as 'market commodities' rather than 'family members' that they are led to adapt their behavior; rather, it is the knowledge of what practical consequences such characterizations entail. Conversely, institutional design based on economic theory would be impossible were the latter not formulated and/or disseminated in some form, and it is easy to imagine that the exact nature of some institutional design could differ were the style of formulation and/or dissemination significantly altered. In any case, the claims examined in chapter two do not seem to suppose that either of these notions of 'use' is inherently more important than the other for scientific self-fulfillment, and certainly offer us no reason to restrict a general account to either kind.

A subtler and, for our purposes, more significant distinction emerges from the debate between Buck and Romanos concerning the former's acting-on-beliefs model of reflexive prediction. Recall that Buck's (1963, 360–362) definition included necessary conditions stating that the causal effect of dissemination must be "mediated by the formation of beliefs on the part of the various actors on the social scene, and by their behaving in a way which can be reasonably described as 'acting on' those beliefs," and that, furthermore, the mediating beliefs must include a belief in the truth of the prediction. Recall also that Romanos criticizes these restrictions because they are motivated only by an observation that certain standard examples of reflexive prediction seem to conform to them. Treating these restrictions as necessary conditions thus, he argues, problematically rules out the possibility of non-standard examples that do not include such mediating beliefs.

Romanos is correct that Buck's arguments for the acting-on-beliefs restrictions are problematic. However, in developing an account that attempts to do away entirely with some restriction of this kind, Romanos goes too far. Recall that on the standard account only one condition must be met for a prediction to be reflexive: "the formulation/dissemination style of the prediction must be a causal factor relative to the prediction's coming out true or false" (Romanos 1973, 106). This indeed avoids Buck's undermotivated restrictions. But trouble arises when we consider Romanos' notions of formulation and dissemination, which are not restricted to natural language, but rather may consist of "electric impulses, bodily movements, puffs of smoke, or *anything else which may be interpreted as expressing a prediction*" (Romanos 1973, 105, emphasis added). Owing to the ambiguity of the phrase 'may be interpreted as expressing a prediction', I argue that Romanos' account may be read as suggesting an overly broad account of 'practical use'.

To see this, consider the following fanciful, yet instructive, situation. A train passenger is asked to play a game in which they are to make a prediction concerning whether or not the train will stop within the next minute. The prediction is to be expressed by pressing one of two buttons, one labelled 'The train will stop within the next minute,' the other 'The train will not stop within the next minute.' The passenger presses the 'will stop' button, and lo, the train promptly halts. It seems the passenger has predicted correctly. Unbeknownst to onlookers, however, are two important facts. First, the passenger is illiterate and only pressed a button in order to avoid the embarrassment of revealing this fact. Second, the 'stop' button was in fact a trigger for the train's emergency braking system. Supposing that the passenger's pressing of the button 'may be interpreted as expressing a prediction', this prediction ends up being self-fulfilling on Romanos' definition, given that the manner of its 'dissemination' was a causal factor in bringing about the predicted event.

However, this seems problematic. In this case, it is *merely* the electromechanical act of pressing the button that sets the relevant causal chain in motion. Given the passenger's illiteracy, the buttons' labelling had no real influence on which button was pressed. The content of the representational entity itself is nothing more than an inert accessory to the action here. This being the case, it would be misleading to claim that the 'prediction' *qua prediction* had anything to do with its own fulfillment. What the situation demonstrates, it seems, is simply the arbitrary nature of symbolic expression: any action may be, in the proper circumstances, interpretable as expressing any arbitrary prediction or other representation. But when the consequences of such an action only *happen to* align with the represented state of affairs, where the content itself has no influence on the performance of the action or the subsequent causal chain resulting from it, there is no reflexive prediction but rather mere coincidence.

Romanos might object that the button pressing is in fact not interpretable as expressing a prediction in the first place, perhaps on the grounds that the passenger lacks a proper understanding and intention required to elevate the physical action to an act of dissemination. However, this plays into Buck's hands by requiring the introduction of mediating beliefs into the causal chain. Perhaps another justification can be offered for refusing this action the status of 'prediction expressing'. But without a clearer notion of what Romanos means by the locution 'may be interpreted as expressing a prediction,' it is difficult to state what this might be. In any case, the above discussion shows that we should avoid any ambiguity on the matter, and must explicitly include some restriction in our concept of 'practical use' that ensures that self-fulfillment is the result of representations' content and not *merely* what is 'done with them'.

Of course, this is entailed by the acting-on-beliefs account: by treating mediating beliefs in the truth of a prediction as a necessary component of the causal chain leading to its self-fulfillment, Buck ensures that content is not merely incidental. However, bringing the discussion back to Ferraro et al.'s proposed mechanisms of self-fulfillment reveals the acting-on-beliefs conditions to be too strong to include as a necessary condition of self-fulfillment.

For one, there is a lack of clarity concerning the nature and scope of the "social actors involved" who on Buck's (1963, 361–362) account must hold a causally efficacious belief in the truth of the representation in question.[33] If we require the holding of such beliefs on the part of *all* or even most of the 'relevant social actors' involved, then many of the cases we have been considering will fail to qualify. As already pointed out, in cases of economic theory's influence on institutional design, it is very unlikely that the majority of those whose behavior is influenced and is most directly relevant to the accuracy of the representations in question are even aware of the representations or their content. At the other extreme, if we require only a *single* belief-mediated action in the causal chain, we open the door to strange 'butterfly effect' scenarios, in which an initial belief-mediated action leads to a long chain of further events that ultimately culminate in the represented state of affairs but are themselves no longer connected in any significant manner to the content of the representation in question.

A more serious issue is that by requiring a belief in the *truth* of the representation itself, the acting-on-beliefs account presupposes that relevant social actors are not only aware of the existence of some representation, but also have a good grasp of and adopt a specific cognitive attitude toward its content. This rules out, among others, cases in which action is undertaken on the basis of partial or flawed understanding of a representation, or on more circumspect cognitive attitudes than outright belief in its truth. However, this is precisely the kind of 'use' we might expect to find when it comes to the ways in which non-scientists, in particular, act upon their (mis)understanding of complex scientific representations. Managers' decisions to implement performance-based pay or other extrinsic rewards for desired behavior are quite plausibly not grounded in deep understanding of and conviction in the truth of economic theories, but rather in reaction to the general impression gleaned from their business school studies.

So, although some restriction is required such that the content of purportedly self-fulfilling representations cannot be entirely superfluous, Buck's acting-on-belief conditions rule out some of the mechanisms by which self-fulfillment might plausibly be enacted, Ferraro et al.'s included. In light of these arguments, it seems that the influence of scientific representations should be restricted neither to actions performed on the basis of belief that their specific content is true

---

[33] One can retain an acting-on-beliefs requirement formulated in terms of truth despite having abandoned truth as a criterion of self-fulfillment itself. The former is a suggested restriction on the kinds of causal chains that may bring about self-fulfillment, whereas the latter concerns the relevant type of content-world relation that must in fact hold in cases thereof.

nor to their 'implementation' in technological or other practical applications. Instead, I propose that we think of this influence in terms of *content-responsive action*, where an action is considered content-responsive if its performance is a consequence of an agent's understanding of the content of some scientific representation. In order for a representation to count as *self*-fulfilling, changes brought about in its target system must be mediated to a significant degree by content-responsive actions.

Note that the relevant notion of 'understanding' at stake here is meant to imply only a very minimal degree of successful comprehension. Saying that an action is content-*responsive* requires that the acting agent is not *entirely* confused concerning the nature of the content in question. Actions undertaken by one who mistakenly interprets *On the Origin of Species* as a thinly-veiled account of alien abductions in Victorian England are not content-responsive to evolutionary theory. However, as already pointed out, if we are to capture many cases in which representational content intuitively seems to play an important role in the relevant causal chains, we must allow for a good deal of leniency concerning partial or even mistaken understandings. Someone who interprets the central tenet of microeconomic theory to be that all actions by all agents at all times are motivated only by self-interest may be mistaken in this understanding, but actions undertaken on the basis of this misunderstanding would yet rightfully be considered content-responsive.

It might be argued that content-responsiveness as described above is too broad a notion to pick out paradigmatic cases of self-fulfilling science.[34] Consider the following hypothetical situation. An economic model claimed by its proponents to show, among other things, that studying economics tends to make people happier is targeted by a group of rival economists, who publish a satirical article about it, hoping to convince readers of the model's flaws by force of wit as much as argument. If the article is witty enough, it might be shared widely among university economists and their students and could perhaps even come to contribute significantly to their happiness. In this case, it would seem that the postulation of the original representation has led to some degree of self-fulfillment through content-responsive actions. After all, the skeptical satirists wrote and published their article specifically because they took issue with (part of) the content of the original representation. Thus, on this account of content-responsiveness, and in direct contrast to the conditions that made up part of Buck's acting-on-beliefs account, even actions undertaken on the basis of explic-

---

34 My thanks to Torsten Wilholt for helpfully formulating this critique and the following example used to support it.

it *disbelief* in the truth or accuracy of a given representation may make up part of the causal chains leading to its self-fulfillment.

Does this overextend the notion of self-fulfillment? In any case, we can readily admit that the above does not represent what we think of as a paradigmatic action leading to self-fulfillment. Even if such actions don't necessarily involve a belief in the *truth* of a representation (and all that entails), they are at least usually grounded in some attitude of assent towards the representation's aptness, even if the assent may be tentative and the understanding partial. Noting this, should we then include such a restriction in the definition of content-responsiveness and thus self-fulfillment itself?

Consider another possible example of a self-fulfillment effect seemingly based in disbelief rather than an attitude of assent. In recent years, occasional acts of purposeful, conspicuous environmental pollution have been carried out by groups of climate change skeptics, ostensibly in protest against what are perceived as exaggerated scientific accounts of anthropogenic climate change. One such form of protest can be seen in the recent trend of so-called 'rolling coal' in the United States: a small, yet vocal group of pickup truck owners have garnered notoriety for modifying their diesel engines to spew out large, billowing clouds of black smoke at the flick of a switch. National news stories relate how pedestrians, cyclists, drivers of electric-hybrid cars, and environmental activists are purposefully 'smoked out' by 'coal-rollers,' at times with the stated aim of taking "a stand against rampant environmentalism" (Tabuchi 2016). While the true motivations of the 'rollers' are likely complex, it appears their actions are in no small part a response to their (likely limited) understanding *and rejection* of scientific accounts of the role of human action in causing climate change. And, although the total increased contribution to carbon emissions brought about in response to disbelief in this case are, on the whole, negligible, we could imagine this to be just one example of a broader class of anti-environmental-science protest actions that could, at least in theory, result in a higher relative contribution of human factors to climate change than might otherwise exist.

In pondering the question of whether or not the concept of content-responsiveness should be restricted to cases including attitudes of assent, it would do well to recall Romanos' reply to Buck's proposed restrictions: if we are to include such a condition on the basis that it seems to be met in paradigmatic cases of scientific self-fulfillment, then we are essentially stipulating that non-paradigmatic cases do not exist. Thus, the effect at work in the example above and others like it would not, given the proposed condition, be sensibly or helpfully described in terms of 'scientific self-fulfillment'.

However, I don't believe that a general pronouncement of this sort is warranted. One of the central motivations for identifying cases of self-fulfillment has always been to point out unexpected and idiosyncratic (causal) connections between a representation and the states of affairs it depicts. By making at least partial understanding of the content of a representation a necessary condition for content-responsiveness, we've already assured that such connections are indeed due to the content of the representation and not merely its method of dissemination. In the example just described, such a connection between representational content and the resulting state of affairs is postulated to exist, albeit only to a minor degree in the grand scheme of things. Furthermore, this particular connection is certainly unexpected and idiosyncratic in nature, and these facts make it seem especially worthwhile to point out and consider. Focusing on these similarities between effects based in either assent or disbelief, I suggest it would be better to admit the latter as a non-paradigmatic type of self-fulfillment that is of particular interest specifically because of the way it differs from more standard examples. It is still quite possible to come to the conclusion that the framework of self-fulfillment does little to illuminate any particular non-paradigmatic case, but I see little reason to preempt such considerations by defining them out of the picture from the start.

More generally, just as it doesn't attempt to preempt discussion concerning non-paradigmatic cases, this account also does not try to provide explicit guidance on the question of 'how much' of a given causal chain must be made up of content-responsive actions in order for the stated condition of 'mediation to a significant degree' to be met. In a sense, we are faced here with a problem similar to that faced by Buck's account. Requiring that *all* actions in a given causal chain be content-responsive results in very few, if any, cases of self-fulfillment; requiring only *one* such action opens the door to butterfly effects. However, there are cases in which we intuitively feel that the condition in question is clearly met or not. Beyond this, if there is any criterion to be unearthed whereby edge cases lying between these poles may be clearly distinguished, I am unaware of it.

There are several reactions one could have in response to this issue. One could: completely ignore it, as Buck does; continue to search for the principled distinction that eludes me here; or explicitly acknowledge it as a problem that may arise in discussions of specific purported cases of scientific self-fulfillment, but leave its resolution to the discussants. I adopt the latter position here. Of course, this once again means leaving room for disagreement concerning whether or not the cases discussed in chapter two qualify as scientific self-fulfillment. Some may, in particular, be unconvinced by the arguments presented above and believe that Buck's acting-on-beliefs account provides the only reasonable manner of cashing out the relevant notion of 'use'. If this is the case, it would have to be concluded that many if not most of the representations discussed by Ferraro et al. are unlikely to qualify as self-fulfilling. Buck's justification for this restriction was based on the claim that a selected set of 'standard examples' displays such features. However, in the newer literature, the phenomena examined by Ferraro et al. and performativity scholars are considered paradigmatic cases of self-fulfillment, and many of these clearly do not qualify on the acting-on-beliefs model – perhaps we now have a wider pool of standard examples than Buck once did.

3.4.3 'More like' as increased conformation

Our investigation began with the intriguing suggestion that the mechanisms of self-correction usually thought to account for the special epistemic success of science could be complemented by one in which it is not our scientific representations, but rather the parts of the world they target, that undergo modification. The basic conception considered presupposes that, in order for some representation to be self-fulfilling, it must be properly subject to evaluations of success concerning the 'fit' of its content to a target system. I've argued at length that the truth criterion of reflexive prediction is ill-suited to capture the kind of fit implicated in what are now considered by many to be paradigmatic claims of scientific self-fulfillment. MacKenzie's account, on the other hand, refers simply to economic processes' becoming 'more like' their depiction by economic science, but does not further elucidate the notion of 'likeness' employed. Can we identify a kind of content-world relation that avoids the narrowness of reflexive prediction while providing more detail than Barnesian performativity?

As already noted, the recent literature on scientific representations takes seriously the notion that different kinds of representations employ different types of accuracy standards. Much discussion has been dedicated to exploring specific contenders for the relevant notion of content-world fit, most prominently *similarity* (cf. Giere 2004) and various forms of (structural) *morphism* (cf. Bartels 2006; Ubbink 1960). According to the former accounts, entities, both scientific and otherwise, represent their target systems in virtue of being similar to them, where similarity is typically conceived of in terms of the sharing of (relevant) properties to some (relevant) degree. This raises problems, however, including some of those discussed previously: similarity in terms of shared properties does not seem to capture the directionality of representation and seems to make non-representations, rather than misrepresentations, out of entities lacking shared properties. Furthermore, it is unclear if entities of different ontological kinds (e. g. abstract mathematical equations vs. the concrete weather phenomena they are meant to represent) can be similar in the required sense (cf. Frigg and Nguyen 2016, 14–18).

In light of such issues, other authors have instead suggested we understand both representations and their target systems as being (set-theoretic) structures, and conceive of successful representation in terms of the existence of relation-preserving mappings between the two. These mappings are called morphisms, and various types thereof – most commonly isomorphism, partial isomorphism, or homomorphism – have been proposed to account for what it is that makes some entity a representation and what representational accuracy (or lack thereof) amounts to. Although they avoid some of the issues just identified, for example that concerning the possibility of similarity between ontologically dissimilar entities, accounts of structural morphism run into other problems. They seem to be overly inclusive: mathematical structures are sometimes discovered long before their use in empirical science, but it seems odd to claim that e.g. mathematicians who developed non-Euclidean geometries in fact thereby created representations of spacetime just on the basis that Einstein later developed theories employing morphic mappings between the two. They also seem to have difficulty distinguishing misrepresentations from non-representations: if some postulated target does not exist, then a model or other representational structure cannot be isomorphic to it. Depending on the notion of morphism involved, they may also fall afoul of the directionality condition (cf. Frigg and Nguyen 2016, 22–30).

Despite these issues, however, the above accounts have at least one thing that definitely speaks in their favor. Both provide quite straightforward answers to the question of how representations may be used in successful surrogative reasoning concerning target systems. If a representation and its target share some set of relevant properties or there exists a relation-preserving mapping between them, then reasoning carried out on the former can be expected to yield hypotheses and claims about the latter.

Apart from debates concerning the suitability of each suggested type of relation, which are complex and continue unabated, there is also the more general question of whether or not we should expect to find a *universalist* account, one that holds "that the diversity of styles dissolves under analysis and at bottom all instances of scientific/epistemic representation function in the same way and are covered by the same overarching account," though, on the whole, it appears that "there are few, if any, thoroughgoing universalists" (Frigg and Nguyen 2016, 9).

Given the status of the current discussion, rather than attempting to settle on any specific conception here, I think we should instead focus on our initial intuition, namely that there is a specific type of (epistemic) success that depends significantly upon there being *some* kind of relation of fit between representational content and targets in the world. What exactly this relation consists in can be left an open question; for now, we are perhaps best advised to employ an explicitly inclusive notion, if not in the sense of accepting a pluralistic account, then at least as a placeholder concept that acknowledges the significant difficulties that seem to face universalistic accounts in light of the recent literature on scientific representation.

Although it was developed with other purposes in mind, Helen Longino's notion of *conformation*[35] fits this bill rather well. Longino (2002, 116–117) introduces this as a "general term for epistemological success of content" that explicitly encompasses other, more specific, senses such as truth and similarity, among others:

> I am proposing to treat conformation as a general term for a family of epistemological success concepts including truth, but also isomorphism, homomorphism, similarity, fit, alignment, and other such notions.

Interestingly, her reasons for introducing this notion resemble some of those concerning the limiting features of the truth criterion for reflexive prediction discussed previously:

> Classical truth is a limiting concept in a category of evaluation that in general admits of degree and requires the specification of respects. Truth is where degree and respects fall away. This approach avoids the crudity of a binary evaluation, and hence avoids one of the problems attributed to true or false. (Longino 2002, 117)

Beyond this, conformation is also conceived of as having a number of other features that seem desirable in light of the issues faced by accounts of reflexive prediction:

> It can apply to laws and to statistical claims that are not literally true, but that capture the relations in which we are interested. [...] Idealizations like laws are not, strictly speaking, true because there is not a particular situation that they accurately and precisely represent, but they conform to the range of phenomena over which they are idealizations in the way a map conforms to its terrain. [...] Conformation is also more suitable than true or false for expressing the ways in which complex content, such as a theory or model, is successful representation. [...] We often want to say of a whole complex—for example, the theory of optics, the theory of special relativity, or the synthetic theory of evolution—that it constitutes knowledge. It conforms, even though its components conform in different respects and to different degrees. Its components are not all, strictly speaking, true, but as long as the whole conforms to its object in this sense, it constitutes knowledge. (Longino 2002, 115–118)

---

[35] Note that this is conf**o**rmation with an "o" and not conf**i**rmation with an "i".

The notion of conformation is thus quite broad and inclusive, but crucially, it is explicitly so. Part of the point of invoking conformation is to relieve us from the task of identifying a single type of world-representation relation that may be universally (co-)constitutive of epistemic success. Perhaps such a universal perspective is plausible; perhaps not. One of Longino's insights is that the types of relations seen as constituting epistemic success often differ in the context of specific disciplines, research programs and communities, and objects of study. Arguably, such discussions are better carried out in these more local contexts. In any case, we do not require an answer to these questions to make sense of the claims that concern us here.

The important point about such cases is that there has been a change in the world or, more specifically, the object of study, such that the (genuine) epistemic success of the representation in question is greater than it would otherwise (likely) be. That is, the outcome of some causal chain stemming from the use of some scientific representation is increased conformation between the content of the representation and the object(s) of study it concerns. Recognizing this requires neither supposing that the specific form of conformation always be of the same type, nor may it even require that we clearly identify the exact type of relation involved in any particular case of self-fulfillment in order for our claims to get off the ground.

3.4.4 Applying the concept

Combining the above elements results in a concept of (genuine) scientific self-fulfillment that, although resembling in certain respects both the preliminary characterization with which we began as well as several of the alternative notions discussed above, moves beyond each in significant ways:

Scientific self-fulfillment

> A scientific representation S is self-fulfilling to the degree that S-content-responsive actions contribute to bringing about states of affairs such that a higher degree of conformation between S and S's target system T exists than would have existed in absence of such actions.

As argued above, self-fulfillment of representations should be clearly distinguished from self-fulfillment of predictions made on the basis of such representations. Both of these phenomena must, in turn, be clearly distinguished from what I've called illusory self-confirmation, which may also be helpfully reformulated using the above notions:

Illusory self-confirmation

> A scientific representation is illusorily self-confirming to the degree that S-content-responsive actions contribute to bringing about states of affairs such that a higher degree of conformation between S and S's target system T appears to exist a) than in fact exists and b) than would have appeared to exist in absence of such actions.

With these notions in place, we can now turn once more to examine claims concerning the purported 'self-fulfillment' of economic theories of *homo economicus*.[36]

The first, and most crucial, thing to note is that nothing about the new account negates the fact of content contingency. In order to make any sort of judgment concerning the degree to which actions are content-responsive relative to some representation or what degree of conformation exists between a representation and its target system, we must have at least a somewhat clear idea concerning the content in question. As already suggested, one salient point of contention in the current case concerns whether *homo economicus* is to be conceived of primarily as a model of self-interested human *behaviors* or *motivations*. Knowing which of these is to serve as the target system in question is crucial for distinguishing cases of genuine self-fulfillment from those of illusory self-confirmation.

If the representation in question targets only certain kinds of behavior, then some of the lines of research cited in chapter two can be interpreted as providing fairly clear-cut evidence of genuine scientific self-fulfillment. For example, relation-preserving mappings between model parameters and the real-world objects with which they are associated (e.g. situational factors, agents, behaviors) might be created, strengthened, or made more robust due to the establishment of social norms or conceptual frameworks via content-responsive actions relative to economic theorizing. If, on the other hand, motivations figure centrally in the target system, then much of the research concerning norms, language, and institution-

---

[36] Note that, as defined, genuine scientific self-fulfillment and illusory self-confirmation are not mutually exclusive. It is theoretically possible for a representation to give rise to actions that both genuinely bring about a greater degree of conformation as well as bringing about a state of affairs in which the apparent degree of conformation is greater than the actual degree. I do not consider such complex hypothetical cases in this book.

al design may be interpreted as supporting *either* a claim of illusory self-confirmation *or* of genuine self-fulfillment.

In favor of the former, it may be argued that the effects observed in studies such as those carried out by Marwell and Ames or Frank et al. are the result of self-fulfilling *predictions* that, although perhaps developed via surrogative reasoning performed on models of *homo economicus*, do not themselves entail the self-fulfillment of the models. This would be in line with our revised reading of Merton's account of self-fulfilling prophecies in the history of racialized trade unions. It might also be argued that content-responsive actions influence institutional design in ways that make performance of self-interested behaviors necessary for success or survival without mediation by self-fulfilling predictions. This, in turn, would be in line with Polanyi's account of the 'economic fallacy' and the economistic transformation of society.

Alternatively, an interpretation favoring genuine self-fulfillment might be supported by arguing that the kinds of behavior observed in the various studies cited in chapter two are, in fact, indicative of the inducement of self-interested motivations. Of course, this connection itself would require significant argumentative support, given that accounts like Polanyi's call attention specifically to the possibility of a disconnect between behavior and (apparent) motivation. One way of supporting the claim might be to emphasize the research on motivation crowding-out, which seemed to offer a psychologically plausible account of altered behavioral patterns grounded in altered motivations. But there are at least two issues here. First, motivation crowding-out was presented as just one possible pathway to self-fulfillment, and it is unclear if the other results and pathways identified can be reasonably explained on this basis. Second, and more directly relevant to the discussion of contingent contingency, even if motivation crowding-out is present, we may still be faced with a situation similar to that plausibly encountered in the case of the trade unions. If models of *homo economicus* are understood as representing not only a widespread prevalence of self-interested motivations in humans, but as imputing the *naturalness* thereof, then the very fact that such motivations might be induced through crowding-out might serve as an indication of the illusory self-confirmation of this representation rather than its self-fulfillment. Such distinctions are crucial for evaluating the significance of both self-fulfillment *and* illusory self-confirmation, and will be considered in more detail in chapter six.

Ferraro et al. (2005, 20–21) have underlined the need for further historical and empirical research to "provide complementary insights on the nuances of how theories become self-fulfilling," and similar calls have been made by Ghoshal and Moran (1996) and other prominent proponents of self-fulfillment claims. This is surely correct: further empirical research is required to sort out thorny issues such as whether or not the observation of self-interested behaviors can be reasonably attributed to the presence of self-interested motivations. However, all of the points just outlined make clear that more empirical research, though necessary, will not itself be enough to establish claims of self-fulfillment. In order to interpret the empirical facts clearly as constituting a case of self-fulfillment or illusory self-confirmation (or neither), it is of vital importance that at least certain central facets of the intended target system are clearly identified. Claims of self-fulfillment that fail to do this are, in a significant sense, incomplete and ambiguous, and the novel account of self-fulfillment developed here, though in certain senses 'looser' than its rivals, does not obviate this requirement.

However, once the content in question has been sufficiently established, the new account does in fact help to ease a good deal of the remaining discomfort otherwise brought about by content contingency. Conceptualizations employing strong truth or belief conditions cannot allow for much, if any, subtlety in evaluating claims of scientific self-fulfillment. Truth is a strict master that abides no inexactitude, as we saw in the case of the bank run that culminated in insolvency one minute later than expected. Notions based on probable truth fare better, but still require representations to be truth-apt and the states of affairs figuring in their content to be possible to bring about. This seems to render claims of the self-fulfillment of *homo economicus* understood as an idealizing assumption or of a generalized 'economic theory' understood as a complex of more specific representational components either incoherent or false by definition. A strong belief condition, on the other hand, means many of the actions we intuitively take to be consequences of scientific theorizing will fail to be relevant to evaluating claims of self-fulfillment, because the agents in question have only a partial understanding of or adopt some other cognitive attitude toward the representational content identified.

The new account provides resources for a more nuanced evaluation of such claims. By invoking recent views of scientific representation that are not premised on the centrality of theories, linguistic description, and truth, we see how entities such as idealizations and representational complexes can both genuinely represent their target systems and be subject to standards of accuracy more flexible than binary truth and falsity. In conceiving of content-relative action in terms of agents' (perhaps partial or even mistaken) understanding of representational content, we avoid ruling out by definition seemingly relevant cases in which it is the contact with some representation, rather than explicit belief in its precise content, that provides causal impetus. At the same time, the requirement of minimum understanding for content-responsiveness ensures that the representations in question are *self*-fulfilling *qua representations*. And finally, by purposefully building gradability into both the notions of content-responsive action and relations of conformation, we explicitly allow that causal influence and representational success are matters of degree, while also acknowledging that judgments of the significance of scientific self-fulfillment will almost certainly hinge on the strength of the effect in question, rather than its mere presence.

Discussion of the shortcomings of reflexive prediction revealed the need for a 'looser' account, one that does not define self-fulfillment in terms of a single, clearly stipulated type of representation, pathway of causal efficiency, or content-world relation. The above account meets these requirements. However, it may be challenged that the increased flexibility of such looseness is offset by, or is even perhaps better understood as, a problematic lack of precision. I believe this charge to be unwarranted. Comparison with other views boasting looseness and flexibility, such as MacKenzie's superficially similar formulation of Barnesian performativity, demonstrates both the fact and nature of the novel account's precision. Unlike MacKenzie's, this account explicitly lays out the *range* of options available regarding each central notion involved, the kinds of assumptions that must be made concerning them in order for (specific) claims of self-fulfillment to appear cogent or plausible, and the various strands of current research in philosophy of science concerning the plausibility of these assumptions. The thus identified range of options leaves a good deal of room for discussion concerning not only the empirical facts surrounding specific purported cases of self-fulfillment, but also concerning whether or not they should be understood to constitute a case thereof or if the strength of the effect is sufficient to warrant further consideration. Crucially, in leaving room for such discussions, the novel account clearly and helpfully lays out their terms.

In this chapter, I developed a novel account of self-fulfillment (and illusory self-confirmation) that builds on the strengths of previous accounts while attempting to avoid their weaknesses. Answering the question of conceptualization in this manner not only provides the means for a more nuanced reading of self-fulfillment claims surrounding economic theories of *homo economicus*, but also provides helpful guidance concerning questions of prevalence and significance more generally. It is to these questions that the following chapters now turn.

4 Assessing prevalence

With a more adequate conceptualization of scientific self-fulfillment in hand, we can now turn to what I've called the questions of prevalence and significance. Recall from the first chapter that one plausible explanation for the neglect of scientific self-fulfillment among philosophers of science may be a conviction that the phenomenon, though conceivable, either does not actually exist or is not prevalent enough to merit much attention. Alternatively, it could be thought that although extant or even prevalent, self-fulfillment is nonetheless of little philosophical significance. Adequately challenging such assumptions would require extensive engagement with a wide spectrum of specific scientific disciplines and/or representations, on the one hand, and with specific topics of interest in philosophy of science, on the other. A comprehensive treatment of questions of prevalence and significance would thus extend far beyond the scope of this book.

Rather than present what would necessarily be a superficial overview of a few selected topics, in this chapter, I consider several general strategies that might be adopted when considering questions of self-fulfillment's prevalence. In particular, I identify several unfortunate tendencies that can be observed in previous discussions of such issues, and suggest how the account of self-fulfillment developed in the previous chapter can help us avoid them. The following chapters then take up suggestions concerning the phenomenon's philosophical significance.

4.1 An *a priori* boundary

The example and discussion of *homo economicus* has already given us some idea about the kind and extent of evidence and analysis required to support a claim of self-fulfillment concerning some scientific representation. When considering the possible or actual prevalence of the phenomenon more generally, however, a natural question to begin with is whether there are clear limits that can be established on more or less *a priori* grounds and thus serve as boundaries to specific self-fulfillment claims and inquiries (cf. Henshel 1982). And indeed, one of the most longstanding and oft-repeated assertions concerning such phenomena proposes a broad demarcation of just this sort: self-fulfillment, it is asserted, is possible only in the context of the social sciences, not the natural sciences.

Were this true, we would already have an important partial answer to questions of prevalence and significance, as we would thereby seemingly be justified in excluding entire scientific disciplines and domains, and the philosophical issues that pertain to them, from the purview of our investigations.[37] However, I argue that the proposed demarcation of possibility along a social/natural science divide is untenable. As will become clear, the most common argument presented in its favor rests upon a faulty inference from a (in one sense correct) thesis concerning the uniqueness of self-fulfillment to 'human affairs' to the incorrect thesis that self-fulfillment cannot occur in the social sciences. Pulling these two theses apart allows us to capture the intuition that has seemingly guided so many social scientists and philosophers to make such claims without repeating the faulty inference from one to the other.

4.1.1 Uniqueness to human affairs

Clear statements supporting the notion that self-fulfillment (or self-defeat) is limited to human affairs and/or the social sciences can be found going all the way back to a very early paper by Merton (1936, 904, emphasis added):

> There is one other circumstance, peculiar to human conduct, which stands in the way of successful social prediction and planning. Public predictions of future social developments are frequently not sustained precisely because the prediction has become a new element in the concrete situation, thus tending to change the initial course of developments. *This is not true of prediction in fields which do not pertain to human conduct.* Thus, the prediction of the return of Halley's comet does not in any way influence the orbit of that comet; but, to take a concrete social example, Marx's prediction of the progressive concentration of wealth and increasing misery of the masses did influence the very process predicted.

This idea is formulated in similar terms in Merton's (1948, 195, emphasis added) more influential paper on the self-fulfilling prophecy:

> The [bank run] parable tells us that public definitions of a situation (prophecies or predictions) become an integral part of the situation and thus affect subsequent developments. *This is peculiar to human affairs. It is not found in the world of nature.*

---

[37] Both philosophers and social scientists have also suggested that we would thereby learn something of interest about an important methodological difference between the natural and social sciences (cf. Henshel 1982). Such theses bear on discussions of naturalism in the philosophy of social sciences, which ask if the targets of social scientific research can be reasonably studied using the tools of ('positivist') natural science (cf. Guala 2016b). I do not consider such issues much further here, given that I argue against the plausibility of a strict demarcation along these lines. Nevertheless, this serves as one further possible topic of interest to philosophers of science arising from claims concerning scientific self-fulfillment.

Whereas these assertions remain largely unargued and unexamined in Merton's work, Krishna (1971) attempts to ground them in a deep distinction between the 'world of nature' and the 'world of men'. I quote at length here both because the passage in question is representative of a common line of reasoning and, more importantly, will serve below to show clearly where this reasoning fails:

> [Merton] has not tried to probe into the reasons for this difference between the situation concerning predictions about the world of nature on the one hand and the world of social reality on the other. Had he done so, he would have discovered that the differences derive primarily from the fact that what we think about nature does not affect it in any sense, except the purely technological one. This gives us freedom to form whatever hypotheses we want to make about nature, for we are certain that the phenomenon about which we are forming the hypothesis would remain whatever it is and shall in no way be affected by what we have thought or postulated about it. The world of nature is essentially unconscious and thus impervious to any influence except those that are purely physical in nature.
>
> The world of men, on the other hand, constituted as it is of beings who are conscious, both of themselves and of others, is liable to be affected and influenced by factors other than the purely physical ones. It can become aware of what is thought or postulated about it, and this very awareness can affect or influence it in a certain direction. A conscious being, just because it is conscious, cannot remain unaffected or indifferent by its awareness of what is conceived or thought about it. The difference, therefore, between the world of nature and the world of social reality, or what Merton has called 'the world of human affairs,' is rooted in the absence or presence of the capacity for self-consciousness on the part of that which is the object of study.
>
> This possibility of an object's being affected by the way it is conceived, or thought to be, is at the heart of both the self-fulfilling and the suicidal prophecies. (Krishna 1971, 1104)

Very similar sentiments were subsequently expressed concerning the fields of economics[38] and psychology[39], among others, and remain common into the pre-

---

38 E.g., Morgenstern (1972, 706–707):
Nature does not care–so we assume–whether we penetrate her secrets and establish successful theories about her workings and apply these theories successfully in predictions. In the social sciences, the matter is more complicated and in the following fact lies one of the fundamental differences between these two types of theories: the kind of economic theory that is known to the participants in the economy has an effect on the economy itself, provided the participants can observe the economy, i.e., determine its present state. [...] There is thus a 'back-coupling' or 'feedback' between the theory and the object of the theory, an interrelation which is definitely lacking in the natural sciences.

39 E.g., Buss (1978, 58–59):
[C]ertain structural changes [characterize] past and present paradigmatic changes within psychology – structural changes *not* indigenous to the natural sciences, but very much *intrinsic* and *unique* to psychology. [...] Such a characterization of revolutionary paradigms within psychology is unique to the human or social sciences since they are reflexive stud-

sent. According to one updated sociological take on self-fulfilling prophecies, "what distinguishes social science from natural science is the potential for reality to be altered by theory," thus "a theory of society could, in principle, prove self-fulfilling" (Biggs 2009, 299). Even Ferraro et al. (2009, 671) assume that "for a theory to be self-fulfilling, the objects of the theory must *know* about it so they can potentially act on its dictates" and thus that they will not affect objects of natural scientific study. Hacking's (1995; 1999; 2007) work on looping effects, as we shall see below, has led to increased philosophical discussion of such issues in recent years. Perhaps the most focused analysis, however, is to be found, once again, in the short-lived reflexive prediction literature.

One of the main issues taken up in Buck's (1963, 360) initial paper on reflexive prediction concerns what he calls the *unique-to-human-affairs thesis*, the "explicit suggestion that 'this characteristic of predictions [i.e. self-fulfillment or self-defeat] is peculiar to human affairs' and the implicit suggestion that this peculiarity marks a philosophically significant difference between the social and natural sciences." Buck critically examines a proposed counterexample to this thesis put forward by Grünbaum (1956, 239–240), who, responding directly to Merton's earlier statements about the indifference of Halley's comet and other natural phenomena to our attempts to understand them, suggests moving beyond "commonplace meteorological and astronomical phenomena" to instead "consider the goal-directed behavior of a servo-mechanism like a homing device," which is operated by purely "physical principles":

> Yet the following situation is allowed by these very principles: a computer predicts that, in its present course, the missile will miss its target, and the communication of this information to the missile in the form of a new set of instructions induces it to alter its course and thereby to reach its target, contrary to the computer's original prediction. (Grünbaum 1956, 239–240)

This situation, argues Grünbaum, does not differ substantially from a commonly cited example of reflexive prediction in the social realm, namely an economist's prediction of an oversupply of some good that leads producers to reduce output and create undersupply. Thus, the homing missile system is argued to constitute an instance of a self-defeating prediction instantiated in an entirely non-human system. Merton (1957, 129), convinced, subsequently amended his previous state-

---

ies. The objects of study in the social sciences (people) are also subjects. They can therefore reflect upon their objectivity, and subsequently change it in light of previous research findings and new information.

ment to read that self-fulfillment is peculiar to human affairs and "is not found among predictions about the world of nature (except as natural phenomena are technologically shaped by men)," referring to Grünbaum's homing missile by way of explanation.

Buck, however, rejects Merton's concession as unwarranted, arguing that such systems, although perhaps capable of 'acting on orders' based on information provided to them, cannot be reasonably seen as acting on belief in its truth. This, of course, means that such cases run afoul of the necessary conditions for reflexive predictions required by Buck's acting-on-beliefs account. Thus, he rejects the proposed counterexample. It is perhaps no surprise that Romanos, who drops any reference to beliefs from his own definition of reflexive prediction, does not so much accept Grünbaum's counterexample as he does reject Buck's criteria for ruling it out. At best, Buck's "demand that we bring our reflexive prediction analogues from the natural sciences up to his standards appears as quite arbitrary" (1973, 104). Of course, as we saw in the previous chapter, Romanos' account is not without its own problems and is perhaps even susceptible the same charge of circularity he levels at Buck's.

4.1.2 A faulty inference

Following this line of discussion, from Merton, to Grünbaum, to Buck and Romanos, instills the impression that the answer to the boundary question with which we began – is scientific self-fulfillment restricted to the social sciences? – depends upon our willingness to accept the unique-to-human-affairs thesis. Buck (1963, 360) initially writes of the "implicit suggestion" that the peculiarity to human affairs also "marks a philosophically significant difference between the social and natural sciences." But how do these questions actually relate to one another?

The assumption suggested by much of the rhetoric in these discussions is that the possibility for self-fulfillment stands or falls with the ability of the objects of study in some scientific domain to believe in or otherwise understand and react to their representation by science. Although we typically assume that the objects of natural scientific study lack such capacities, suggestions like Grünbaum's challenge this supposition, while discussions like that between Buck and Romanos can be seen as staking out the conceptual positions required to accept or reject such challenges. Despite the lasting influence of the supposed connection between capacities for belief, understanding, etc. and the possibility of self-fulfillment, however, more careful examination exposes it for the red herring it is.

When turning to examine the uniqueness thesis in more detail later in his paper, Buck (1963, 366, emphasis added) states that "the essential question is *whether the beliefs and actions of human beings must be causally relevant* to the truth-value of a reflexive prediction," and that "*it does not matter whether the actual state of affairs predicted*, e.g., so many acres under wheat next July, *is a human action or not.*" Crucially, although neither Buck nor Romanos comment upon it, this offhandedly stated fact undermines the initial 'implicit suggestion' of a strong connection between the unique-to-human-affairs thesis and the unique-to-social-science thesis. Putting it in the terms developed in the previous chapter, the former concerns *only* the questions of whether self-fulfillment requires that content-responsive actions be included in the causal chains leading to increased conformation and whether non-humans can perform content-responsive actions. But it should be clear that how we answer these questions neither entails nor requires that target systems themselves are either capable or incapable of belief, understanding, or content-responsiveness.

The conflation of the two theses and the flaw it begets can be seen more clearly by considering several statements culled from the above quote from Krishna (1971, 1104). He attempts to explain Merton's proposed difference between predictions "about the world of nature on the one hand and the world of social reality on the other" – the unique-to-social-science thesis – by referring to the (assumed) fact that only "the world of men [...] can become aware of what is thought or postulated about it, and this very awareness can affect or influence it in a certain direction" – the unique-to-human-affairs thesis. The flip side of the latter statement is that, because it lacks such awareness, "what we think about nature does not affect it in any sense, except the purely technological one." The misstep occurs when Krishna (1971, 1104) attempts to link the theses. He claims that nature's assumed lack of awareness:

> gives us freedom to form whatever hypotheses we want to make about nature, for we are certain that the phenomenon about which we are forming the hypothesis would remain whatever it is and shall in no way be affected by what we have thought or postulated about it.

But this is belied by the admitted possibility of what Krishna calls 'technological' or 'physical' influences. If a target of some scientific representation can be significantly affected, influenced, altered, or brought about through 'physical' or 'technological' means, then we *cannot* be certain that it "would remain whatever it is and shall in no way be affected by what we have thought or postulated about it," for our thoughts and postulations may give rise to just such techno-physical influences by way of content-responsive action.

If it is true that only humans are capable of content-responsiveness, then the unique-to-human-affairs thesis is correct just in the sense that the connection between scientific representations and changes brought about in their target systems must be mediated by human understanding and action. However, none of the authors discussed above offer any justification for restricting self-fulfillment to cases in which it is content-responsive actions *on the part of the target system itself* that bring about increased conformation. Tellingly, even purported cases of self-fulfilling social scientific representations do not necessarily display this feature. As we have seen, managers' content-responsive actions may give rise to increased conformation via motivation crowding-out among employees who are completely unaware that their behavior and/or motivations are the target of economic representation. Arguably, even Merton's original notion and example of self-fulfillment cannot bear the restriction: in the classic example of the bank run, it is not the bank or its financial standing, but the bank's customers, that become aware of and act upon the prediction of insolvency.

In any case, such a restriction cannot be grounded in the unique-to-human-affairs thesis itself, but would have to be argued for on independent grounds. One could, of course, grant all of the above yet still restrict focus to cases in which awareness or understanding on the part of target systems is necessary simply on the basis that there is something particularly interesting about such cases. In fact, Hacking (1999, 105–106) can be seen as making just such a move when, in the context of a discussion that bears striking resemblances to those above, he rejects the notion that non-human lifeforms may engage in looping effects on the basis that their 'responses' to our attempts at classification are not grounded in awareness:

> Microbes, not individually but as a class, may well interact with the way in which we intervene in the life of microbes. [...] Disease microbes that we try to kill may as a class, a species, respond to our murderous onslaught. [...] Do not microbes adapt themselves to us, quickly evolving strains that resist our antibacterial medications? Is there not a looping effect between the microbe and our knowledge? My simple-minded reply is that microbes do not do all these things because, either individually or collectively, they are aware of what we are doing to them. The classification microbe is indifferent, not interactive, although we are certainly not indifferent to microbes, and they do interact with us. But not because they know what they are doing.

Hacking's restriction of focus might be justified given his primary goal of understanding the role of scientific classification in what he calls 'making up people' – he simply isn't concerned with the 'making up' of microbes and other such 'unaware' things, and thus excludes them from his investigation.[40] But I can identify no similar justification relative to the goal of understanding the significance of scientific self-fulfillment from the perspective of philosophy of science.

Thus, although (a specific sense of) the unique-to-human-affairs thesis seems to be correct, this offers us no reason to accept the unique-to-social-science thesis. It is also difficult to see what other justification might be given for an *a priori* boundary along these lines. If there is indeed a clear dividing line between the domains of self-fulfillment's possibility and impossibility, it does not seem to lie at the boundary between natural and social science. Are there any other alternatives?

4.1.3 Criterion of malleability

Ironically, Krishna's (1971, 1104) statements can be read as containing a nugget of truth concerning a genuine demarcation criterion. He writes that the "possibility of an object's being affected by the way it is conceived, or thought to be, is at the heart of both the self-fulfilling and the suicidal prophecies." We have seen that Krishna intends 'being affected' to be read as implying awareness or understanding, however, if we instead read this simply as the ability to be affected *as a consequence* of the way it is thought to be, then we arrive at a meaningful *a priori* distinction. It must be possible for human actions to significantly influence, alter, or shape the states of affairs that make up the target system of some representation (through 'technological' or 'physical' means) in order for it to be a candidate for self-fulfillment. This follows from the definition developed in the previous chapter, and a similar restriction clearly applies to the other characterizations considered as well. Predictions of bank insolvency could not become self-fulfilling if the financial standing of banks were something that cannot, even in principle, be altered via human action. Economic models of human behavior or motivation could not become self-fulfilling if the same were true of these objects of study. The boundary between those scientific domains in which self-fulfillment can possibly occur and those in which it cannot is thus neither that between natural and social science, or that between the 'world of nature' and 'social reality,' but rather that between the (humanly) *malleable* and non-malleable.

---

40 However, Khalidi (2010) considers a number of arguments for limiting what Hacking calls 'interactive kinds' to the "human domain," including Hacking's awareness restriction, but finds them all wanting even in light of Hacking's stated goals.

Rejecting the proposed natural/social boundary and replacing it with a criterion of malleability has several significant consequences. First, there are still scientific representations and even some fields of study for which self-fulfillment can be ruled out on *a priori* grounds, namely any in which the relevant target systems are in principle unamenable to change through human action. Most saliently, this includes representations of target systems that are by definition unamenable to change (e.g. the immutable laws of nature thought to be studied by much of physics) or those that existed only in the prescientific past (e.g. most of archeology, historical anthropology, cosmology, paleontology, and a number of other fields), although there are surely others as well. Second, although the malleability criterion itself can be established, and can be used to rule out self-fulfillment in some fields of study, on *a priori* grounds, its adoption means that the question of self-fulfillment's possibility in many other (natural or social scientific) fields is an *a posteriori* inquiry. The degree and manner in which human action may cause significant changes in the target systems of biological or climatological representations, for example, is a matter of ongoing empirical inquiry. Third, the practical malleability of many target systems is not fixed, but instead may grow with broadly 'technological' advances.[41] While the extent of human influence on e.g. species diversity or global warming is still being investigated, it is beyond question that our ability to influence these target systems has increased over time, for better or (as now seems likely) worse. The boundaries of the space of possibility for scientific self-fulfillment will thus likely grow with time, although there are still clear limits.

4.2 Two strategies of assessment

Refuting the unique-to-social-science thesis is an important first step toward serious consideration of questions of prevalence, but the picture developed in its stead does not offer much in the way of a positive answer. In-principle possibility is relatively cheap and in no way implies plausibility. It is easy enough to dream up a farfetched scenario in which even the orbit of Halley's comet, Merton's favored foil, could be significantly affected by content-responsive actions sometime in the future. Indeed, self-fulfilling prophecies and closely related phenomena have long been a favored trope in science fiction, where they are often

---

[41] We may also come to learn that certain things we once believed to be beyond our control were in fact, in significant part, products of our own actions, as is argued by many social constructionists concerning purportedly biologically determined features of race and gender.

portrayed as capable of even more astounding feats that serve to highlight unanticipated and often unsettling consequences of scientific prediction.[42] However, such flights of fancy have little to tell us about current scientific practice. What we want to know is how common self-fulfillment really is and how we might best go about establishing its plausibility and/or existence.

4.2.1 Meta-theories

One straightforward suggestion for assessing prevalence is to develop what Bergenholtz and Busch (2016, 36) term *meta-theories* in their discussion of self-fulfilling social science theories:

> A meta-theory is here defined as a theory that takes theories about empirical phenomena as its subject of explanation. A meta-theory is, thus, a second-order theory, concerned with the development of first-order theories and their impact. [...] [I]t should, at least theoretically, be possible to create a (second-order) meta-theory that not only (a) predicts if there is a self-fulfilling impact of the adoptions of (first-order) theories, but also (b) identifies the specific theoretical mechanisms that constitute this impact.[43]

The research examined in chapter two could be seen as contributing to the development of meta-theories about first-order economic theories of *homo econom-*

---

[42] Philip K. Dick's (1956) short story "The Minority Report" explores the dangers of predictive policing in a future dystopian society. Three precognizant mutants linked by computer are used to generate predictions concerning future crimes, which are used to justify arrest of the (not-yet) 'criminals,' apparently stopping crime before it starts. The assumed foolproofness of this new forensic science is called into question when the head of 'Precrime' himself is implicated in a future murder. This leads, first, to his realization that there are often serious discrepancies between the reports issued by the three 'precogs' and, second, to his conscious decision to carry out the crime in order to maintain the system's authority, thus culminating in the self-fulfillment of the original prediction of murder.

Isaac Asimov's (1951) *Foundation* series follows the unfolding of a set of predictions put forward by 'psychohistorian' Hari Seldon concerning the broad flow of human development over thousands of years. Each time the so-called 'Seldon Plan' seems to be subverted by some apparently unexpected turn of events, a prerecorded hologram of the long dead scientist appears to inform everyone that this had, in fact, been part of the plan all along. The story explores the complexities of the concept and trope, introducing multiple lines of iterated predictions and leaving the reader questioning whether the Plan is genuinely self-fulfilling, illusorily self-confirming, or something more complex.

[43] Although the authors refer here specifically to the 'prediction' of self-fulfilling impacts, the rest of their discussion strongly suggests that they intend this to cover the establishment of past impacts as well; I use the term to refer to both.

icus. Empirical research concerning the apparent inducement of self-interested behaviors through direct economic training attempts to establish a self-fulfilling impact of adoption. The three types of mechanism presented by Ferraro et al. (2005) – social norms, institutional design, and language – are intended to account for this impact.

But we have also already seen some of the difficulties that may arise when attempting to develop an adequate meta-theory. Content contingency requires a sufficiently clear conception of the representational content in question. Evidence must put forward that is not only suggestive of increased conformation, but is capable of distinguishing between self-fulfillment and illusory self-confirmation. Claims of self-fulfillment also entail claims about the likely course of events in counterfactual situations in which content-responsive actions were not carried out; such claims are difficult to assess empirically. Other difficulties surely exist, but these are some of the most pressing.

Perhaps surprisingly, Bergenholtz and Busch are unconcerned with the practical possibility of developing meta-theories. This is because the notion is introduced largely as an answer to questions of self-fulfillment's philosophical significance rather than prevalence. For example, the authors consider the possibility that self-fulfillment presents a challenge to scientific realism, but claim that the in-principle possibility of meta-theories renders this purported challenge toothless. It is, they write, irrelevant to their "analytical point about self-fulfillment and the threat to realism that the sense in which [development of meta-theories] is 'possible' may be fairly remote in terms of our actual epistemic situation" (Bergenholtz and Busch 2016, 37). Of course, the same cannot be said in relation to questions of prevalence. So, what, if any, are the prospects for tackling the kinds of difficulties outlined above?

As we have seen, the specific content we ascribe to some representation affects our judgments about whether certain actions should be considered content-responsive as well as whether changes brought about by such actions constitute genuine self-fulfillment, illusory self-confirmation, or neither. Thus, it is easy to get caught up in the thought that the problem of content contingency must be solved by clearly identifying the content of a first-order representation before the task of developing a meta-theory can get underway in earnest. In fact, however, this seems to get things backwards. Before getting down to the task of analyzing the impact of some representation, we should first seek to establish or at least make plausible that some impact has occurred or may come to occur in the future.⁴⁴

To this purpose, it will usually be more helpful to begin by considering some object of scientific scrutiny itself rather than the representation(s) that may target it. As shown above, many self-fulfillment claims or inquiries can be ruled out on (largely) *a priori* grounds, most saliently when the object of study is unmalleable by human action either in principle or in light of our current (or future) 'technological' capabilities. If malleability is granted, we can then investigate whether or not the object or state of affairs has been (or could be) brought about or significantly influenced by human actions and, if so, in what manner and to which degree. Finally, we can ask whether the identified actions can be considered content-responsive to some representation that seems to target the object or state of affairs in question. Of course, this process also implies that we have at least a vague idea of what kinds of things are the target of scientific scrutiny in the first place. But this level of understanding is often more easily achieved than establishing the specific content of a particular representation.

Empirical investigations like most of those outlined in chapter two enter into this process at the stage of considering the extent and nature of influences brought about via human action. Ideally, data will be acquired that can eventually distinguish self-fulfillment from illusory self-confirmation and establish a plausible counterfactual claim. One important part of this challenge can be approached by consciously designing studies capable of distinguishing which specific mechanisms account for a given impact. For example, a few of the studies cited in chapter two sought not only to establish that contact with economic theorizing led to certain types of behavior, but to ascertain whether the observed effects were due to e.g. particular syllabi and teaching styles (Frank et al. 1993) or particular names assigned to decision-making games played between experimental subjects (Liberman et al. 2004). The required counterfactual claims can sometimes be rendered plausible by designing studies that specifically attempt to (re-)create the relevant counterfactual situations (cf. Salganik and Watts 2008) or by relying on cross-cultural observational data that paints a picture of typical behaviors in parts of the world that have had little to no direct contact with the scientific representations in question (cf. Henrich et al. 2005).

Of course, none of these suggestions guarantee that relevant evidence is either available or can be ascertained with any degree of certainty. Biggs (2009) argues that experimental designs meant to probe the counterfactual counter-

---

44 Biggs (2009) considers a somewhat similar procedure for analyzing dynamic processes as cases of self-fulfilling prophecies.

parts of purported real-world impacts can be exceedingly difficult to implement in many domains, despite the straightforward logic on which they are grounded. For example, experiments designed to test potential self-fulfilling effects of false beliefs on behavior in placebo and education research have shown that it is, in fact, quite difficult to reliably induce the false beliefs that, in these contexts, constitute the relevant counterfactual situation. For fields and representations that have been particularly successful in generating content-responsive actions – *homo economicus* arguably being a prime example – it may be difficult to find any 'untreated' control group to observe. If society has indeed undergone some kind of 'economistic transformation' as suggested by Polanyi, then it may be impossible to find subjects who have remained entirely untouched by content-responsive actions performed on the basis of such theories. Whether or not such difficulties arise depends to a large degree on the particulars of the domain, object of study, and representations in question.

If, in spite of the difficulties, we manage to obtain reasonable evidence of some (likely) impact, we can then more fruitfully turn to analysis in terms of self-fulfillment and illusory self-confirmation. Eventually, as argued in the previous chapter, we must still decide upon some sufficiently clear representational content if we are to make a definitive self-fulfillment claim. However, as it turns out, making definitive claims of this sort may be of interest only to those who wish to answer questions of prevalence in isolation of questions of (epistemic) significance. As we will see in chapter six, content contingency does not appear so much as a 'problem' to be 'solved' when considering the implications of self-fulfillment for scientific practice, but rather as an analytical tool to be kept handy. For epistemic purposes, it will usually suffice to operate with conditionalized claims such as 'if S's content is C, then its impact via C-content-responsive action Y constitutes scientific self-fulfillment'. Ultimately, the question of whether some impact constitutes self-fulfillment, illusory self-confirmation, or neither takes back seat to the overarching question of all empirical inquiry: what is the case?

Development of meta-theories is an obvious and necessary strategy if we are to seriously address questions of prevalence. However, there are a few ways in which even successful meta-theories, at least as conceived by Bergenholtz and Busch, leave something to be desired. First, meta-theories aim at the description or prediction of actual or likely self-fulfilling impacts of *particular* first-order representations. But restricting focus to such a strategy seemingly presents us with little direction of where *else* we should be on the lookout for scientific self-fulfillment. Much of the empirical research cited in favor of self-fulfillment claims concerning *homo economicus* was carried out largely in response to an unexpected fluke result of Marwell and Ames' 1981 study, which gave rise to the notion that there was 'something different' about economics students that deserved further attention. It would be beneficial to have some means of anticipating avenues for research into potential (future) cases of self-fulfillment without being reliant on windfalls of this sort. Second, in addressing single first-order representations, even positive meta-theories give us little information about the prevalence of self-fulfillment more generally. A strategy that allows for more generalization would be required to support judgments of this type. And finally, the picture developed by Bergenholtz and Busch strongly suggests that investigation of meta-theories might occur largely in isolation from development of the first-order theories they target. However, in chapter six, I argue that this encourages a distorted view of the epistemic significance of scientific self-fulfillment.

Given these issues, in the next section, I consider a complementary strategy to addressing questions of prevalence that places more emphasis on the identification of general mechanisms and processes that may encourage or hinder self-fulfillment rather than establishment of specific impacts.

4.2.2 Mechanisms and mid-range theories

In one respect, namely their suggested focus on particular impacts of particular first-order theories, Bergenholtz and Busch's suggested meta-theories recall Hacking's studies on looping effects. As outlined in the first chapter, Hacking is highly skeptical that a 'general theory' of looping can be developed, given both the supposedly unpredictable nature of human responses to scientific classification and the influence of unexpected and contingent sociocultural factors. This has led him to focus on detailed historical analysis of a series of particular cases while (for the most part[45]) eschewing attempts at abstracting any general principles that might be used to predict the course of yet unexplored (or unfinished) cases of looping. As previously argued, the phenomenon of scientific self-fulfillment cannot be equated with looping effects, which are broader in encompassing impacts of theory that do not lead to increased conformation and narrower in restricting focus to mechanisms of change involving awareness on the part of target systems. Despite this, there is some overlap between the phenomena, and the methodological discussion surrounding Hacking's skeptical as-

---

[45] Arguably, the 'engines of making up people' examined in Hacking's most recent work on looping can be understood as general mechanisms that might be found in many specific cases. Even here, however, Hacking (2007, 315) is quick to point out that although his detail-rich "probes" are "driven by general speculation," that "every case is different" and his "chosen topics do not lend themselves to generalisations."

sertions is relevant to the worries articulated about sole reliance on meta-theories.

The rich detail and thick description of Hacking's stories – this is what they are, even if grounded in historical fact – make up much of their appeal and interest. However, in recent years, his anti-theoretical stance has come increasingly under attack. Kuorikoski and Pöyhönen (2012, 188), although praising Hacking's case studies as "groundbreaking and fascinating," lament that they "only point toward an interesting phenomenon without providing the resources for systematic modeling, analysis, and ultimately, explanation." Not only this, reluctance to develop such resources, combined with the account's prominence, has led it to be widely cited in support of "sweeping social-constructionist claims" that are "ambiguous and have connotations more likely to lead to conceptual and methodological pseudo-problems than to increased understanding" (Kuorikoski and Pöyhönen 2012, 187). The solution to these problems, they think, lies in the space between Hacking's particularity and the sweeping generalizations it has (unwillingly) enabled: a more theoretically satisfying account of looping requires development of mechanism-based, mid-range theories.

Beside his work on self-fulfilling prophecies, one of Merton's (1967, 39) lasting contributions is the notion that scientific sociology should aim at the development of *theories of the middle range*, theories:

> that lie between the minor but necessary working hypotheses that evolve in abundance during day-to-day research and the all-inclusive systematic efforts to develop a unified theory that will explain all the observed uniformities of social behavior, social organization and social change.

This type of theorizing, Merton (1967, 40) explains, "is principally used in sociology to guide empirical inquiry," which it achieves by, first, abstracting some "characteristically simple" idea or image on the basis of empirical observations that can then be used to generate empirically testable inferences about a range of relevant situations. Such a methodological strategy has already proven its value many times over in the natural sciences, writes Merton, as when Pascal famously conceived of atmosphere as a 'sea of air' and, on this basis, inferred the testable (and quickly proven) hypothesis that air pressure at the top of a mountain should be lower than at its base.

Similarly, the sociological theories of reference groups and relative deprivation were initially grounded on the simple idea that people often adopt the standards of (significant) others as a basis for their own evaluations of some situation. This idea was used to generate the counterintuitive hypothesis that the sense of loss experienced by disaster survivors does not grow linearly with their objective losses, but is instead evaluated relative to the losses of some pertinent reference group they view as comparable to themselves. Subsequent testing supported the theory of relative deprivation over the common-sense assumption of linear correlation between objective and experienced loss. Most relevant to our discussion is the fact that the theories of reference groups and relative deprivation seem to apply not only to the case of disaster survivors, but rather guide empirical inquiry on a "particular *class* of behavior" that we might expect to find in other structurally similar situations (Merton 1967, 40–41).

Such 'simple ideas' are only a starting point, however. Successful mid-range theories, continues Merton (1967, 42–43), generate not only hypotheses for some domain, but also specify and explain the operation of the "social mechanisms" that bring about the behaviors in question. This mechanistic aspect of mid-range theories is mentioned only briefly by Merton; however, it has been adopted and further refined in recent years by proponents of so-called 'analytical sociology,' who argue that mechanistic explanations and mechanism-based mid-range theories should be the central concern of sociological theorizing (cf. Hedström and Udehn 2009).

There is relatively little consensus concerning the precise meaning of 'mechanism' among analytical sociologists. Noting this, Hedström and Bearman (2009) argue that the currently most promising conception is that of Machamer, Darden, and Craver (2000). Despite the fact that the latter are concerned primarily with mechanistic explanations in the life sciences,[46] Hedström and Bearman (2009, 5) abstract from their account the notion that a mechanism is, roughly speaking:

> a constellation of entities and activities that are organized such that they regularly bring about a particular type of outcome, and we explain an observed outcome by referring to the mechanism by which such outcomes are regularly brought about.

Although disagreement exists beyond such broad characterizations, analytical sociologists typically share the view that their approach represents a crucial (likely complementary) alternative to much contemporary mainstream sociology, which, it is claimed, often restricts focus to the establishment of statistical correlations rather than investigation of the mechanisms that might explain their presence.

Kuorikoski and Pöyhönen bring these ideas to bear on looping effects. Rather than stopping with the grouping of the disparate set of cases examined

---

[46] There seem to be large discrepancies between the mechanism concepts employed by analytical sociologists and those currently discussed in the philosophy of life sciences. These differences are, however, largely irrelevant for the methodological point developed here.

by Hacking under the general heading of 'looping,' "instead, the causal processes behind the propagation of scientific representations and psychological and sociological reactions to them ought to be examined in such detail so as to enable reasonable inferences to possible alternative courses of events and even predictions" (Kuorikoski and Pöyhönen 2012, 194–195). They suggest the development of a typology of feedback mechanisms encompassing not only Hacking's favored mechanisms of awareness-based responses leading to 'destabilization' of classified 'kinds of people,' but also a set of positive feedback mechanisms that might stabilize the behavior in question and ultimately lead to self-fulfillment.[47] Kuorikoski and Pöyhönen refer by way of example specifically to the case of *homo economicus* and some of the mechanisms put forward by Ferraro et al. (2005): motivation crowding-out, social norms, and specific types of selection and filtering mechanisms instantiated through institutional design.

Crucially, when considered in light of the foregoing discussions of mid-range theories, it becomes clear that mechanisms such as those suggested by Ferraro et al. might serve not only as explanatory components of meta-theories targeting specific self-fulfilling representations, but may also guide inquiry into yet unconsidered cases in contexts displaying conditions under which those mechanisms have been known to act. Thus, in addressing questions of prevalence, we needn't rely only on the development of meta-theories concerning specific first-order representations, but can instead refer to (and expand upon) a general typology of

---

[47] Relaxing the restriction to mechanisms involving awareness of classified individuals and explicitly including stabilizing rather than merely destabilizing elements would seem to bring the notion of looping effects suggested by Kuorikoski and Pöyhönen much closer to that of scientific self-fulfillment developed in this work. However, there are still important differences between the two approaches.

First, the resulting notion of looping still encompasses types of change that do not result in increased conformation. Crucially, it must be noted that, although the two may often occur in tandem, that increased stabilization will not necessarily constitute increased conformation relative to some representation, which depends, as always, on the specific content in question.

Second, Kuorikoski and Pöyhönen's discussion is still largely restricted to the effects of 'classifications' in the 'human sciences,' whereas the account developed here broadens the scope to consideration of any kind of scientific representation that takes as its target system entities malleable by human action, including those of the natural sciences. Given the tone of their paper and their rejection of the purported anti-naturalist consequences of looping, it seems likely that these authors would be open to such a broadening of scope. However, they neither explicitly comment on the possibility of looping in the natural sciences nor discuss mechanisms that might account for increased conformation in natural science domains. Furthermore, despite the possibility of reconciliation between looping and self-fulfillment hinted at here, I remain convinced of the utility of treating the two perspectives as friendly rivals, as suggested in chapter one.

mechanisms that might promote or hinder self-fulfillment in some particular domain or across a variety of situations. We've already seen a number of general mechanisms that would make up part of this typology, most saliently those investigated by Ferraro et al. Further development of such a typology goes beyond the scope of this work. However, by elaborating on the discussion in chapter three and drawing on the notion of malleability introduced in this chapter, we can begin to envisage in a general way how such a project might be successfully developed.

4.3 Applying the strategies

When attempting to apply these strategies, it is helpful to imagine processes of self-fulfillment as being broken down into two 'halves' along the lines suggested by the definition developed in chapter three. The first concerns the generation of content-responsive actions on the basis of some representation, while the second concerns the manner in which these actions bring about increased conformation. Speaking in very general terms, if we want to know where to look to potentially discover novel instances of scientific self-fulfillment, we can reflect upon the mechanisms that might account for such connections, the conditions in which they are likely to come about, and specific domains of inquiry in which such conditions seem to be given. If we wish to assess the prevalence of self-fulfillment more generally, we might consider whether the types of mechanisms and associated conditions we have discovered in relatively clear cases of self-fulfillment seem to be common or exceptional.

4.3.1 Examples

In some cases, one general mechanism or several closely related ones may plausibly be implicated in both halves of a single case of self-fulfillment. For example, the various psychological and sociological mechanisms whereby self-interest comes to be adopted as a *normative* standard of behavior (cf. Miller 1999) might help explain both the fact and manner of economic representations' presentation in educational settings (content-responsive action) as well as the ability of this presentation to induce self-interested motivations or behaviors in economics students (increased conformation). In other cases, however, and particularly in the context of the natural sciences, the mechanisms in question will likely differ greatly between the two halves of the process.

Ferraro et al.'s discussion of the impacts of institutional design provided examples of mechanisms that may serve to link content-responsive actions to increased conformation with regard to economic theories. However, they present only a limited account of how such representations come to issue in the content-responsive actions that lead to or constitute their institutional embedding in the first place. A recent paper by Marti and Gond (2018), however, can be read as more directly addressing this 'half' of the self-fulfillment of *homo economicus*.[48] Noting that much recent work promoting self-fulfillment claims tends to exhibit a 'success bias' by considering only theories that have successfully transformed society, they seek to establish the boundaries of the phenomenon by identifying a three step process through which theories must pass in order to become self-fulfilling, based loosely on MacKenzie's notions of generic, effective, and Barnesian performativity, respectively:

> (1) actors start experimenting with new theories, (2) their experimentation produces anomalies, and (3) these anomalies convince initially unconvinced actors that the new theory is indeed valid and thereby lead to a practice shift. (Marti and Gond 2018, 493)

This is already a more detailed account than that provided by Ferraro et al., but it is still quite abstract. However, each of these steps is further characterized by two 'boundary conditions' which determine whether or not they will occur. 'Experimentation,' the trying out of new possibilities for action suggested by a representation (e.g. new financial trading strategies suggested by the Black-Scholes-Merton equations), requires the representation's implementation into *material devices* and/or promotion by *powerful initial backers*. Production of 'anomalies,' observable violations of common expectations that conform with the novel theory (e.g. occasional successes of the adopted trading strategies in violation of expectations of market unpredictability), requires the *visibility of effects* of experimentation for those not yet convinced of the representation's aptness, as well as the absence of *counteracting behavior* capable of effectively halting experimentation. Finally, anomalies lead to 'practice shifts,' widespread changes in actors' behavior (e.g. those enabling emergence of organized exchanges for stock derivatives), only if sufficient *discontent with the status quo* exists to encourage at-

---

[48] In fact, the model presented below could also constitute the *entire* process of self-fulfillment in some cases, namely those in which the 'practice shift' identified in the third step itself constitutes increased conformation. However, in other cases, the practice shifts in question will be just part of the causal chain that eventually pushes a target system in this direction. I present the model after this fashion.

tempts at *sensegiving by convinced actors* who attempt to provide the yet unconvinced with theory-conforming explanations for anomalies.

Marti and Gond's account presents a good example of a mid-range theory of the link between scientific representations and content-responsive actions (in the domain of economics and/or management). Although their use of the term 'boundary conditions' suggests that the italicized terms in the preceding paragraph represent conditions that must *necessarily* be present in order for self-fulfillment to occur, it is more useful to think of them as mechanisms that can enable or support the generation of content-responsive actions, and which might be found across a variety of structurally similar situations. Coupled with a mid-range theory that links the 'practice shifts' in question to increased conformation between a relevant representation and its target system, this provides a kind of 'how-possible' account of a specific case of self-fulfillment that might eventually become the target of an empirically supported meta-theory.

As a proof of concept, let us also consider how such a set of mid-range theories might be put forward for a potential case of self-fulfillment in a natural science. It should be noted from the outset that this example is highly speculative, and represents merely an attempt to show how inquiry along these lines could be carried out. Biologists and taxonomists sometimes discover that what we long took to be a single species of animal is actually several distinct species. In the cases I refer to, such arguments are not grounded in the use of shifting or vague species conceptions, but rather the uncovering of new information about the (usually genetic) traits present in one or more animal populations. Thus, we encounter news headlines in *Nature* proclaiming that "African elephants are two distinct species" (Gilbert 2010) and "DNA reveals that giraffes are four species – not one" (Woolston 2016). After briefly explaining the genetic findings leading to the new classification, these articles typically move on to consider the findings' possible implications for conservation efforts. For example, Gilbert (2010) writes that all African elephants are "conserved as the same species. But the evidence that they are two distinct species suggests that they may be facing different pressures and require different conservation strategies." Drawing inspiration from such discoveries, I wish to consider the counterintuitive idea that scientific representations that *mistakenly* depict some population of organisms as actually consisting of multiple distinct species could potentially become self-fulfilling.[49]

---

[49] There are admittedly issues here with determining what exact content of a representation of this sort might render self-fulfillment claims cogent. A false, yet clearly time-indexed statement such as 'on December 21, 2010, it is the case that the population of animals commonly referred

We must first consider if the target system in question is something plausibly malleable via human action. In this case, the question is whether we are capable of instigating a *speciation event*, the emergence of one or more new species that occurs when an existing "lineage splits into multiple reproductively isolated, genetically distinct sub-populations (cladogenesis)" (Bull and Maron 2016, 2). Clearly, we cannot alter the past genetic history of some organism. However, the success of selective breeding of organisms throughout human history and the recent explosion of genetic engineering are testament to our ability to alter some population's genetic future. It is perhaps difficult to imagine how these *intentional* forms of manipulation might reliably issue from the type of representation in question. However, it has also been argued that human actions might *unintentionally* act as mechanisms supporting speciation events. Although human action is often presented only as a threat to biodiversity, Bull and Maron (2016, 3) argue that human activities

> can directly or indirectly result in reproductive barriers of various kinds (e. g. geographical, physical) being created between sub-populations of an existing species—or, in different selective pressures being applied to specific members of a species (e. g. by age, size). In both cases, the development of new traits could occur in sub-populations. Given sufficient time this could, at least in some cases, result in cladogenesis [i.e. a speciation event]. We also assume that there will be some scenarios in which the emergence of new traits, or even full speciation, can be attributed primarily to reproductive isolation or selective pressure caused by human activities, rather than a combination of anthropogenic and non-anthropogenic factors.

Bull and Maron (2016, 3–5) also present a number of more specific mechanisms that might drive anthropogenic speciation: *relocation* of species to new ecosystems, which has been documented in some cases to drive "rapid evolution following introduction, in some cases within 10 years"; *domestication*, which introduces both "deliberate and incidental" selective pressures that have at times "resulted in the documented emergence of novel species"; *hunting*, which "drives new trait development in wild animal populations, influencing broader ecological dynamics, which could eventually be a precursor to speciation"; creation

---

to 'African elephants' consists of two distinct species' will not be made true even if it were to somehow lead to a future speciation event. However, models of such animal populations needn't make explicit reference to a specific timeframe in which they are to hold, and might include general structural features meant to map to features of their target system related to taxonomic diversity, such as reproductive isolation and genetic distinctness. As we have seen, such difficulties are not unique to this example, but relate to (the problem of) content contingency more generally, and will thus be put aside here.

of *novel ecosystems*, such as new bioclimatic habitats brought on by climate change, and even urban environments, which have already been observed to be capable of generating new species of insects.

> The common house mosquito (*Culex pipiens*) adapted to the environment of the underground railway system in London, UK, establishing a subterranean population. Now named the 'London Underground mosquito', *Culex pipiens molestus* can no longer interbreed with its above-ground counterpart. (Bull and Maron 2016, 5)

Also contemplated is the possibility of future speciation-driving mechanisms such as direct genomic manipulation, re-creation of extinct species, or even the facilitation of organisms to extra-terrestrial bodies. Finally, the authors note that microorganisms might undergo rapid diversification not only through the mechanisms outlined above, but also in relation to disease, medicine, and the human 'micro-biome'.

Bull and Maron provide us with a range of mechanisms that plausibly link a variety of human actions to increased conformation with biological representations depicting reproductive isolation and genetic distinctness in some population(s) of organism(s). The question then becomes how these actions might be generated in response to the content of such representations. One mechanism might consist in their impact on conservation efforts. These might include relocation of subpopulations posited to constitute separate species or other so-called '*ex-situ*' methods in the hopes of avoiding loss of genetic integrity through hybridization (cf. Wolf et al. 2001). On the other hand, reports describing the discovery of new species are read not only by scientists and conservationists, but by collectors, hobbyists, and sellers of exotic species as well. Taxonomists Stuart et al. (2006, 1137) express dismay at the realization that their previously published descriptions of several new species of reptiles and amphibians have "tragically aided their commercial exploitation." Plausibly, the creation of a market for such new species might lead to a number of the different activities identified above, including a sort of 'pet store' domestication employing selective breeding for desirable traits. Finally, with the rise of relatively cheap and simple methods for targeted genome editing in recent years, such as the greatly hyped CRISPR-Cas9 system, have come suggestions of employing genetic engineering directly in species conservation efforts. Thomas et al. (2013, 485) weigh the pros and cons of a strategy they call "facilitated adaptation," which "involves rescuing a target population or species by endowing it with adaptive alleles, or gene variants, using genetic engineering."

The above suggests it is possible to develop mid-range theories accounting for both 'halves' of a speculative case of self-fulfillment in the natural sciences.

In order to move beyond speculation, a meta-theory providing evidence of a particular impact of some taxonomic representation of this kind would be required. Of course, even granting the in-principle possibility of a case of self-fulfillment along these lines, we might feel that the actual possibility of the postulated chain of events is so remote as to render this a mythological story of 'marvelous coincidence' on par with Oedipus Rex or the man who dreamt of finding his fortune in Cairo. Part of this impression may be due to the relatively narrowly defined representational content we have considered, namely distinctness of species within one specific population of organisms. We might tell a more plausible story employing many of the same mechanisms described above if the target systems in question concerned the biodiversity of species more generally. For example, Bull and his colleagues also investigate how incentives employed in biodiversity offsetting policies might result in the self-fulfillment of estimated rates of diversity decline (Gordon et al. 2015). However, it should be admitted without hesitation that it is at least equally likely that such a chain of events has never and will never actually occur.

4.3.2 Challenges

On this note, let us close this chapter by reflecting explicitly upon the fact that the strategies outlined above are just that: strategies for investigating the prevalence of scientific self-fulfillment and not a guarantee that employing them will deliver credible claims of prevalence. I have largely focused on the possibilities for making a positive case here. However, it is crucial that our attention is not restricted to those mechanisms that may enable or promote self-fulfillment if we are to acquire a realistic picture. As stated in the introduction, avoiding unwarranted exaggeration is as much a part of taking the phenomenon seriously as is avoiding its out-of-hand dismissal. With this in mind, I briefly consider three serious challenges to self-fulfillment's prevalence (or our ability to detect it) that may fall out of the approach outlined above.

First, the identification of a mechanism or mid-range theory supporting self-fulfillment in some domain warrants only investigation of further cases in structurally similar situations – it does not warrant the assumption that self-fulfillment is in fact present in these situations. Jussim (2012) details how the (apparent) discovery of self-fulfilling expectancy effects in educational and professional settings led to an explosion of social psychological research that initially seemed to demonstrate not only the existence, but the near ubiquity and extreme power of self-fulfilling prophecies in interpersonal relationships of all types. Ultimately, however, the vast majority of these strong claims relied upon the presupposition that mechanisms of self-fulfillment were the only candidate explanations for the observed effects. Researchers ignored what Jussim presents as a (more) plausible alternative explanation based on the mechanism of *accuracy:* when students of teachers with low expectations for their academic outcomes come to manifest the expected deficits, this may be due to the simple fact that teachers are generally good judges of academic talent rather than the insidious effects of the expectations themselves. In this case, overemphasis and presupposition of a single type of mechanism led to shoddy meta-theories.

Second, the effectivity of certain mechanisms in promoting self-fulfillment might derive from the fact that self-fulfillment in general is quite rare. This is considered by Biggs (2009, 296) in the context of self-fulfilling prophecies, which he defines in opposition to a dynamic process he calls an *inductively derived prophecy* (IDP), presented in schematic form as an interaction between a teacher, X, and their pupil, Y:

(0) Y is p.
Student is academically talented.
(1) Because of (0), X believes that 'Y is p.'
Because Student is talented, Teacher believes that 'Student is academically talented.'
(2) X therefore does b.
Teacher therefore places Student in a study group for academic high-achievers.
(3) Because of (0), Y manifests p.
Because Student is academically talented, Student manifests academic talent (i.e. displays high academic achievement.)

Self-fulfilling prophecies are then defined as processes in which a) it is actually the action carried out in (2) that causes Y to manifest p, and b) this fact is misapprehended by either X or Y, who believe the causal order is as represented by the IDP. The critical point for us is Biggs' (2009, 311) suggestion that it is not only reasonable for actors to assume the causal order of IDP, given how common it undoubtedly is, but that:

> it is arguable that SFPs can exist because they are unusual, being 'parasitic' on the frequency of IDP. These two processes would stand in the same relation as forged to authentic banknotes; the former are more likely to go undetected when rare.

Arguably, scientific self-fulfillment might also be dependent upon mechanisms of representational uptake that presuppose the commonality of accurate science and the relative rarity of 'success' brought about via increased conformation.

Finally, there is Hacking's insistence that the objects of study in the human sciences are 'moving targets' that consistently defy and outstrip attempts at scientific description. So insistent is he in this point that Mallon (2016, 171) christens the central thesis of much work on looping in his honor: "*Hacking Instability:* Theories of human categories lead the humans who putatively fall into such categories to react in ways that disconfirm those theories." Interestingly, although Hacking (2007, 311) prefers to present his work as avoiding generalizations, he often explains the tendency toward disconfirmation by reference to a favored mechanism of his own, namely concerted *resistance* on the part of classified groups:

> Kinds of people who are medicalised, normalised, and administered, increasingly try to take back control from the experts and the institutions, sometimes by creating new experts, new institutions. The famous case is homosexuality [...] Gay pride and its predecessors restored to homosexuals control of the classifications into which they fall.

Resistance, as postulated by Hacking, arises out of a (shared) feeling of needing to 'escape' one's scientific classification, either by consciously avoiding ascribed behaviors and traits or, perhaps more importantly, altering or dismantling existing institutions that forced the manifestation of those behaviors and traits in the first place.

According to the strategy outlined here, resistance should be considered a potentially powerful mechanism that can *hinder* self-fulfillment (or, rather: promote self-defeat). However, the true extent to which resistance might cast doubt on the prevalence of scientific self-fulfillment more generally comes when we note its clear parallels with Marti and Gond's notion of 'discontent with the status quo,' which was presented as a mechanism that tends to promote self-fulfillment. Such parallels might lend credence to the idea that one and the same mechanism may tend to either promote or hinder self-fulfillment, self-defeat, or something else entirely, depending on the specific circumstances in which it becomes active – and with this, we arrive at something very like the antigeneralization thesis that Hacking has been insisting upon the whole time.

5 Challenges of performativity

This book began by introducing a general intuition concerning the possibility of self-fulfilling science: although scientific representations are usually thought to become more accurate over time due to processes of self-correction, it is conceivable that increased accuracy could result from changes in the world instigated by the representations themselves. It was noted that, despite garnering some attention by a small group of philosophers of science following World War II, the topic of scientific self-fulfillment has since been largely ignored. This tailing off of interest was attributed to, among other things, a relative lack of conceptual clarity concerning the phenomenon in question, justified skepticism concerning its existence and prevalence, and, finally, a tendency among many of those who have at times discussed this or other closely related phenomena to either overestimate or underestimate their philosophical significance. The previous chapters constitute an attempt to clear up what I take to be a number of widespread misconceptions concerning questions of conceptualization and prevalence and replace them with a more secure base from which a sober analysis of the phenomenon's philosophical significance might begin.

In this chapter, I turn to examine these issues. I begin with a brief general consideration of questions of significance and how the popularity of performativity approaches has influenced their discussion in recent years. Two specific suggestions are considered concerning the philosophical import of self-fulfillment as seen through the lens of performativity. First, I present an example of how the perceived association between performativity, anti-realism, and social constructionism has tended to direct what little philosophical attention has been paid to claims of the self-fulfillment of *homo economicus* toward their impact for debates concerning scientific realism. Though such claims are undoubtedly important, I address them only briefly, and further argue that the focus on broadly metaphysical issues has tended to unduly overshadow other legitimate, and possibly more pressing, questions concerning, broadly speaking, epistemic and ethical/practical issues. The remainder of the chapter is devoted to critically examining the drastic epistemic claim that the possibility of self-fulfillment somehow renders representations entirely unamenable to our usual notions of scientific success and evaluation. I examine two possible lines of argument for such claims, which are often grounded in a suggestive analogy between linguistic performatives and reality-altering scientific representations, but ultimately find both unconvincing.

5.1 Assessing significance

The question of whether or not scientific self-fulfillment is significant for philosophy of science must be understood as a placeholder for more specific inquiries about if and how the possibility, existence, or prevalence of the phenomenon either generate new philosophical problems or contribute something novel to existing ones. Answers to questions of significance thus depend not only on what we think self-fulfillment is and what evidence we have for its prevalence, but on what issues we take to be relevant to philosophy of science itself. In this section, I briefly consider how differing notions of the proper purview of the field may encourage or discourage inquiry into specific issues and how the recent trend of framing self-fulfillment in terms of 'performativity' has shaped perceptions of its possible significance.

5.1.1 The purview of philosophy of science

Arguably, the decline of interest in scientific self-fulfillment and related phenomena in mainstream philosophy of science following debates on reflexive prediction was encouraged by the view that the field's proper purview is restricted to elucidation of, broadly speaking, the 'logical' aspects of science and scientific reasoning. This view was partially enshrined by Reichenbach's (1938, 6–7) distinction between the contexts of discovery and justification and the common insistence that philosophy of science is concerned only with (the rational aspects of) the latter. Many took this distinction to express not only a shared set of interests, but rather to provide "the very foundation of philosophy of science" by guaranteeing its existence as "an autonomous enterprise, independent of other disciplines that address the sciences from different angles" (Hoyningen-Heune 1987, 501).

Such views seem to guide Romanos' (1973, 98–99) contention that, although Buck was correct in concluding that reflexive prediction poses no insurmountable problems for social scientists, he did not sufficiently stress the implication of this fact, namely "that there is no logical connection between a prediction's being reflexive and its being a problem for the scientist in the process of theory testing, and therefore that the problem presented, to begin with, is only *technical* and not *methodological* at all." This distinction is important because only the latter would support a claim of a "*methodological* (and as a result 'philosophically interesting') distinction between the natural and social sciences" (Romanos 1973, 100). Both Buck and Romanos seem content to drop the issue on the basis that the challenges identified are solvable *in principle*, indicating that, although they may require consideration by working scientists in specific fields, reflexive predictions are of little concern to philosophers of science.

Accompanying the longstanding focus on logical issues of epistemic import was a widespread view that broadly 'ethical' or 'practical' issues arising from science's role in society, although undoubtedly important, were the proper concern of scientists, politicians, and ethicists, but not philosophers of science. One half of this position consisted in the notion that philosophy of science should avoid not only the context of discovery (a stricture that was increasingly challenged in the wake of Kuhn's influence on the field) but, especially, the so-called context of application (cf. Carrier and Nordmann 2011). The other half consisted in the conviction that ethical or other 'non-epistemic' considerations should ideally play no role in the context of (rational) justification. Douglas (2009, chapter three) traces the development of the so-called 'value-free ideal' that became dominant in 20th century mainstream philosophy of science, attributing its ascent to a combination of factors including both the lasting impact of the logical positivists as well as pressures to professionalize and depoliticize the field of philosophy of science in the context of the Cold War.

Again, we can sense the influence of such views on the reflexive prediction debate. Buck (1963, 362–363) characterizes Merton's suggestion that self-fulfilling prophecies perpetuate a 'reign of error' as resulting from a "confusing blend of moral and methodological appraisal," noting that although we might join Merton in deploring moral errors, "we should insist on keeping morals and methodology distinct." We, as later observers of the reflexive prediction literature, might likewise join Buck in appreciating the wisdom of keeping these issues conceptually separate while simultaneously making note of the telling fact that neither Buck nor Romanos present any such 'moral' issues as possible avenues of inquiry from the perspective of philosophy of science.

While such outlooks were not ubiquitous, they were highly influential in shaping many philosophers' views concerning suitable topics of investigation and, through this impact, the *de facto* boundaries of the field itself. The intervening years, however, have seen significant departures from such views. An explosion of debate surrounding scientific realism in the late 1970s and '80s signaled the return of metaphysical issues to the limelight decades after their veritable banishment in accordance with positivist strictures. Growing skepticism concerning the existence of a logic of scientific justification and the utility of a strict discovery/justification distinction more generally, both spurned on by the historicizing work of Kuhn (1962; 1977), greatly expanded the range of epistemic issues considered proper and worthy of philosophical analysis. More recently, powerful arguments have been put forward against both the plausibility and desirability of entirely excluding non-epistemic goals and value judgments from even the heart of scientific reasoning, thus requiring more careful consideration of such issues by philosophers of science (cf. Douglas 2016; Elliott 2017; Wilholt 2009). These arguments have often also been accompanied by calls for increased engagement with the ethical or otherwise 'practical' aspects of science, such as those arising in the context of application (cf. Douglas 2010; 2014).

Given the opening up of mainstream philosophy of science that has occurred since the earlier discussions of reflexive predictions and other such phenomena fizzled out, one might expect recent claims concerning purportedly self-fulfilling representations in the social sciences, such as those discussed in chapter two, to generate a good deal of interest. As of yet, however, consideration of such claims by philosophers of science has been quite limited,[50] being restricted almost entirely to specialized literature on the philosophy of economics (cf. Mäki 2012) or, in a few instances, overview works comparing philosophy of natural and social science (cf. Guala 2016b).

One emerging trend of this limited, yet slowly growing, body of literature seems to be to conceive of the central phenomenon in question in terms of 'performativity'. This is relevant for our attempt to address questions of significance, as the manner in which we conceptualize and describe self-fulfillment can have a substantial impact on our intuitions concerning its ability to generate new philosophical problems or contribute something novel to existing ones. For example, as briefly suggested in chapter three, there is a good case to be made that the perceived association between performativity and anti-realism (along with certain forms of social constructionism) has tended to direct what little philosophical attention has been paid to claims concerning the self-fulfillment of *homo economicus* toward their possible significance for debates surrounding 'realism' (in one or another of the term's many senses). The following section seeks to present an example of this impact this by examining a dispute between Ferraro et al. and critics Felin and Foss (2009a, 2009b), and subsequent commentary by Bergenholtz and Busch (2016), about the potential consequences of self-fulfilling science. Unfortunately, I argue, this narrow focus has resulted in the overshadowing of other legitimate, and possibly more fruitful, perspectives on questions of significance.

---

[50] Cases of looping effects that include or constitute self-fulfilling science present an exception. My reasons for considering these strands of research separately are outlined in chapter one.

5.1.2 Self-fulfillment vs. 'realism'?

Because the primary aim of Ferraro et al.'s (2005) original paper was to operationalize more general claims about self-fulfilling theories by identifying specific mechanisms, their initial discussion of the *implications* of their findings was quite limited. Critics Felin and Foss (2009a), on the other hand, in addition to calling many of Ferraro et al.'s findings themselves into question, also stress the potentially dire consequences of claims concerning self-fulfilling science. As they see it, "the strong forms of the self-fulfilling nature of theories and language are sobering because, if true, they threaten the fundamental definition of science and theory as an attempt to understand and predict objective reality" (Felin and Foss 2009a, 655).

This critique led to a brief response by Ferraro et al. (2009, 673), in which they reflect more explicitly upon the theoretical and practical consequences they see as arising from their descriptive claims. They highlight three issues. First, they suggest that scientific self-fulfillment generates a special kind of responsibility for researchers working in disciplines in which such effects may occur. This goes beyond what is advocated by standard research and business ethics approaches by requiring researchers to consider the "ethical consequences of theory"; it "focuses on the ethical and moral consequences of what we teach and how we do our research" (Ferraro et al. 2009, 673). Second, they identify possible consequences for the evaluation of evidence. Testing potentially self-fulfilling theories requires "more subtlety and more attention to the mechanisms that may make them appear true even if they are not" (Ferraro et al. 2009, 673). Finally, they consider that, if multiple potentially self-fulfilling theories contend with one another, "multiple futures and realities are possible." From this, they draw the conclusion that, in such cases, "we have the opportunity to both envision and create a different and maybe even better, more humane, and just world" (Ferraro et al. 2009, 673). Summing up, Ferraro et al. identify three avenues for further research concerning the possible theoretical and practical consequences of self-fulfilling science: issues of moral responsibility, evidence evaluation, and issues surrounding what we might call the thesis of 'multiple possible futures'.

Each of these issues can be seen as relating to established or emerging topics of discussion in philosophy of science. Douglas (2010) argues that consideration of the moral responsibility of scientists was once considered a proper and natural task for philosophy of science, and urges a return to a more socially engaged understanding of the field. Almost mirroring Ferraro et al.'s suggestion, Douglas (2014) even places special emphasis on the need to go beyond the standard approaches of research ethics by considering the consequences of scientists' theories and actions in order to achieve a full mapping of the "moral terrain of science." Evidence evaluation has, of course, long been a canonical topic in the field. As already noted, Kopec and earlier discussants of reflexive prediction have examined issues of this sort specific to self-fulfilling science.[51] Finally, the notion that scientists might help bring about a better world by choosing to promote potentially self-fulfilling theories with preferable outcomes can be related to recent discussions concerning the balancing of epistemic and non-epistemic interests and values in science (cf. Elliott and McKaughan 2014; Douglas 2016).

Despite the variety of issues suggested by Ferraro et al., however, commentators have primarily focused on the perceived threat of performativity-based accounts of self-fulfilling theories to scientific realism. This can be seen, first of all, in the way Felin and Foss (2009b) filter their responses to Ferraro et al.'s suggestions through the specter of the anti-realism they see as inherent to the performativity approach. Based on their reading of several classics in the field, Felin and Foss (2009b, 676) claim that "according to the performativity perspective, then, we cannot even meaningfully speak of the ex ante 'truth' or 'reality' of theories, because theories themselves participate in defining and creating what is truthful and what is real." But then what sense does it make to speak of testing such theories in an attempt to assess their correctness? "If not truth," they ask, "what then should be the basis for choosing one theory over another?" (Felin and Foss 2009b, 676). By denying the notion of 'ex ante truth,' they continue, performativity implies a radical reinterpretation and repurposing of science itself from advancing knowledge about the world to attempting to bring about "the best of all possible worlds" (Felin and Foss 2009b, 676). In a final blow, they charge Ferraro et al. with (perhaps unintentionally) courting anti-scientific social constructionist views prominent in the science wars by "heavily anchoring their arguments on the performativity perspective" (Felin and Foss 2009b, 677).

Felin and Foss, and other commentators who share their concerns, do not typically engage seriously with the philosophical literature on scientific realism. However, certain statements that may be culled from this literature do seem to offer at least some initial support for their concerns. Indeed, philosophers of science have often declared the notion of 'mind-independence' (or sometimes 'human-independence') to be a criterion and/or necessary condition of realism about some phenomenon. Devitt (2005, 786), for example, characterizes the doctrine of realism as being "committed not only to the existence of this world but also to its 'mind-independence'," meaning it does "does not depend for its existence and nature on the cognitive activities and capacities of our

---

[51] I examine two issues related to such suggestions in the following chapter.

minds." Chakravartty (2007, 212), in a similar fashion, describes realism as the view that "our best scientific theories give approximately true descriptions of both observable and unobservable aspects of a mind-independent world." Such statements have long been a staple of many positions taken up in debates concerning natural kinds and realism more generally, and might seem to lend credence to the worries described above, given that claims of self-fulfillment entail that the nature and/or existence of some state of affairs is in fact *dependent* upon what some people have thought about it at some time. If this is correct, then self-fulfilling science may indeed seem to pose a significant problem for our usual beliefs about science and its epistemic success, insofar as these notions are tied to the concept of scientific realism.

However, other philosophers of science have recently argued that the notion of mind-independence implied by such positions is unclear at best and a red herring at worst. Khalidi (2016), for example, motivates such an argument by initially noting that, if we were to posit an unqualified connection between some phenomenon's being mind-dependent and its being 'non-real' in some sense, then the reality of psychological and social properties and entities must be denied. Perhaps even more concerning, even such seemingly robust things as manmade chemicals and genetically-modified organisms seem to be ruled out if we adopt a strict formulation of the mind-independence thesis. In response to such considerations, many authors have attempted to further refine and qualify the central notions involved. Khalidi critically examines several prominent variants of the criterion of mind-dependence and finds them wanting for the purpose of establishing anything significant about some phenomenon's existence. Comparing the notion of mind-independence with a related notion of life-independence, he asks his readers to consider the seemingly preposterous analogous claim that biological entities and kinds are somehow 'non-real' because they fail the test of life-independence:

> Metaphysically speaking, there is no reason to think that being dependent on the mind in the sense of mental sustenance would impugn the reality of a kind any more than dependence on life would. Biological kinds like cells, organisms, and species, are life-dependent in the sense that each of their instances requires the phenomenon of life for sustenance. To say that social (and psychological) kinds are mind-dependent is no more significant than saying that biological kinds are life-dependent. It marks a difference in domain. True enough, natural kinds in physics and chemistry are usually not mind-dependent, but this is hardly different from saying that natural kinds in physics and chemistry are usually not life-dependent. (Khalidi 2016, 244)

Similar arguments may be found in the social construction literature, where proponents of naturalistic approaches to social construction have increasingly argued that constructionist claims, which are sometimes entailed by claims of scientific self-fulfillment and may also contribute to the impression of a conflict with realism, in fact in no way query the 'reality' of the entities to which they are applied (cf. Haslanger 2012).[52]

In addition to these general attempts to cast doubt on any significant connection between mind-independence and realism, several authors have argued along similar lines against the purported threat to realism presented by self-fulfillment and/or performativity. Bergenholtz and Busch (2016), the only extended treatment of the debate between Ferraro et al. and Felin and Foss published in a dedicated mainstream philosophy of science journal (of which I am aware)[53], aims to "cool the fire" in this debate by examining the supposed challenge to realism as well as the suggestion of a special kind of moral responsibility for individual scientists. Echoing Felin and Foss, Bergenholtz and Busch (2016, 25) begin by stating that "the overall terminology and structure of this debate is, in part, derived from the classical debate between (social) constructionism at one end of the spectrum and realism on the other." After explaining Barnesian performativity and briefly laying out the notion of induced self-interest, Bergenholtz and Busch (2016, 29) characterize what they take to be the crux of the debate thusly:

> This example highlights the main issue at stake; not only will the behavior of individuals change to some degree due to the adoption of a scientific theory, but some underlying empirical regularities (Felin and Foss 2009a) will also change, which might turn the theories from false to true. Self-fulfillment is, thus, threatening to undermine objectivity in general and a fundamental premise of scientific realism in particular: that there are some sort of theoretical mechanisms [...] and regularities out there in the world not directly affected by our theorizing about them.[54]

Noting the ambiguity of the term '(scientific) realism' as it is sometimes employed in such debates, the bulk of Bergenholtz and Busch's paper is then devoted to presenting four commonly discussed types (or aspects) of scientific realism and arguing that the purported threat to each by self-fulfillment is largely illusory. Like Khalidi, these authors argue that metaphysical realism in the domain of the psychological and social cannot rely upon an unqualified notion of mind-in-

---

52 See also footnote 30.
53 Aside from my own recent addition, Lowe (2018), from which much of this section is derived.
54 It should be noted that the final sentence of this quote actually expresses a much stronger claim than proponents of self-fulfillment claims must be committed to. The existence of phenomena affected by our theorizing in no way entails that there are no phenomena not thusly affected, nor do any of the authors discussed in chapter two suggest otherwise.

5.1 Assessing significance — 129

dependence. Instead, Bergenholtz and Busch (2016, 33) stress the intuitive connection between the notions of metaphysical realism and objectivity, and conclude that the relevant criterion of the former should be understood in terms of observer-independence:

> In summary, theories within social science are developed by scientists studying social phenomena (minds studying mind dependent phenomena). It is not the mind dependent nature of the subject *per se* that poses a challenge to realism about social science. The issue is rather whether the phenomenon is dependent on the mind of the observer. As long as the dependency relation is between groups or individuals, not identical with or in part constituted by the observer, objectivity need not be compromised.

As mentioned in the previous chapter, Bergenholtz and Busch ultimately go on to argue that the in-principle possibility of studying self-fulfillment effects and developing meta-theories to account for them is sufficient to ensure the required degree of observer-independence. They conclude that "no realist of any kind should have any problems with a situation where a first-order theory changes people's behavior if this change can be predicted by a meta-theory—and being a realist, the realist would merely need to argue that this is possible."

Similarly, Mäki (2012, 21) argues that the primarily causal effects described by performativity scholars do not conflict with any reasonable account of realism concerning economics or the social sciences more generally:

> It is no threat to scientific realism about economics to acknowledge the possibility of causal economics-dependence of some items in the real-world economy. After all, economics as an academic discipline is itself social activity exercised within society, so such connections are a natural feature of social reality. Good social science will investigate such connections together with other causal connections in society at large.

If accounts such as these are correct, then the dramatic implications of self-fulfillment for realism suggested by Felin and Foss seem to be either ill-founded or grossly exaggerated. Suffice it to say, recent contributions to the philosophy of science literature raise significant challenges to any simple connection between the notions of mind-dependence and non-reality. Of course, they also leave many questions unanswered, and further discussion concerning the significance of scientific self-fulfillment for issues of scientific realism is undoubtedly needed.

Unfortunately, however, questions of self-fulfillment's significance to our understanding of science have thus far been largely restricted to such (broadly metaphysical) topics, sometimes at the cost of failing to take seriously other possible avenues for research. As I argue elsewhere, this tendency may be attributable in part to the common association between anti-realism and the performativity approach in terms of which self-fulfillment has often been treated of late (cf. Lowe

2018). For example, both Felin and Foss as well as Bergenholtz and Busch, who explicitly relate Ferraro et al.'s claims to those of performativity scholars, restrict their critical focus almost entirely to the purported threat of self-fulfillment to scientific realism, rather than considering any of the other various possible implications suggested by Ferraro et al. themselves.[55] As we saw above, these authors draw a number of consequences from their claims that seem to relate to other established or emerging topics of discussion in philosophy of science.

In the remainder of this and the following chapter, I begin to examine several of the more broadly 'epistemic' issues suggested by Ferraro et al.'s contention that the possibility of self-fulfillment means we need to pay special attention to the mechanisms that may be involved in bringing about some representation's accuracy (or the mistaken appearance thereof). Before moving on to what I take to be some truly significant epistemic consequences of scientific self-fulfillment in the following chapter, I first wish to analyze – and ultimately put aside – one further purported general threat to our usual notions about science that has arisen in connection with performativity scholarship in recent years. According to this view, the notion of scientific self-fulfillment, understood in terms of performativity, somehow renders our usual notions of scientific success and epistemic evaluation inapplicable or incomprehensible. I will argue that such views are mistaken. Before defending the general compatibility of the possibility of self-fulfillment with our usual notions of science, however, we must first reflect upon what these 'usual notions' amount to.

5.2 Epistemic success and evaluation in science

5.2.1 Epistemic success

It is a commonplace that science displays an unparalleled degree of what may be aptly called 'epistemic success'. Even those who attempt to cast doubt on the justifiability of this view typically begin by acknowledging its pervasiveness. But while most have little trouble accepting that science is (seen as) an epistemic overachiever, it is considerably more difficult to spell out exactly what this

---

[55] Although Bergenholtz and Busch (2016, 37–39) do briefly address the specific "ethical challenge" presented by Ferraro et al., according to whom awareness of the possibility for scientific self-fulfillment implies a special ethical responsibility on the part of scientists for what they teach and write. However, compared to their handling of the 'threat to realism', their treatment of this ethical issue comes across almost as an afterthought, both in terms of dedicated space as well as argumentative rigor. I touch on this issue again briefly in chapter seven.

means or what it is that makes it the case. Explicating and critically examining the special epistemic credentials of science and scientific knowledge as they are often taken for granted in our broader epistemic, social, and ethical deliberations and projects is commonly considered one of the perennial and central issues facing (general) philosophy of science (cf. Psillos 2016).

Like a number of other philosophers of science who have pondered such issues, Laudan (1984, 87) argues that evaluation of success in general is always relative to some set of goals: "To say that an activity is successful is simply to say that it promotes the ends of (at least some of) those engaged in it [or] those judging it to be successful." The question then becomes one of identifying the relevant goals and how they are best promoted. Laudan (1984, 89) himself considers the following "typical list" of "cognitive outcomes" frequently associated with success in science:

a) to acquire *predictive control* over those parts of one's experience of the world which seem especially chaotic and disordered;
b) to acquire *manipulative control* over portions of one's experience so as to be able to intervene in the usual order of events so as to modify that order in particular respects;
c) to increase the *precision* of the parameters which feature as initial and boundary conditions in our explanations of natural phenomena;
d) to integrate and *simplify* the various components of our picture of the world, reducing them where possible to a common set of explanatory principles.

On this view, to call science successful is to claim that it is, to a significant degree, *well-suited* to help us achieve goals just such as these. To say that science enjoys a special status in our broader projects and deliberations is to claim that science is significantly *better* at helping us to achieve these goals than other types of human activity and inquiry. And to evaluate the success of science, either as an idealized institution, a concrete set of practices, or in the form of a particular theory, model, etc., is to judge the degree to which it seems to meet or facilitate the meeting of just such goals.

Laudan claims that the particular goals he identifies "concern themselves with certain interesting *epistemic* and *pragmatic* attributes" (1984, 89, emphasis added). In fact, however, his list is notable specifically because of its relative lack of emphasis on the kind of 'purely' epistemic goals that are often associated with scientific success, such as generating true statements or knowledge about and facilitating our understanding of the world around us. In what sense, then, is the type of success suggested here of a specifically *epistemic* nature?

In some domains of human experience, at least some of the goal states on Laudan's list could clearly be achieved through non-scientific means. Consider the goal to acquire *manipulative control* over portions of one's experience so as to be able to intervene in the usual order of events. If I am bothered by the fact that my neighbors trespass upon my property, I might erect a gated fence in order to gain some measure of manipulative control over who may enter. Acquiring control in such situations doesn't usually require the type of inquiry we typically associate with science. However, for many other domains of human experience, particularly those, as Laudan (1984, 89) says, "which seem especially chaotic and disordered," the path to manipulative control is decidedly less straightforward. Recent advances in nanotechnology, for example, have made it possible to 'erect fences' at the molecular scale in order to, among other things, prevent pathogens from 'trespassing' into places we feel they do not belong – most notably, our food (cf. Bajpai et al. 2018).

In such cases, the most effective if not only path to control runs through an increase of knowledge or understanding. The advent of the 'molecular machines' used in nanotechnology would have been impossible without significant advances in knowledge in the fields of physics, chemistry, and biology, among others. There is a sense, then, in which the success of science must be construed as a specifically *epistemic* kind of success even on what are usually called 'instrumentalist' accounts, of which Laudan's might reasonably be considered an example. The goals relative to which science's success is ultimately to be measured may be largely pragmatic in nature, but the nature of scientific success itself is essentially epistemic, because it is through distinctly *epistemic* means or progress that it helps us attain such goals. On this view, attaining truth, knowledge, or understanding is a constitutive goal of science, but it is only a proximal goal on the way to other ultimate ones.

Of course, even such an 'epistemically friendly' reading of instrumentalism will be seen by many as vastly underplaying the importance of the epistemic dimension of scientific success. Truth, knowledge, or understanding are not merely the means by which science helps us attain some set of largely non-epistemic goals, those of more realist dispositions may contend; rather, their attainment is an important, if not *the*, ultimate aim of science itself. It is not uncommon to hear people explicitly endorse *truth* as the ultimate or optimum aim of scientific inquiry. For reasons I discuss below, however, many philosophers of science are weary of doing so. Those who reject instrumentalism but are cautious of directly equating success in science with the attainment of truth sometimes instead contrast the *explanatory success* of science with its *predictive* or, more broadly, *descriptive success*, and emphasize the centrality of the former for a specific notion of *scientific* success (cf. McMullin 1996). There are, of course, many different accounts of explanation in science, and not all necessarily entail attainment of truth, knowledge, or understanding. However, such notions are clearly intertwined with the explanatory dimension of scientific success as understood by those who explicitly contrast (merely) descriptive and explanatory aims of science.

5.2.2 Epistemic evaluation

Whether as end or means (or more precisely, in the latter case: proximal ends that serve as means to other ultimate ends), epistemic notions figure centrally in our usual understanding of scientific success. It is one thing, however, to identify a condition of success and another to evaluate whether or not it has been fulfilled. At its broadest, *epistemic evaluation* of some aspect of science or scientific practice is the process of judging whether or not, or to which degree, or in what manner the aspect in question contributes to the attainment of the relevant condition(s) of epistemic success. The various 'aspects' under consideration may vary considerably (cf. Humphreys 2016 for overviews of many of the following issues). One of the key projects of 20th century philosophy of science consisted in attempting to evaluate various general *methods* of scientific inquiry in relation to such goals. Early sociologists of science such as Merton investigated the effect of the *norms* of institutionalized science on its ability to meet its epistemic goals. More recently, feminist philosophers of science and social epistemologists have stressed the role of the *social organization* of scientific communities in either promoting or hindering epistemic success. And we can also ask how development of new *concepts, frameworks, questions, styles of reasoning,* or *forms of representation*, among other aspects of science, contribute to the meeting of such goals.

Perhaps the most direct form of epistemic evaluation, however, consists in judgments concerning the degree to which *specific scientific representations*, especially theories and models, either constitute or move us toward our (proximal or distal) goals of truth, knowledge, or understanding. How such judgments might be best (or at least rationally) carried out has long been a central question for philosophers of science. Often, issues arising in connection with judgments of this sort are discussed under the heading of 'theory appraisal' or, because the type of judgments in question are typically of a comparative nature, 'theory choice'.

One of the first things to notice when considering how such judgments may be made is that they are unlikely to consist in the simple application of the success conditions themselves as evaluative standards. Sometimes it is possible to simply 'see' if some success condition has been met or not. If a student wants to know whether or not their attempt to pass a test was successful, they need only be aware of what percentage of correct answers is required for passing and what percentage of correct answers they have given. Because the instructor knows which answers are correct and which are not, evaluating whether or not the condition of success has been fulfilled in this case requires nothing more, we might say, than simply 'looking'. The conditions of success can themselves be employed directly as an evaluative standard in such cases.

In science, however, we do not have the benefit of an answer key. This is nearly definitional – if we already had the answers, we would have no need for the kind of extended, structured inquiry that seems to define scientific activity.[56] Thus, we should expect neither that the evaluative standards employed in gauging the epistemic success of specific scientific representations are just the success conditions themselves, nor that the process of evaluation can consist in simply 'looking' to see if these conditions are met.

This is perhaps most clear when we consider how the epistemic goal of (attainment of) *truth* might be used as an evaluative standard for assessing scientific representations. As already pointed out, such representations are, almost by definition, concerned with matters at the boundaries of human knowledge, those about which we are to some degree ignorant. Thus, even if one accepts attainment of truth as an or even the ultimate aim of science, it is clear that this cannot serve directly as an *evaluative* standard for the epistemic success of representations, because this would presuppose that we already know the truth that such representations are supposed to aid us in discovering.

---

56 There are, of course, many cases in which we feel that we now have a more or less definitive answer to a question that was once the subject of intense scientific debate. Two things should be noted here.

First, the process of epistemic evaluation interesting to philosophers of science is foremost one that is employed when faced with open questions and live options. Science is (again, almost by definition) concerned with pushing the boundaries of knowledge. Of course, it is possible to consider the epistemic qualifications of beliefs we usually take to be unproblematically testable or true; this is one of the hallmarks traditional epistemology. Philosophers of science, however, are not generally interested in unmasking the epistemic vulnerabilities of what we usually take to be easily won knowledge, but rather in understanding how epistemic evaluation can be reasonably carried out when there is no obvious way forward. Observations such as 'the cat is on the mat' may present interesting issues for some epistemologists, but they do not typically worry philosophers of science.

Second, one of the main insights of much history and philosophy of science is that even longstanding and apparently definitive answers won through the struggles of science may be less secure than we typically take for granted. The various failures of previously well-corroborated theories demonstrate to us the importance of explicitly acknowledging the fallibilistic nature of scientific claims. Furthermore, concerns about the theory-ladenness of observation are meant to give us pause in our usual assumption that statements concerning the 'observable' aspects of some theory, at least, can be easily shown to be true or false. The cat on the mat may not bother us, but perhaps the mite on the cat, when observed through a microscope, should.

This is one reason some philosophers of science are reluctant to directly equate scientific success with the attainment of truth. Another stems from the observation that most of the scientific theories that have been proposed in the past are now taken to be clearly false. If truth were a necessary condition for epistemic success in science, then it seems we must conclude that there has been, despite appearances, little success of this sort. And, given that we have no particularly good reason to believe that the trend of postulating perhaps helpful yet ultimately false theories has or will come to an end, we also have little reason to believe that science will become more successful in this respect in the future. So, at least, runs the influential line of argument often called the 'pessimistic induction' developed by, among others, Laudan (1981).

In the face of arguments such as these, many authors have recognized the implausibility of employing truth directly as an evaluative standard. However, they have drawn very different conclusions about how to proceed from this point. The positivists' goal of establishing correspondence rules capable of cashing out theoretical statements in terms of more directly evaluable observational statements can be seen as a kind of workaround that still attempts to employ truth as a direct evaluative standard, albeit in an indirect manner. The widespread conviction that this project ultimately failed provided much of the impetus for the various responses that followed. Instrumentalists might proceed by largely removing such lofty epistemic notions from their conception of scientific success altogether. Those of a more realist bent have at times attempted to 'save' truth by restricting evaluation to *parts* of larger theories or the underlying *structures* of reality they might represent despite including e.g. non-referring entities (cf. Ladyman 2016). Popper (1963) and his followers famously entertained the notion that truth in such evaluations may be replaced with truthlikeness, or verisimilitude. And, as discussed in chapter three, many recent approaches focus on types of representations the accuracy of which is not easily or most naturally measured in terms of their truth or falsity in the first place.

Other authors have noted that what applies to truth must equally apply to notions of knowledge or understanding that include truth as a necessary condition, such as the standard analysis of knowledge as justified true belief. Again, different responses are observable. As already seen, Longino (2002, 108–123) continues to speak of 'scientific knowledge' but advocates the replacement of a strict truth condition by the more pluralistic notion of *conformation*. This denotes a family of 'epistemological success concepts' that may exist as relations between the content of scientific representations and some object(s) distinct from that content. Truth, in fact, figures as *one* of the relations in question, but the inclusion of others such as isomorphism, similarity, fit, and alignment show that we are dealing here with something other than the standard notion of knowledge familiar to epistemologists. Elgin (2017, 9–32), on the other hand, sees such challenges as a motivation for abandoning talk of 'knowledge', 'assertion', and 'belief' in matters of epistemic evaluation in science altogether. This doesn't mean denying the possibility or importance of such evaluation, however. Instead, she suggests such evaluations be examined (and carried out) in terms of 'understanding', 'profession', and 'acceptance' instead.

Such debates continue with little sign of abatement, and are a testament to the difficulty of coming up with a definitive evaluative standard of epistemic success of scientific representations. Since the rise of post-Kuhnian philosophy of science, however, many discussions of theory appraisal have stressed the role of so-called 'theoretical virtues' or 'values' in carrying out comparative evaluations between rival explanatory accounts. This has become one of the most widely discussed perspectives on the epistemic evaluation of scientific representations – in fact, many of the approaches discussed in the proceeding paragraphs employ some version of it.

The 'virtues' in question are characteristics of scientific representations that either constitute or at least strongly indicate its epistemic 'goodness' or success. Chief among them is what is often called 'empirical adequacy,' or sometimes simply 'accuracy,' which I discuss below in more detail. Beyond this, accounts differ concerning what other virtues might be relevant, but perhaps the most widely cited list comes from Kuhn (1977) himself: consistency, scope, simplicity, and fruitfulness. Kuhn famously argued that such features should be understood as values (rather than hard and fast criteria or rules) because their presence should *influence* and *guide* our decisions concerning which theories to accept without ever being capable of completely *determining* which of them we must rationally choose. More recently, it has been argued that the range of values considered germane to such decisions must be widened to include not only the above, so-called 'epistemic' values, but also a host of ethical or otherwise 'non-epistemic' ones.

Disagreement abounds concerning which potential features of theories should actually be considered 'virtuous,' how exactly to interpret and apply the virtues in epistemic evaluation, and what conclusions may be reasonably drawn from their presence. However, there is one 'virtue' of good theories that all the perspectives discussed thus far seem to agree upon. Whether instrumentalist, realist, positivist, empiricist, or most things in between, there is near universal agreement that good theories must be to some degree *empirically adequate*.

Considerably less agreement is to be found concerning the question of what empirical adequacy amounts to. Perhaps most commonly, it is cashed out in the terms laid out by van Fraassen (1980), according to whom a theory is empirically adequate just in case the claims it makes or warrants concerning *observable* objects or states of affairs are correct. But there are issues with this formulation, given e.g. the well-known problem of clearly distinguishing observational from theoretical statements and the theory-ladenness of observations more generally. Noting the problems with this formulation and the lack of explicit alternatives in the literature, Bhakthavatsalam and Cartwright (2017, 446) suggest the following characterization for what is usually meant by those who emphasize the importance of empirical adequacy:

> a theory (or model or set of scientific claims) is empirically adequate when the claims it makes about empirical phenomena – or at least the bulk of these claims, or the central ones – are correct, or approximately correct enough, where some distinction between empirical and theoretical phenomena is supposed.

Many, if not most, philosophers of science treat something like this as a *sine qua non* of successful, or at least acceptable, scientific representations. Bhakthavatsalam and Cartwright argue against treating empirical adequacy as a necessary condition for theoretical success; however, the apparent and acknowledged radicality of their suggestion reveals their approach to be the proverbial exception that proves the rule. In general, empirical adequacy is taken to have pride of place among the theoretical virtues, and serves as a central (though not exclusive)[57] evaluative standard against which the epistemic success of science is to be measured.

Beyond this, there is substantial disagreement on a number of more specific issues concerning empirical adequacy. For example, how much weight should this theoretical virtue be ascribed compared to the others mentioned above? Upon reflection it is clear that a theory that maximizes empirical adequacy through ad hoc adjustments almost inevitably sacrifices simplicity and, likely enough, other values found on most philosophers' lists of theoretic virtues. But a maximally simple and coherent theory that fails entirely in the point of empirical adequacy is clearly defective. Furthermore, realists and anti-realists might disagree concerning why exactly this particular virtue is so important. Whereas the former tend to take its presence to be a necessary condition for and an indicator of the truth they see as the ultimate epistemic goal of science, the latter contend that empirical adequacy is simply as good as it gets for inquirers like

---

[57] The following chapter includes discussion of the phenomenon known to philosophers of science as the thesis of *underdetermination of theory by data*, which argues that evaluation based on empirical adequacy alone is insufficient to decide which of a number of theoretical alternatives should be preferred even in light of purely epistemic goals.

us. These differences of perspective, however, arise only against the background of a shared commitment to the importance of empirical adequacy as an evaluative standard for the epistemic success of scientific representations.

5.3 Self-fulfillment vs. epistemic evaluation?

Epistemic evaluation of scientific representations is, on most readings of the accounts just discussed, a constitutive part of science. Judgments concerning empirical adequacy are accorded a central role in the evaluative process, even when they are necessarily accompanied by other theoretic virtues.

Some of the authors and research programs discussed in previous chapters have at times, however, expressed worry that recognizing the potential for scientific self-fulfillment poses serious issues for our usual notions of epistemic evaluation. According to one version of this worry, showing that some specific scientific representation is self-fulfilling or even that an entire discipline is prone to self-fulfillment is tantamount to demonstrating the impossibility of engaging in genuine epistemic evaluation thereof. Considering that epistemic evaluation of the sort just described is a constitutive part of (empirical) science, this amounts to the claim that such representations or disciplines might not, despite appearances, be properly considered part of science at all. It is, we might say, to question the *scientificity* of the representation or discipline in question.

One central impetus for such views seems to stem from performativity scholarship in general and the work of the acknowledged 'father' of this approach, Michel Callon, in particular. Those who see the suggestion of an incompatibility between self-fulfillment and epistemic evaluation on the basis of this work do not typically go so far as to present explicit arguments. Rather, such a notion may be read off of any number of suggestive statements by Callon and his followers and is further bolstered by an evocative analogy between linguistic performatives and self-fulfilling scientific representations. Given the growing prominence of the performativity approach and the impression that it might license such drastic claims concerning more traditional notions of scientific success, in the following sections, I consider two lines of explicit argument that attempt to cash out this supposed incompatibility. Ultimately, I conclude that neither succeeds, and that the underlying analogy that suggests them is misleading.

To begin, consider the following collection of suggestive quotes from Callon concerning the lessons ostensibly to be drawn from the realization that (economic) theory shapes or, in his preferred terminology, 'performs' (economic) reality:

5.3 Self-fulfillment vs. epistemic evaluation?

> [W]e have to abandon [...] the idea of critique of hard economists, which is intended to show them that they are wrong. [...] We recognize the right of economists to contribute to performing markets, but at the same time we claim our own right to do the same but from a different perspective. [...] What is very important is to abandon the critical position, and to stop denouncing economists and capitalists and so on. (Callon et al. 2002, 301)

> The anthropology characterizing [neo-classical] economics [...] which sees any individual as an autonomous subject capable of intentions and a free will, responsible for his or her acts, is becoming pervasive. The question is no longer 'Is this anthropology true or false?', but 'Is this anthropology able (Where? How? For how long and in which spaces?) to perform, to enact, a reality corresponding to what it says?' (Callon 2005, 10)

> One of the main benefits of the notion of performativity is that it rids us of [...] the representational idiom, in terms of which the purpose of science is to create representations of reality. (Callon 2007, 321)

> Scientific theories, models, and statements are not constative; they are performative, that is, actively engaged in the constitution of the reality that they describe. (Callon 2007, 318)

> We can now see why the concept of performativity has led to the replacement of the concept of truth (or nontruth) by that of success or failure. (Callon 2007, 320)

> We are no longer in the register of truth as a reference but–to stick to the same word–in that of truth as success or failure, in truth as fulfilled conditions of felicity. (Callon 2007, 321)

Such quotes seem to posit a serious conflict between the (potentially) self-fulfilling nature of economic theory and the employment of our usual notions of epistemic evaluation and success when considering the field and its theoretical products. There seem to be at least three ways of interpreting the apparently suggested tension.

On the first, the possibility of subjecting (potentially) self-fulfilling scientific representations to epistemic evaluation as typically conceived is granted, yet the utility or advisability of doing so is questioned. On the second, the possibility of epistemic evaluation is granted, however, the type of epistemic evaluation in question will necessarily differ in significant ways from our usual conception because of the influence of self-fulfillment. Finally, on the third and most radical reading, (the potential for) self-fulfillment somehow renders scientific representations unamenable to any kind of genuinely epistemic evaluation – epistemic evaluation is not just ill-advised or in need of modification, but is rather impossible in light of scientific self-fulfillment. In the remainder of this chapter, I focus exclusively on this latter radical claim. Forms of the other two are discussed in the following chapter.

On what basis might one come to develop a view that self-fulfillment is somehow fundamentally incompatible with epistemic evaluation? There are, I think, two paths by which performativity scholars or their readers might come to this conclusion. The first uses an analogy between linguistic performatives and reality-shaping scientific representations to argue that the latter are lacking in the proper type of empirical content required for genuine epistemic evaluation. The second, somewhat less obvious path, proceeds from the assumption that self-fulfillment can be predicted with (near) certainty, and thus that the representations in question lack the proper kind of genuinely hypothetical content required for epistemic evaluation.

5.3.1 Performatives and epistemically evaluable content

Recall that the notion of performativity as employed by Callon, MacKenzie, and others is based, at least in spirit, upon Austin's notion of linguistic performatives. The most well-known examples of this phenomenon include things like making a bet, a formal agreement, or a promise, such as 'I promise to write you every day.' Although they apparently share the same grammatical form as statements, writes Austin (1962, 5), such utterances seemingly belong to a different category of discourse – the so-called *performatives* – in that:

> A. they do not 'describe' or 'report' or constate anything at all, are not 'true or false'; and
> B. the uttering of the sentence is, or is a part of, the doing of an action, which again would not *normally* be described as, or as 'just', saying something.

In explicitly drawing on Austin's account and terminology, Callon and his followers have at times been seen as suggesting in passages like those quoted above that what usually pass for scientific statements or other representations are, in fact, significantly similar to linguistic performatives. The basic intuition fueling the analogy is easy enough to follow. Regarding linguistic performatives, we have utterances that appear, at first glance, to be simple statements that describe the world but are, upon closer examination, actually better understood as being part of an action that changes it in some manner. In light of the evidence for induced self-interest discussed in chapter two, we might feel that something quite similar is afoot regarding certain scientific representations: what initially appeared to be theories or models describing self-interested human behavior or motivations turned out, upon closer examination, to be (part of an act of) influencing or even bringing about the phenomena in question.

If the general analogy between linguistic performatives and self-fulfilling scientific representations holds, then perhaps Austin's statements A and B above apply to the scientific representations in question as much as they do to linguistic performatives. Thus, one might think, what originally appeared to be genuine scientific representations turn out not to be truth-apt or to lack descriptive content entirely. Whether or not Callon or other performativity scholars would endorse this view explicitly is not entirely clear, despite the suggestive nature of the quotes presented above. Given this unclarity, I explicitly refrain from attributing the views discussed in the remainder of this chapter directly to Callon or his followers.

What is clear, however, is the fact that these authors have at least been understood by others as making just such claims. For example, in a recent introductory book on the philosophy of the social sciences, Mark Risjord (2014, 266) writes that:

> In its strong form, performativity is rather controversial. Insofar as it would deny that social scientific theories are descriptive, it denies that they are true or false. Like promises, social scientific theories create what they describe. Promises are successful or unsuccessful, not literally true or false.

Santos and Rodrigues (2009, 986–987) write of the "performativity programme" that

> it replaces the traditional conception of science as a descriptive form of knowledge by one that conceives of economics as a set of instruments and practices that act upon economic players and economic institutions. [...]
> The implication of this, in Callon's view, is that the relevant criterion to assess economics is success, rather than truth, where success is measured by the extent to which reality conforms[58] to what is described by economic theories.

Given that recent work on scientific representations has not been restricted to consideration of truth-apt theories conceived of primarily in terms of sets of sentences, the notion that performativity casts the truth-aptness of representations into question might not necessarily pose a significant threat to the possibility of epistemic evaluation. However, if the representations in question were indeed lacking in any and all descriptive content, as the suggestion often seems to be, this would indeed be a serious problem for anybody who views science as a genuinely epistemic endeavor in the sense introduced in the previous section. This is because, with a few notable exceptions, these approaches all subscribe to the notion that empirical adequacy is a central standard to be used in epistemic

---

[58] This should, I think, be read as 'the extent to which reality *comes to conform* to what is described by economic theories', given that conformation with reality is usually understood as the primary, if not only, criterion of truth.

evaluation. Recall once more Bhakthavatsalam and Cartwright's definition of empirical adequacy:

> a theory (or model or set of scientific claims) is empirically adequate *when the claims it makes about empirical phenomena* – or at least the bulk of these claims, or the central ones – *are correct, or approximately correct enough*, where some distinction between empirical and theoretical phenomena is supposed. (Bhakthavatsalam and Cartwright 2017, emphasis added)

No matter how we are to understand what it could mean for theories, models, etc. to be non-descriptive or to lack descriptive content, it would seem to entail, at the least, that such 'representations' neither consist of nor entail or otherwise warrant claims about empirical phenomena that could be (approximately) correct or not. And this, in turn, would seem to render the representation in question unamenable to epistemic evaluation, conceived of as necessarily including judgments of empirical adequacy. In lacking descriptive content, such representations would lack any epistemically evaluable content. In fact, it would seem a mistake to refer to these as 'representations' at all (as suggested by Callon's quip about 'ridding us of the representational idiom'). Instead, they appear as *pseudorepresentations*, entities created by science that, despite initial appearances, lack the sort of content that would allow them to serve in a representational capacity. For ease of presentation, I will nevertheless mostly employ the term 'representation' for both genuine representations and non-descriptive entities in the following, clarifying the exact intended sense only when potentially unclear.

Thus, we seem to be presented with an argument against the applicability of our usual notions of epistemic evaluation based on an analogy between linguistic performatives and self-fulfilling representations, and the implication that the purportedly non-descriptive nature of the former equally holds for the latter. Left at this intuitive level, this suggestion may seem to warrant the worry that self-fulfillment poses a drastic epistemic threat. However, upon closer inspection, this line of reasoning faces serious issues.

First, the assumption that linguistic performatives are necessarily entirely lacking in descriptive content, upon which the above inference is based, is highly questionable at best. Notably, not even Austin himself ultimately claims this. Although he does attempt to draw a clear distinction between constatives and performatives, nowhere does he suggest that all utterances are necessarily either one or the other. After introducing the distinction and several intuitive examples of each class, he goes on to note that, in fact, it is difficult to identify any examples that are clearly evaluable by *only* truth or falsity, on the one hand, or *only* felicity or infelicity, on the other. For example, apparently performative utterances that constitute a *warning* seem to be clearly evaluable along both dimensions:

> [C]onnected with the performative (I presume it is one) 'I warn you that the bull is about to charge' is the fact, if it is one, that the bull is about to charge: if the bull is *not*, then indeed the utterance 'I warn you that the bull is about to charge' is open to criticism–but not in any of the ways we have hitherto characterized as varieties of unhappiness. We should not in this case say the warning was void–i.e. that he did not warn but only went through a form of warning–nor that it was insincere: we should feel much more inclined to say the warning was false or (better) mistaken, as with a statement. (Austin 1975, 55)

From such examples and others that seem to blur the distinction, Austin (1975, 55) draws the conclusion that "considerations of the happiness and unhappiness type may infect statements (or some statements) and considerations of the type of truth and falsity may infect performatives (or some performatives)."

If this is correct, then there are at least some performatives that seem to possess descriptive content.[59] Establishing just any analogy between performatives and self-fulfilling scientific representations would thus not be enough to warrant the conclusion that the latter lack such content. Rather, it would have to be established that the latter are (analogous to) a specific subset of performatives that in fact lack descriptive content. However, this seems quite unlikely in the case of the claimed examples of self-fulfilling science discussed thus far. Consider statements such as 'every agent is actuated only by self-interest,' 'the price of derivative options equals (some output of the Black-Scholes-Merton model),' or 'there are two distinct species of (animal family)'. These seem clearly to be, in fact, of the same character as Austin's warning about the bull. Despite whatever effect may be brought about by the 'utterance' (i.e. practical use) of such representations, and their evaluability along the dimension of their 'success' in doing so, they also seem to be clearly evaluable as claims concerning empirical phenomena that may be judged to be more or less accurate. And this is all that is required for amenability to epistemic evaluation as typically conceived.

The second major problem facing the above line of reasoning is that the analogy between linguistic performatives and self-fulfilling scientific representa-

---

[59] In fact, we can probably safely go far beyond this weak statement by noting that the felicity conditions of even those speech acts that do not take the grammatical form of assertions usually include the obtainment of a certain state of affairs. My demand that you 'Leave my house immediately!' does not have the same grammatical form as 'You are currently in my house and I would like you to leave it.' but the state of affairs described in the latter assertion must obtain if the demand is to be felicitous. However, this suggestion would require further explication, and the weaker point is sufficient for my argument.

tions is itself flawed. The intuition underlying the analogy was founded upon the notion that both, despite initial appearances, 'do something' to the world, rather than merely describing it. However, to the extent that the latter change the world, it is in a manner quite different from that in which performatives do, at least as they are traditionally understood. To see why this is so, let us first examine how Austin proceeds after recognizing the problems arising from his initial constative/performative distinction.

The difficulties of identifying clear criteria whereby constatives and performatives could be properly distinguished led Austin to the conclusion that a fresh start was needed. Instead of beginning with a supposed distinction between types of utterances, he would instead explore the "circumstances of 'issuing an utterance'" more generally (Austin 1975, 92). This exploration is grounded in a distinction between three different aspects of any utterance.

The *locutionary* aspect of an utterance consists in saying *something*, in the sense of using words with sense and reference, very often expressing some propositional content we might very roughly call the 'literal meaning' of the utterance. In performing a locutionary act, however, one also performs an *illocutionary* act, such as "giving some information or an assurance or a warning; announcing a verdict or an intention; [...] making an identification or giving a description, and the numerous like" (Austin 1975, 98–99). The distinction between these two aspects may be expressed by saying that locution is "performance *of* an act of saying something," whereas illocution is "performance of an act *in* saying something" (Austin 1975, 99–100). Only the latter captures most of what was supposed to be interesting about the original notion of performatives: the idea that 'words' may 'do things' in the sense that certain actions are carried out in our performance of an utterance. It is *in* saying 'I promise,' 'I bet,' and the like, that we promise, bet, and so on. However, notes Austin, this is not the only sense in which the performance of an utterance can also be said to 'do something'. Indeed, there is a third aspect, the *perlocutionary*, which he describes as the performance of an act *by* saying something. By this, Austin (1975, 101) means the production of "certain consequential effects upon the feelings, thoughts, or actions of the audience, or of the speaker, or of other persons" by one's saying something.

Austin (1975, 102) offers the following example to illustrate the distinction between locutionary, illocutionary, and perlocutionary aspects:

Locution: He said to me, 'You can't do that.'
Illocution: He protested against my doing it.
Perlocution: He stopped me, he brought me to my senses, etc.

In uttering 'You can't do that,' the speaker articulates a series of words with a more or less definite meaning. Depending primarily on how the word 'can't' is cashed out, we may be dealing with a (likely truth-apt) statement concerning the legality, appropriateness, morality, etc. of the hearer's behavior. Alternatively, the speaker's words may be interpreted as (merely) expressing a normative judgment, the content of which itself is neither true nor false, strictly speaking. In either case, however, the performance of the utterance in question constitutes part of an action the speaker is performing *in* articulating these words, namely a protestation directed at the hearer's behavior. This is the illocutionary force of the utterance. The hearer, in this case, is brought to discontinue their unwelcome behavior *by* (the perlocutionary force of) the speaker's words. But it is clear that this outcome was not inevitable; the speaker could have successfully protested in the sense of making their misgivings known, while at the same time failing to curtail the unwanted behavior. The perlocutionary effects of an utterance, whatever they may be in any given case, are not part of the action performed in uttering; they are, instead, the consequences that follow the performed action.

This brief summary glosses over many of the difficulties that arise when attempting to spell out the distinction between illocutionary and perlocutionary aspects more carefully. Austin himself was keenly aware of these difficulties, and many later commentators have struggled to sharpen the distinction. However, this should suffice to demonstrate the weakness of the purported analogy between linguistic performatives and self-fulfilling scientific representations.

As we saw in chapter three, Mäki (2013, 447) argues that in order for economic theorizing to work in a manner truly analogous to linguistic performatives, it would have to be the case "that uttering or writing down an economic model for an audience (that understands the model and perceives the uttering as genuine and done in appropriate circumstances) establishes the model world as part of the real world." Because the connection between economic theory and reality envisioned by performativity scholars requires practical use that goes far beyond simply uttering, Mäki argues, their claims must in fact be understood to refer to causal rather than constitutive processes. Or, in the vocabulary devised by Austin, we might say that for cases like induced self-interest, the changes in question are not brought about directly through an action performed *in* uttering or otherwise 'using' economic theory (illocutionary force) but rather indirectly through a chain of causal events set into motion *by* its use (perlocutionary force). Traditionally, most of the interest in linguistic performatives has been motivated by their apparently powerful illocutionary effects. Given that the kind of self-fulfilling scientific representations discussed thus far affect their changes through perlocutionary effects, however, the purported analogy between the two phenomena is ultimately unconvincing. As we saw, Mäki views this as reason enough to abandon talk of 'performativity' in connection with the kinds of effects typically investigated by performativity scholars.

Others, however, have been keen to reaffirm the analogy. For example, Guala (2016a) argues that Mäki's attempt to 'save Austin from MacKenzie' is, while understandable, ultimately flawed. His critique, it is argued, depends centrally upon the claim that none of the meanings attached to the term 'performativity' as used by performativity scholars is faithful to Austin's original notion. And this claim, as we have just seen, depends upon the distinction between illocutionary and perlocutionary effects, and perhaps a corresponding, more ontologically laden one, between constitutive and causal processes, respectively. Guala (2016a, 30), however, develops and defends a "deflationary interpretation, according to which illocutionary effects do not have any major ontological implications," in order to defend the claim that Austin's original notion of performativity may have more in common with its usage by Callon, MacKenzie, and other performativity scholars than Mäki supposes.

However, Guala's line of argument provides no solace for those who would use the analogy between linguistic performatives and self-fulfilling scientific representations to claim that the latter are unamenable to epistemic evaluation. For it is based on a revisionist reading of Austin on which (causal) perlocutionary, rather than illocutionary, effects take center stage. Even concerning such paradigmatic examples of performatives such as promising, Guala (2016a, 43–48) claims that the real work is done entirely by the causal impact of an utterance rather than any ontologically significant act of constitution enacted in its uttering. On this picture, whatever illocutionary effects remain are (merely) semantic, rather than ontological, in nature.

Furthermore, on Guala's account, the primary manner in which both performatives and performative economic theory exert causal influence is by creating and coordinating beliefs and expectations. Presumably, a large part of the power of representations to do this arises from the impression that they provide reliable information about some target system in the world. And although it is perhaps conceivable that this impression is systematically mistaken (in some domains), it seems fair to place the burden of proof for such a claim on those who would make it. Guala, for one, does not propose anything of the sort; thus, rather than undermining the idea that performativity implies a lack of descriptive content, his account seems to give such content pride of place in explaining the inner workings of performativity.[60]

---

[60] Perhaps it could still be objected that the connection between scientific representations and self-fulfilling causal effects of their practical use somehow show us that we should view them as

The notion that (the possibility of) self-fulfillment renders scientific representation unamenable to epistemic evaluation because of a purported analogy with linguistic performatives is thus shown to be ill-conceived from front to back. If we adopt a reading on which the latter 'do things' through an ontologically-laden constitutive process that works primarily through illocutionary force, then the analogy simply fails to hold for the examples of self-fulfilling science considered thus far. If we adopt a deflationary reading such as Guala's, then the analogy between linguistic performatives and self-fulfilling scientific representations may yet hold, but at the cost of giving up on the intuition that there is anything particularly odd or mysterious afoot that would rule out the amenability to epistemic evaluation of either. And if the analogy cannot be employed to call into question the possibility of descriptive content concerning specific self-fulfilling representations, then it clearly cannot be used to motivate a more thoroughgoing and widespread skepticism concerning the scientificity of entire disciplines or fields on this accord.

5.3.2 Meta-theories and hypothetical content

Brissett (2019), in a critical examination of the history of modern performativity scholarship, identifies another common feature of its claims that may lay bare a subtler line of argument unpinning the purported threat to epistemic evaluation. Callon and other founding figures developed the performativity approach as an attempt to employ the insights of Austin's work while at the same time distinguishing their project from others sharing this common ancestor. In doing so, claims Brissett, performativity scholars end up rejecting certain features inherent to both Austin's account and their competitors', with the result that the prevalence or probability of strong performativity effects is often wildly overestimated. At times, this overestimation looms so large that scientific statements come to be viewed as *inevitably* bringing about the states of affairs to which they relate. I show why this belief might generate worries about epistemic evaluation (in the context of ongoing inquiry) below; for now, let us have a brief look at the history in question and the problematic assumptions to which, Brissett claims, it gave rise.

---

having normative, rather than descriptive, content. However, this would be to confuse the notion that our truth-apt and otherwise descriptive-content-bearing beliefs, expectations, theories, etc. often exert significant normative force upon our dealings with the notion that the content of the representations themselves is normative, rather than descriptive, in nature.

One important predecessor project of performativity is that of Bourdieu (1991), who appreciated the importance of Austin's insights while rejecting that they should be restricted to the domain of linguistics. Rather, he conceives of Austin's performatives as just one, often relatively small, component of broader *acts of institution* that unfold over longer timeframes and include more moving parts than focus on a specific utterance might reveal. Brissett (2019, 25) sees Bourdieu as extending Austin's project by placing much more emphasis on various non-linguistic features of the rites in which performatives are enacted, the institutional structures required to grant them their power, and the uptake of such acts of elocution by others.

In developing the performativity approach, Callon positions these non-linguistic aspects at the center of the attempt to understand how economic theory may come to shape economic reality. As we have seen, performativity scholars have focused on the role of technical and technological devices as mediators between economic theories and agents' behavior. Perhaps the most famous example of such devices are the 'cheat sheets' and computer programs that implemented the Black-Scholes-Merton pricing equations for derivative options, as discussed by MacKenzie (2006a). The move to a focus on such devices rather than linguistic performatives was just one of a number of explicit attempts to distance performativity scholarship from other approaches that acknowledge the impact of theorizing only in more direct and obvious ways.

Muniesa and Callon (2009)[61] describe several distinctions or 'tensions' between their preferred approach and those that came before. Whereas more traditional sociological approaches have tended to focus on the direct influence of academic *theorizing* on behavior, performativity attempts to open our eyes to the arguably more influential impact of extra-academic *engineering* that, while often based on academic theorizing, aims at the resolution of concrete problems rather than the pure furthering of knowledge. Going hand in hand with this distinction is another between *psychogenic* influences – broadly, those mediated by (collective) beliefs and conventions – and *material* effects, which create and promote new possibilities and motivations for action through the creation of tools, artifacts, and (institutional) spaces. These and other closely related distinctions are exemplified by the differences between the more or less 'classic' examples of self-fulfilling prophecy-like phenomena – bank runs, bandwagon effects, and the like – and a case like the self-fulfillment of the Black-Scholes-Merton equations.

---

[61] I rely upon Brissett's (2019, 34–39) translation and summary of the original French text.

Let us briefly pause to note once again that, from the perspective developed in the preceding chapters, the decision of performativity scholars to focus on non-linguistic, material, and less obvious and/or direct effects and uses of scientific representations is not only acceptable, but highly welcome. Such studies support one important finding concerning an adequate conceptualization of scientific self-fulfillment: namely that requiring all or most actors in the causal chains involved in such effects to be aware of, understand, and believe in the truth of the relevant scientific representations is much too strong a condition. For this would rule out many apparently relevant cases, despite the fact that they otherwise fulfill the general structural requirements of self-fulfillment claims and the clear intuition that they, if anything, should qualify as examples thereof. Historical and sociological investigation of specific phenomena may reveal the subtle causal mechanisms whereby scientific representations can become self-fulfilling, and their identification gives us reason to suspect that similar mechanisms could be at play in situations that are structurally similar. As such, performativity scholars' empirical research on such issues has the potential to provide an essential contribution to furthering our understanding of scientific self-fulfillment and its prevalence.

The trouble begins, argues Brissett, when in focusing so strongly on the role of technical devices, performativity research also comes to largely ignore the social conditions – language games, conventions, norms, shared beliefs, etc. – that must be present in order for the technical devices in question to impact economic reality as they sometimes do. And this, in turn, undermines one of the key insights of Austin's original notion of linguistic performatives: namely, that would-be performative utterances may in fact fail when the proper conditions are not met.

> It is particularly interesting to note that performativist sociology breaks away from Austin's original definition. Remember that the starting point for the philosopher was the fact that certain statements fail when they have no impact on the world. This leads him to place the performative felicity conditions at the heart of the definition, and therefore, the possibility of failure. (Brissett 2019, 108)

In contrast to this,

> the Callonian approach, with its technicist vision, expels the ideas of social felicity conditions that exclude performative failure. So here we are, beyond a simple constructivism that could both admit that economists could participate in the construction of social reality and fail to do so, in a hyper-constructivist perspective: nothing seems to prevent performativity. (Brissett 2019, 108)

Again, it is difficult to assess the degree to which performativity scholars actually (implicitly) adopt such a view, given that they do not typically state it explicitly. However, a general tendency to focus on mechanisms that facilitate performativity has been noted by several authors, as when Felin and Foss (2009a, 654) suggest that the "general logic of the self-fulling nature of (false economic) theories has not been questioned or challenged" by performativity scholars, or when Marti and Gond (2018, 487) posit the existence of a "success bias" based in the proclivity to focus exclusively on cases in which positive effects are found. All of these authors, Brissett included, thus set out to elucidate the various limits or 'boundary conditions' of effective transformations of reality based in (economic) theorizing.

For our purposes, it is enough to note that the existence of such a tendency might help explain how one could come to the conclusion that purportedly self-fulfilling scientific entities are rendered unamenable to proper epistemic evaluation. Losing sight of all the ways in which scientific theorizing *may* fail to change the world might lead one to (implicitly) assume that it cannot, in fact, fail to do so. The initial analogy to Austinian linguistic performatives suggested that the proper category of analysis for scientific entities should not be truth or falsity, but rather successfulness or unsuccessfulness. However, if Brissett's analysis is correct, then performativity theorists have, at times, lost sight even of the possibility of assessing the economic theories they study in the latter terms.

If we (implicitly) assume that our uttering, believing in the truth of, or otherwise 'using' an apparently descriptive statement or representation cannot fail to bring about the state of affairs it targets, then we will feel secure in our knowledge that it will in fact do so. But this, in turn, may seem to rule out the possibility (or reasonableness) of continuing to think of that representation as possessing a genuinely *hypothetical* character. The type of epistemic evaluation at stake in empirical science, however, is concerned only with statements, theories, models, etc. that are genuinely hypothetical in nature. To take an extreme case, statements expressing logical truths are truth-apt and may be 'evaluated' in the sense of being subjected to judgements concerning their truth, however it is clear that the type of epistemic evaluation at issue in empirical science is not concerned with or applied to such statements. Similarly, we might admit that some representation is capable of generating empirical statements in relation to which epistemic evaluation could take place but feel certain that use of the representation would bring about exactly those states of affairs that would confirm it (because it cannot fail to do so). In such a case, it might seem acceptable to speak of 'evaluations of accuracy' yet odd to think that such evaluations have anything in common with the type of epistemic evaluation germane to empirical science. (Indeed, we might rightfully wonder why we should undertake such evaluations at all.) On such a picture, what the performativity approach reveals is not the non-descriptive nature of self-fulfilling scientific representations, but rather their non-hypothetical nature, and thus the ridiculousness of attempting to subject them to epistemic evaluation as traditionally understood.

To illustrate, a defender of this line of reasoning might have us imagine a computer program that asks the user to predict what color a lightbulb, currently unlit and hidden behind a curtain, will be lit when the curtain is removed. In fact, the program is written such that the lightbulb takes on whatever color is entered before being revealed. If unaware of this causal connection, both user and onlookers may reasonably take the former's input to constitute a genuine prediction, and might even decide to make bets before the curtain is lifted concerning whether or not the prediction will turn out true or false. If, however, someone were to examine the code and learn the truth, such behavior becomes unfathomable. The performativity theorist, the defender might claim, reveals this source code, thus making us aware that continuing in the fashion we have until now practiced would be ill-advised at best.

Note that the above scenario relates most directly to the notion of self-fulfilling *predictions* rather than self-fulfilling theories, models, or other types of representations. In chapter three, I argued that we should analyze these phenomena separately for a number of reasons. Here we find one more: it is far less clear how the type of story told above might apply to such representations or whether the intuitive challenge concerning a genuinely hypothetical character is equally given in such cases. Putting it in the terms developed in the previous chapter, the question seems to be: can we have (near) certain knowledge of the correctness of some meta-theory while remaining uncertain as to the degree of accuracy (or epistemic success more generally) of the first-order theory to which it pertains?

We may, in some cases, feel more secure in our knowledge concerning *some kind* of effect a representation will exert on its target system than we are of the representation's own accuracy. For example, someone who is on the fence about whether or not some animal population constitutes one or two species might feel quite certain that conservation efforts enacted in response to the content of a two-species model will result in a speciation event if it has not, in fact, already occurred. Initially, it seems as if the space between judgments concerning what *will be* the case given some future chain of events and what *is* the case before such events take place allows us to continue to view the epistemic success of the first-order theory as an open question.

Trouble might seem to loom, however, when we consider how secure knowledge of a strong *self-fulfillment* effect as defined in chapter three might be compatible with suspending judgment in this manner, given the inclusion of the counterfactual condition that content-responsive actions generate increased conformation relative to a hypothetical situation in which such actions did not occur. Making such a judgment with (near) certitude would seemingly require that we already have an excellent understanding of the actual state of the target system in question, arguably enough so as to preclude treating the representation in question as possessing genuinely hypothetical character.

However, two considerations serve to defang this apparent threat. First, such tension as exists here derives entirely from the inclusion of the counterfactual condition. Second, performativity research, despite its usefulness in elucidating the phenomenon of self-fulfillment, cannot give us the postulated *certain* knowledge of counterfactual (future) situations. One might be led by the tendencies identified by Brissett, Felin and Foss, or Marti and Gond to adopt the assumption that 'nothing seems to prevent performativity,' but the discussions presented in the previous chapter clearly indicate otherwise. In the majority of cases, the best we are likely to manage regarding possible future cases of self-fulfillment is identification of a number of mechanisms that have proven to be active in structurally similar situations. Not all of these mechanisms will necessarily encourage self-fulfillment; many may actively hinder it.

Even if we are successful in identifying which particular mechanisms are likely to become active under certain conditions, and which conditions in fact hold in a given case, the fact that we are dealing with causal chains rather than acts of constitution means that we cannot be certain that 'use' of the representation under the specified conditions will in fact be sufficient (in the strong sense) to bring about the postulated effects. Going beyond this would require us to have knowledge that the connections between representation, content-responsive actions, and increased conformation hold with something like the force of nomological, metaphysical, conceptual, or logical necessity, and this seems clearly to outstrip our epistemic capacities.

If the purported connection is weaker than this, we've moved on from the claim that we can have *certain* knowledge that specific content-responsive actions will bring about some specific state of affairs. And it was this strong claim (if any) that might seem to entail the senselessness of treating (future) self-fulfilling representations as possessing the kind of hypothetical character germane to empirical science and, thus, the relevant notion of epistemic evaluation. Crucially, this does not mean that claims concerning the possibility, plausibility, or likelihood of future self-fulfillment are irrelevant to epistemic issues of interest to philosophers of science – indeed, I examine one such issue in detail in the following chapter. It is merely to say that the radical reading of Callon's claims discussed at the outset, according to which self-fulfillment somehow renders scientific representations entirely unamenable to epistemic evaluation, is not tenable.

We have now seen two general ways in which a purported analogy between linguistic performatives and self-fulfilling scientific representations might be utilized in order to argue against the amenability of the latter to epistemic evaluation as traditionally understood. The first worked by denying that such representations have any descriptive content that could be taken into account when assessing their empirical adequacy. The second admitted that descriptive content may be present, but questioned whether or not this content could be seen as having a genuinely hypothetical nature in the first place. Both, we have seen, are flawed in a number of ways, not least because the analogy to which both appeal is undermotivated and misleading. Whatever significance the work of performativity scholars may have for our practice of epistemic evaluation, it does not seem to consist in the kind of all-encompassing threat suggested above. In the following chapter, I explore more moderate theses about how self-fulfillment may affect certain aspects of epistemic evaluation and ongoing scientific inquiry.

6 The epistemic significance of self-fulfillment

The epistemic significance of scientific self-fulfillment or other closely related phenomena has sometimes been overestimated based largely on intuition rather than argument. In the previous chapter, I criticized two strong and potentially destructive claims concerning the epistemic import of self-fulfillment suggested by certain strands of performativity scholarship. It is not the case, I argued, that self-fulfillment entails a lack of empirical or genuinely hypothetical content that would render scientific representations unamenable to epistemic evaluation as typically understood. With the field cleared of such drastic suggestions, I turn now to examine more nuanced ways in which self-fulfillment may be significant for epistemic issues in philosophy of science.

Strictly speaking, though it is convenient to refer simply to the epistemic significance of 'self-fulfillment,' I argue in this chapter that both *genuine self-fulfillment* and *illusory self-confirmation* have important consequences for our practice of epistemic evaluation. I begin by considering the latter phenomenon, noting that some of the epistemic worries expressed by proponents of 'self-fulfillment' claims concerning *homo economicus* are, in fact, better understood as positing its illusory self-confirmation. I then show that these worries are no less interesting from the standpoint of philosophy of science for this misattribution, however, as they have potentially significant implications for certain strands of debate concerning what philosophers of science call the *underdetermination of theory by data*. One consequence of the empirical claims of Ferraro et al. (2005), I argue, is that research performed in hopes of adjudicating scientific disputes between rival theoretical accounts of *homo economicus* may actually make it *more* difficult to acquire the kind of evidence that would be necessary to decide the issue. Such effects may constitute a fortification of what are known as 'weak' or 'transient' cases of underdetermination and represent an epistemically troubling phenomenon that has largely escaped the notice of philosophers of science.

In the second half of the chapter, I turn to examine the consequences of genuine self-fulfillment for epistemic evaluation. I argue that despite the fact that genuine self-fulfillment entails an increase in conformation – epistemological success of content – that is, strictly speaking, at least co-constitutive of an increase in epistemic success, that this needn't worry us overly much from an epistemic perspective. The existence of (perhaps yet undiscovered) alternative representations that incorporate the insights of meta-theories into the first-order theories they study means that the correct epistemic response to the discovery of (possible) self-fulfillment is to seek out these richer models rather than worry about the marginal self-improvement of the associated first-order representations.

6.1 Illusory self-confirmation and underdetermination

6.1.1 Specious validity

In the previous chapter, it was noted that Ferraro et al. (2009) make three suggestions concerning what they take to be the implications of scientific self-fulfillment. One of these suggestions, which were largely ignored by both Felin and Foss as well as Bergenholtz and Busch in favor of more radical sounding claims relating to anti-realism, was that self-fulfillment has "implications for how we test our theories," requiring "more subtlety and more attention to the mechanisms that may make them appear true even if they are not" (Ferraro et al. 2009, 673). Ferraro et al. are correct to harbor this concern in response to the empirical claims of their account; however, they are mistaken in attributing it to the workings of scientific self-fulfillment. Rather, it is a product of illusory self-confirmation. To appreciate this, it will be helpful to return briefly to Merton's work on self-fulfilling prophecies.

When Merton (1948, 195–196) introduced the notion of self-fulfilling prophecy, his intent was not only to call attention to an important yet overlooked facet of human experience, but to criticize it as a pernicious influence on human relations:

> The specious validity of the self-fulfilling prophecy perpetuates a reign of error. For the prophet will cite the actual course of events as proof that he was right from the very beginning. (Yet we know that Millingville's bank was solvent, that it would have survived for many years had not the misleading rumor created the very conditions of its own fulfillment.) Such are the perversities of social logic.

As we have seen, Merton makes such 'perversities' responsible for a number of social ills, including much of the widespread ethnic and racial strife present in the United States. But recognizing the workings of self-fulfilling prophecies is meant to offer not only an explanation of but a potential *corrective* to such 'reigns of error' and the evils they beget: "*the self-fulfilling prophecy, whereby fears are translated into reality, operates only in the absence of deliberate institutional controls*" (Merton 1948, 210).

To illustrate, Merton points out that bank runs, which were fairly common in early 19th century America, virtually disappeared with the introduction of government sponsored deposit insurance and other banking legislation. With an institutionalized guarantee that their deposits were safe in the case of bank failure, depositors no longer had a strong incentive to withdraw their funds 'before it was too late' in response to rumors of impending insolvency. As a further example, more to his central point, Merton asks us to

> return to our instance of widespread hostility of white unionists toward the Negro strikebreakers brought into industry by employers after the close of the very first World War. Once the initial definition of Negroes as not deserving of union membership had largely broken down, the Negro, with a wider range of work opportunities, no longer found it necessary to enter industry through the doors held open by strikebound employers. Again, appropriate institutional change broke through the tragic circle of the self-fulfilling prophecy. Deliberate social change gave the lie to the firm conviction that "it just ain't in the nature of the nigra" to join co-operatively with his white fellows in trade unions. (Merton 1948, 209)[62]

Despite Merton's explicit attribution of 'specious validity' to *self-fulfilling prophecies* and his claim that 'fears are translated into reality' through their workings, careful consideration of passages such as the above reveal that much of his concern is more directly related to the illusory self-confirmation of underlying representations that seemingly warrant such predictions. His is not the claim that rumors of the strikebreaking nature of black workers brought about a state of affairs in which the purported nature was in fact given. Rather, this representation gave rise to content-responsive actions that encouraged the *mistaken impression* of its accuracy. One (but not the only) way in which this might come about is indeed through the deliverance of self-fulfilling prophecies: surrogative reasoning performed over such a model of black workers' inner nature will be seen as licensing the expectation of strikebreaking in many particular situations, and these expectations may in turn contribute to bringing about the expected behavior. However, it is precisely Merton's intended point that the firm conviction underlying such predictions neither was nor became true.

A strikingly similar situation can be observed in connection with self-fulfillment claims surrounding *homo economicus*. Ferraro et al. (2005, 12) declare the topic of their investigation to be self-fulfilling *theories* and purport to identify mechanisms by way of which "the assumptions and ideas of economics come to create a world in which the ideas are true." However, in other places, they apparently vacillate on whether the theories in question actually become true or merely come to seem true, as when they write that:

---

[62] Unfortunately, Merton does not specify which 'appropriate institutional change' he specifically has in mind here.

> theories can 'win' in the marketplace for ideas, independent of their empirical validity, to the extent that their assumptions and language become taken for granted and normatively valued, therefore creating the conditions that make them come 'true'. (Ferraro et al. 2005, 8)[63]

At other times, they write that theories can become self-fulfilling by "creating the behavior they predict" (Ferraro et al. 2005, 8), however, as we saw in Merton's analysis of union segregation, representations can generate self-fulfilling predictions without thereby themselves becoming self-fulfilling. It is only when reflecting more carefully upon the implications of their earlier paper in response to the critiques of Felin and Foss that Ferraro et al. (2009, 673) explicitly recognize, as noted above, that:

> [T]here are implications for how we test our theories. [...] [I]f predictions and theories set off chains of events that can make them self-confirming, testing such theories requires more subtlety and more attention to the mechanisms that may make them appear true even if they are not.

Once we have drawn an explicit distinction between genuine self-fulfillment and illusory self-confirmation, it is difficult to see how the worry articulated here might be read in the terms of the former.

Does this mean Ferraro et al. have gone too far in making the above claim, given that it does not seem to relate directly to the *self-fulfillment* of theories that their account ostensibly concerns? Not necessarily. As repeatedly pointed out, whether content-responsive actions lead to self-fulfillment, illusory self-confirmation, or neither depends not only on the chains of events they set into motion, but on the precise content of the representation that motivated them. The mechanisms identified by Ferraro et al., however, provide a mid-range theory of typical causal chains leading from economic representations, to content-responsive actions, to changes in the world, *regardless of whether these changes lead to self-fulfillment or illusory self-confirmation*. Thus, such accounts, as well as the empirical data cited in their favor, are quite capable, in principle, of contributing to our understanding of the latter phenomenon and the epistemic issues to which it may give rise.

Indeed, I believe Ferraro et al. are correct to conclude that their account has the 'implications for how we test our theories' they postulate. These implications, I argue, are closely related to a well-known topic of philosophical debate concerning the so-called *underdetermination of theory by data*. I introduce some

---

[63] I assume that the scare quotes surrounding 'true,' together with the implication that the theories in question could be 'empirically invalid,' are meant to suggest the mere illusion of truth.

relevant facets of this issue and explain their relation to illusory self-confirmation below. First, however, we need to consider which representation these authors might have in mind when formulating their concerns about theory testing, and how claims of illusory self-confirmation make their own theoretical contribution to understanding the represented phenomena. As we will see, Ferraro et al.'s dispute with Felin and Foss presents a clear picture of these issues.

6.1.2 *Homo economicus* and human nature

Although Ferraro et al. (2005) consider several 'scope conditions' that may affect or hinder the causal efficacy of the mechanisms they identify in their initial paper, critics Felin and Foss (2009a, 656) take them to task for purportedly ignoring the more crucial 'boundary conditions' of "objective reality" and "human nature." Felin and Foss recognize the general ability of theories to influence reality, but are particularly concerned with the idea that "even *false* theories also fulfill themselves," (Felin and Foss 2009a, 655) a claim they strangely see as warranting a "natural extension [...] that *any* (even false) reality can be created through theory" (Felin and Foss 2009a, 656). Falsely attributing the latter claim to Ferraro et al., they then challenge them to explain why it is that core economic assumptions other than self-interest have failed to bring about the reality they depict. For example, *hyperrationality*, the assumption that agents have full knowledge of their own and other agents' preferences, choices, and the consequences these will entail, fails to obtain despite its widespread adoption in economic theory. Felin and Foss have a straightforward explanation for its failure. "[O]bjective reality intervenes: the boundary of objective reality means that not just any false theoretical claims, assumptions, or prophecies can be made, which would subsequently be fulfilled" (Felin and Foss 2009a, 657). Thus, they refute the claim they falsely attribute to Ferraro et al., arguing that certain stubborn facts about the world will simply preclude the possibility of the kinds of changes required to render false theories true.

More directly relevant for our topic is the further claim that taking these boundary conditions seriously shows not only that not just any arbitrary theory can become self-fulfilling, but also that such reality-altering effects of representations as do exist can be explained without reference to the mechanisms suggested by Ferraro et al.:

> We specifically utilize many of the same examples as [Ferraro et al. 2005] (from economics and social psychology) and explain how sensitivity to these boundary conditions fundamentally changes their underlying conclusions. [...] Although this may seem simplistic

and naive, we argue that theories affect reality when they are true [...]. Or put differently, self-fulfilling prophecies based on true predictions, rather than false ones, affect reality. [...] Theories then affect reality because they capture and explain underlying objective realities better than alternative conceptualizations of that reality [...]. (Felin and Foss 2009a, 656.)

Of particular interest is their assertion that a growing body of literature convincingly demonstrates the existence of "an underlying universal human nature" that questions the "strong malleability of human nature" implied in Ferraro et al.'s work (Felin and Foss 2009a, 659).[64] Unfortunately, the exact notion of human nature in question is not clearly stated; however, the main distinction Felin and Foss seemingly intend to capture here is that between the relative contribution of "various dispositional characteristics," on the one hand, and "beliefs or expectations *about* dispositions or human nature," on the other, to bringing about observed behaviors (Felin and Foss 2009a, 658, emphasis added).

After some tiptoeing around the issue, Felin and Foss (2009a, 660) eventually hypothesize that "self-interest–rightly understood–in fact provides a real underlying human motivation, rather than one that is falsely constructed." Thus emerges a picture of self-interested behavior as arising largely from dispositional characteristics that form a part of human nature rather than from the impact of theories or beliefs *about* such dispositions. At this point we might be reminded once again of Edgeworth's (1881, 16) formulation of the supposed first principle of economics, namely that "every agent is actuated only by self-interest." How might such an account be capable of explaining the data and observations Ferraro et al. cite without referring to the mechanisms they posit to account for them?

Consider once again the observed impact of economic training on various types of self-interested behaviors discussed in chapter two. Various studies seemed to support the hypothesis of a treatment effect, meaning roughly that the correlation between contact with economic theory and willingness to behave in self-interested manners is not the product of a selection effect, but rather that the former induces the latter. Recall, however, that some authors refer to this treatment effect as either an 'indoctrination' or a 'learning' effect. In light of the alternative accounts put forward by Ferraro et al. and Felin and Foss, these terms appear not as mere rhetorical flourishes, but as signals of significantly divergent interpretations of what the data show about the plausibility of *homo economicus* as a model of human nature.

---

[64] Their primary sources for this claim seem to be Chomsky (1957), Brown (1991), and Pinker (2002), alongside a few others.

Ferraro et al. seem to take this data, combined with other well-known failures of textbook predictions of microeconomic theory (cf. Caporael et al. 1989; Katzner 2001; Henrich et al. 2005), to indicate that humans *are not*, in fact, actuated only by self-interest, but may be brought to exhibit behaviors suggestive of this notion through (inadvertent) 'indoctrination' with the social norms and language of *homo economicus*. Felin and Foss, on the other hand, can argue that such studies show humans *are* self-interested by nature but may come to exhibit behavior more clearly indicative of this fact once they have 'learned' via economic training how best to pursue such interests in a variety of (economic) situations. Bergenholtz and Busch articulate such an idea in an attempt to reconcile evidence of a treatment effect with the claim made by Felin and Foss (2009a, 656) that "theories affect reality when they are true."

> [I]f economic students become more self-interested after being exposed to economic theories about self-interest, it is simply because self-interest is an effective type of economic behavior that can optimize economic outcomes—just as insight into chemistry can optimize how we handle chemical material. (Bergenholtz and Busch 2016, 30).

There are two things to note about this dispute. First, Ferraro et al.'s account of the data and observations implies that the human nature model of *homo economicus* is illusorily self-confirming. We have thus found at least one target of their epistemic worries, and may now better understand the sense in which "testing such theories requires more subtlety and more attention to the mechanisms that may make them appear true even if they are not" (Ferraro et al. 2009, 673). Second, this claim of illusory self-confirmation does not arrive on the scene *ex nihilo* only to hover above the substantive dispute, diagnosing its ills from the standpoint of the detached observer. Rather, it is a *result* of an alternative account of the phenomenon under investigation that has already, in virtue of the claims it makes, jumped into the scientific fray on the ground. Thus, the relationship we encounter here is not simply one between a first-order theory and a meta-theory, but rather between two rival accounts, one of which happens to make explicit reference to the other's causal impact in its explanation of the available data.[65]

---

[65] In fact, we could imagine that defenders of a human nature model of *homo economicus* could even investigate the impacts of theories such as Ferraro et al.'s on the objects of study in question, potentially giving rise to their own claims of illusory self-confirmation. Perhaps humans can be 'indoctrinated' by the social norms and language of accounts positing the 'strong malleability of human nature' so as to act in conspicuously non-self-interested ways, thus lending illusory confirmation to accounts such as Ferraro et al.'s.

Leaving aside for the moment the question of their more general plausibility, both of the accounts in question seem capable, in principle, of accommodating the observations of a treatment effect. Of course, the effects of direct economic training represent only one strand of evidence that might be cited in favor of or against either conception. Perhaps other evidence exists or could be gathered that one of the two accounts could clearly not accommodate, thus generating a serious challenge to it. For the sake of argument, however, let us assume that, for the moment at least, we are in fact at an epistemic impasse, and that the currently available evidence is insufficient to clearly adjudicate this dispute.

This is not an unusual situation at the cutting edge of research – in fact, it may be definitional thereof. The usual scientific response to such situations, at least ideally, is simply to seek out additional data that might be capable of distinguishing which rival account is more plausible. However, philosophers of science have sometimes entertained the notion that more data (or indeed, *any* data) may be insufficient to clearly support one rival theory over another. Often, they speak of '*the* thesis of underdetermination' in connection with this idea. Despite this labelling, however, the phenomenon of *underdetermination* actually comes in a number of strengths and types. Below, I will argue that the kind of epistemic impasse postulated to exist between the rival accounts of Ferraro et al. and their critics – namely those in which illusory self-confirmation seems likely – may have a surprising fortifying effect on what is often taken by philosophers to be a weak, epistemically unproblematic, and epistemologically uninteresting form of underdetermination. Before this, however, some prefatory remarks on underdetermination more generally are required to set the stage.

6.1.3 Underdetermination

The familiar fact that the empirical evidence currently available to us in some domain is often not enough to decide between theoretical rivals is part of what motivates philosophical discussion of what is often called the *underdetermination of theories by data*. Stanford (2017) suggests that the most basic notion of underdetermination in science may be captured by the common saying that 'correlation does not imply causation'. If violent cartoons cause or encourage violent behavior in children, then we might expect to find a correlation between the amount of cartoons watched and violent playground behavior. However, such a correlation is also predicted by the hypothesis that children predisposed to violent behavior especially enjoy and seek out violent forms of entertainment. Thus, "a high correlation between cartoon viewing and violent playground behavior is evidence that (by itself) simply *underdetermines* what we should believe about the causal relationship between the two" (Stanford 2017).

In a brief introductory article, Newton-Smith (2000, 532) refers to situations like the above as cases of *weak underdetermination* and points out that, in general, philosophers of science have been interested primarily in claims concerning stronger forms of the phenomenon. Such claims maintain not only that our current evidence is often insufficient to determine which of a number of rival accounts is to be preferred, but that there could be rivals between which no amount of data could decide, or even that *all* representations are undetermined by all possible observational data. These arguments are often based on the notion that theoretical rivals can be *empirically equivalent*, meaning they entail (all and only) identical empirical predictions or consequences and therefore cannot be distinguished by any amount or kind of data. Going even further, it is sometimes argued that such rivals not only may exist but that an infinite amount of empirically equivalent alternative theories can be algorithmically generated from any existing theory (cf. Kukla 1996).

Such possibilities might be seen as having dire consequences for scientific rationality. If empirical data are and can never be sufficient to determine which theories or representations we should accept, then something else must fill in the gap. As we saw in the preceding chapter, Kuhn (1977) famously suggested that so-called epistemic virtues such as simplicity, internal and external consistency, scope, and fruitfulness guide – but do not absolutely determine – our judgments in such cases. However, his insistence that each virtue may be legitimately interpreted in multiple ways and that no algorithm exists for determining their relative significance lent many philosophers of science of the day the impression that Kuhn was advocating an essentially irrational, or at least arational, method of theory evaluation. As we saw in the previous chapter, the broader rejection of positivist assumptions in the intervening years has gradually led to something akin to Kuhn's view becoming a relatively uncontroversial picture of epistemic evaluation for many realists and anti-realists alike. More recent work on the sociology of science and the role of so-called non-epistemic values has, however, questioned the genuinely or purely epistemic nature of the theoretic virtues, thus threatening to endanger even this seemingly moderate view of scientific objectivity and rationality (cf. Reiss and Sprenger 2017).

Some authors, on the other hand, have argued that philosophers of science have been too quick to fret about the epistemic significance of underdetermination based on the mere possibility that our theories could have empirical equivalents. In an influential paper, Laudan and Leplin (1991, 459) maintain that the thesis of widespread or universal empirical equivalence is "precarious, at best" and argue that, even if it were to be granted, equivalence is less worrisome than commonly thought. As they put it, "empirical equivalence is chiefly seen as a thesis about the *semantics* of theories," whereas "underdetermination, by contrast, is a thesis about the *epistemology* of theories" (Laudan and Leplin 1991, 460). This distinction is crucial because epistemic evaluation of evidential support for some theory may go beyond mere assessment of the truth of that theory's empirical consequences. A body of evidence might lend more evidential support to one of two empirically equivalent rivals if only one of them can be derived from a more general theory that itself enjoys evidential support. "More generally," writes Stanford (2017) in summarizing Laudan and Leplin's arguments, "the belief-worthiness of an hypothesis depends crucially on how it is connected or related to other things we believe and the evidential support we have for those other beliefs."[66]

On the whole, the majority of discussion concerning the true epistemic significance of underdetermination has focused on whether or not strong forms of such claims can be defended based on arguments for the (widespread) existence of empirical equivalence. Weaker forms, on the other hand, such as that suggested above by the competing models of Ferraro et al. and their critics, are often discounted as being philosophically uninteresting or unproblematic. Newton-Smith (2000) notes that a standard response to weak underdetermination is simply to seek out further evidence or, if we cannot do this for some reason, to either suspend judgment or look to factors other than empirical fit to resolve the issue (e.g. those suggested by Kuhn or Laudan and Leplin). Kitcher (2001, 30–31), in considering the consequences of underdetermination for the ideal of objectivity, points out that such cases are well-known to scientists, as

> [p]art of the routine character of their work consists in recognizing that different hypotheses are equally justified in light of the body of findings so far assembled and in devising experiments or observations that will enable them to resolve the issue. *Transient* underdetermination is familiar and unthreatening. [...] For in the mundane cases of transient underdetermination scientists do resolve the dispute between alternative hypotheses, opting for one and rejecting its rival(s).

In recent years, however, some authors have deemed this general discounting of weaker forms of underdetermination unjustified. Stanford, for example, argues that the transient underdetermination of even non-equivalent theories by only currently available evidence is problematic when *recurrent:* "that is, so long as

---

66 Interestingly, though neither Laudan and Leplin nor Stanford comment upon it, these suggestions bear a good deal of similarity to Kuhn's (1977) thoughts on the role of external consistency and (aspects of) fruitfulness in theory evaluation.

we think that there is (probably) at least one such (fundamentally distinct) alternative available—and thus the transient predicament re-arises—whenever we are faced with a decision about whether to believe a given theory at a given time" (Stanford 2017). The frequency of cases in which previously unconceived of distinct alternative theories have led unexpectedly to novel underdetermination predicaments in the past motivates, claims Stanford (2001, S9), a "New Induction" over the history of science that strongly suggests the recurrent nature of transient underdetermination and the issues it entails.

Biddle (2013) takes a different route to defending the importance of transient underdetermination, directly challenging Kitcher's claim of its being familiar and unthreatening to the ideal of objectivity. In many areas of (policy-relevant) cutting-edge science, argues Biddle (2013, 126), we often cannot wait for full epistemic clarity:

> Suppose, for example, that we need to determine whether a particular chemical used in pesticides is sufficiently safe or has acceptable environmental impact, or whether a drug that is currently on the market should be taken off the market. Suppose, furthermore, that the available evidence does not unambiguously determine which hypothesis should be accepted, or which decision should be made. In these cases, we do not have the luxury of waiting until all of the evidence is in, as postponing a decision could result in severe environmental degradation, loss of life, or other adverse effects. In situations such as this, there is a gap between evidence and hypothesis choice, and this gap is inevitably filled by contextual factors.

Biddle goes on to argue that these contextual factors will often necessarily include value judgments based on non-epistemic – e.g. political or moral – values, and that this 'Argument from Transient Underdetermination' thus undermines the ideal of epistemic purity he takes Kitcher to defend.

6.1.4 Fortifying transient underdetermination

I argue that taking illusory self-confirmation seriously presents us with another reason to believe transient underdetermination may be more problematic than often assumed by philosophers of science. As noted, a standard response to the suggestion of weak underdetermination is to simply suspend judgment until new evidence can be gathered that will adjudicate the dispute. However, claims of illusory self-confirmation seem to suggest that further research may actually make it more difficult to gather the kind of additional data needed to decide such issues.

Merton provides us with an example of how self-fulfilling prophecies might lead to the impression of empirical support for some underlying representation used to generate them without thereby causing the representation itself to become true. The same situation might be observed in the case of *homo economicus*. Surrogative reasoning performed over the picture of human beings as self-interested by nature – i.e. as having a strong, inflexible disposition toward self-interested behavior based on self-interested motivations – warrants expectations that such behaviors will be observable in many specific situations, perhaps whenever there are no contravening influences at work. Sometimes, these expectations might themselves lead to the exhibiting of such behavior where it otherwise would have been absent.

Consider the claim that the use and teaching of economic models encourages individuals to expect self-interested behavior in others whether or not they themselves might be personally inclined to engage in such behaviors. In light of such expectations, it will often appear as if (or actually be the case that) we must ourselves engage in such forms of behavior if we are not to be taken advantage of or fail in our endeavors. If enough people develop such expectations and act accordingly (especially in the context of experiments or other situations scientists look to for relevant evidence) it may come to seem as if the model of human nature upon which they are based is itself correct.

When Ferraro et al. posit that past and ongoing content-responsive actions such as these account for much of the data that are often interpreted as supporting the accuracy of a human nature model of *homo economicus*, they may also imply that continued or future research on the subject will likely continue to bring about or reinforce such effects. Of course, this depends on the specific mechanisms invoked to explain such impacts, as their effects may be postulated to occur only under specific conditions that do not obtain in some domain where differentiating research may yet be carried out. However, if the self-confirming rival has been or becomes very successful in impacting patterns of social norms, linguistic practices, or institutional design in society more broadly, it may become difficult to find subjects that could even potentially generate countervailing evidence, as they no longer provide the set of initial conditions required to perform a crucial test. In order to study the impact of e.g. economic language and conceptual frameworks on the perception of certain situations and behavioral responses to them, we require participants who do not already speak and think in such ways. And if a Polanyi-style 'economistic transformation' of society has already taken place, it may become difficult to impossible to find subjects of which this is true.

From Ferraro et al.'s (2005, 20) perspective, this might provide ample reason to postpone the kind of research that has allegedly led to mistaken impressions concerning the degree of empirical support for human nature models of *homo economicus* at least until we "know more about when and how social science theories affect the world of practice." However, it seems quite unlikely that those already convinced of the approximate correctness of such models will be willing to comply with this suggestion. Perhaps the best Ferraro et al. could hope for is that their rivals take their suggestions seriously and consciously attempt to avoid the behaviors postulated to generate misleading self-fulfilling predictions or 'homogenizing' of the empirical base, at least to a degree that does not impinge upon their ability to carry out further research as they see fit. The hope must be that obfuscation through self-fulfilling predictions can be avoided in the future if only anticipated.

Interestingly, although he does not connect his thoughts on the matter explicitly to issues of underdetermination, Buck briefly considers a similar issue regarding reflexive predictions. Noting the importance of testing predictions derived from theories in the process of epistemic evaluation, Buck (1963, 363) notes that "if you call into question the legitimacy of confirmation following on success in prediction, or of disconfirmation following on failure in prediction, you strike at something very fundamental indeed in science." Ultimately, however, he thinks the epistemological problems arising from this situation can be easily discounted largely on the possibility of developing and acting upon what we've called 'meta-theories':

> How serious, then, is the methodological problem for the social scientist? In my view, not very! He can always investigate the question whether any specific prediction is likely to operate reflexively. Sometimes such considerations may reveal that it is not reflexive. [...] In some cases it may be deemed desirable to deliberately restrict dissemination of the prediction. [...] And even if the reflexivity of a prediction must be merely warned against; even if that warning may in its turn prove reflexive – still something has been achieved. [...] A possible correction of that particular scientific claim has been suggested. (Buck 1963, 365)

Romanos is similarly optimistic about our ability to avoid any truly significant epistemological problems even if reflexivity looms. His account shows, he writes,

> why reflexive predictions are in principle so easily avoided in the process of theory testing; for it is manifestly apparent that there is no *a priori* reason why we should have to produce any prediction in one F/D-style rather than another. (Romanos 1973, 109)

Thus, Buck and Romanos conclude that reflexive predictions can be readily avoided by working scientists and thus hold little interest for philosophers of science (apart from, in Buck's case, their potential to mark an interesting distinction between natural and social sciences). However, there are reasons to question this easy optimism. First, as we saw in chapter four, it is likely quite difficult to develop reliable meta-theories concerning the likely impact of specific first-order theories. More plausible is the development of mid-range theories positing mechanisms that may be active under specific conditions; however, this is also fraught with difficulties and far from a guarantee that specific impacts can be reliably predicted. There are often likely to be both enabling and hindering mechanisms at play, and even one and the same mechanism may produce different effects in different contexts.

Second, even if we feel we have a fairly convincing meta-theory pointing toward the possibility of illusory self-confirmation, it is not clear that the strategies suggested by Buck and Romanos will necessarily help avoiding the problem. The suggestion that scientists might decide simply not to disseminate potentially self-fulfilling predictions presupposes that the scientists themselves are the only ones who might make predictions. Of course, this cannot be assumed, because those who come into contact with the representation are liable to drawn their own (perhaps mistaken) conclusions about what predictions it warrants, and some of these may be self-fulfilling. This might be avoided if not only predictions generated by some representation but the representation itself were never disseminated. However, this seems to present no real option if we wish to continue inquiry into some as of yet unresolved issue.

Romanos' implied suggestion that scientists might mold the formulation, framing, or dissemination of representations so as to avoid expected effects of this kind seems more promising. However, although there may be no *a priori* reason why predictions or representations have to be presented in one F/D style or another, there are plenty of other reasons that working scientists cannot, in fact, simply decide to formulate or present their theories in any arbitrary fashion. The process of performing further research in an attempt to overcome transient underdetermination requires that rival representations be openly discussed, further worked out, and supported by argument. Publishing guidelines, project constraints, norms of scientific communication and community, and a host of other factors present serious *a posteriori* limits on the actual flexibility scientists are likely to possess in carrying out their work. Researchers might preface their work with warnings about the inconclusiveness of the data and discourage content-responsive action until the epistemic situation has become clearer. But this is also far from a guarantee that their postulated representations will not lead to content-responsive actions or illusory self-confirmation.

More crucially, such suggestions suppose that scientists who might have the power to shape a theory's formulation and presentation so as to avoid illusory self-confirmation are aware of and assign some degree of plausibility to the meta-theory in question. However, those whose models make no room for illusory self-confirmation or the mechanisms that may plausibly encourage it have little motivation to warn against such threats. Ferraro et al. might charge that evidence seeming to support the human nature model of *homo economicus* is actually the result of self-fulfilling prophecies, but why should Felin and Foss, whose account of the issue specifically denies this influence, consider how to present their findings so as to avoid it? Doing so would seem at the very least a concession to their rivals' conception, if not simply a problematically misleading statement in and of itself. The in-principle possibility of flexibility in formulation and presentation is little consolation to those whose warnings of perpetuating illusory self-confirmation simply go unheeded by those with the power to do something about it.

Perhaps most intriguing is Buck's final suggestion, that, if nothing else, warning of reflexivity (and illusory self-confirmation) means that at least a possible correction to a particular claim has been achieved. Unfortunately, he does not go into detail about how he imagines this playing out, other than to add that this is the "typical situation in an empirical science offering corrigible claims," and that although "all scientific propositions are corrigible, [...] it certainly is never the case at any one time that all have been tested for possible correction" (Buck 1963, 365). Ferraro et al. would likely see themselves as having performed the service of offering a 'possible correction'. However, once again, this suggestion seems unlikely to be heeded in the manner that, according to their theory, would likely be necessary to prevent further impacts leading to illusory self-confirmation. If things go poorly (from their perspective), we may end up stuck in what would otherwise be a transient form of underdetermination: the claim of illusory self-confirmation presents an account capable of explaining the available data, but is unable to suggest any path toward demystification other than to urge their rivals and observers of the debate to stop employing and relying on a representation that, from the others' perspective, seems to have the full weight of evidence on its side.

One seeming consequence, then, of the kinds of effects identified by Ferraro et al. is that weak forms of underdetermination may be rendered more robust and perhaps even permanent by our attempts to overcome them. This is not Stanford's recurrent transient underdetermination, as it is not the specter of repeated instances of currently unconceived of rival theories that threaten to perpetuate the transient predicament. Rather, current or future attempts to overcome some existing case of actual weak underdetermination may fortify and perpetuate it. Nor is it Biddle's justification for taking underdetermination at the cutting-edge of policy-relevant research seriously, for it is not dependent upon the urgency of acting to effectively meet some non-epistemic goal. Rather, illusory self-confirmation poses a problem even when our goals are purely epistemic and we have, so to speak, all the time in the world.

The above seems to present something close to an epistemic worst-case scenario, in which we eventually become practically incapable of gathering clear disconfirming evidence for some representation even if we are convinced that its apparent epistemic success is in large part an illusion created by its own 'reign of error'. In fact, things could be worse yet. All the preceding presupposes that we actually have some idea of a particular occurrence of illusory self-confirmation or somewhat robust mid-range theories that allow us to at least speculate as to possible effects of this kind in some domain. Despite the issues pertaining to underdetermination that might arise from such awareness, such a situation is seemingly preferable to one in which illusory self-confirmation exists but goes entirely undetected. Conceivably, the extensive workings of mechanisms such as those described above could all but wipe out any possibility of realizing that some taken-for-granted view about the world has in fact created its own spurious validity. This provides, it would seem, at least a *prima facie* argument for vigilance.

Of course, things could also be better than suggested by the pessimistic picture developed above. Although the threat of fortifying underdetermination exists, it is by no means a given. Felin and Foss, we have seen, argue that theories effectively alter reality in virtue of their being true. However, they do admit that self-fulfilling predictions can lead to false impressions *in the short term:*

> Of course, we do not want to completely dismiss self-fulfilling prophecy effects. However, what is important to note is that false beliefs about behavior, which might fulfill themselves in the short term, importantly get dynamically corrected and updated in social contexts. False effects are small and dissipate rather quickly over time as individual behavior gives clues or signals about actual factors and accurate beliefs related to human nature. (Felin and Foss 2009a, 660)

Perhaps Felin and Foss are correct, and illusory self-confirmation tends to eventually wash out over time. Ironically, this may not benefit their side of the dispute. They assume that the accurate beliefs we generate over time will be related to human nature. Of course, there is no reason to suppose this unless one has already bought into this view. It could equally be the case that the postulated illusory self-confirmation of human nature models of *homo economicus* are themselves 'small false effects' that will be eventually be stamped out by the recalcitrant reality of human flexibility.

6.2 Genuine self-fulfillment and epistemic evaluation

6.2.1 Self-fulfillment as self-improvement?

According to the definition developed in chapter three, a scientific representation is self-fulfilling when it gives rise to content-responsive actions that bring about states of affairs such that a higher degree of conformation exists between the representation and its target system than would otherwise have been the case. How should the fact of some representation's self-fulfillment affect our epistemic evaluation thereof (if at all)?

The recent literature on scientific representations, it was noted, discusses different possible candidate notions to account for the accuracy of representations. Some have suggested that it is the sharing of properties between a representation and its target system that renders the former accurate. Others conceive of the relation in terms of structures displaying structural morphism. We chose to invoke the notion of conformation in order to express the likely plurality of types of epistemological success of content required to make sense of the different types of entities of which self-fulfillment claims may be reasonably made.

One thing that should be clear is that this account of representations and representational accuracy is faced with many of the same issues faced by more classical views of theory evaluation. Although the common phrase is 'underdetermination of *theory* by data,' such concerns apply equally in the case of representations more generally. This is why 'accuracy' is not cashed out (entirely) in terms of empirical adequacy on such accounts – what is at stake is not just the confirmation of statements or further representations generated via surrogative reasoning over some representation, but rather e.g. the kind and degree of morphism between the representation's and target system's structures. Thus, when we postulate increased conformation, we are in fact postulating an increase of something considered (co-)constitutive of epistemic success.

The immediate consequence of this would seem to be that genuine self-fulfillment entails an actual, rather than seeming, increase in epistemic success. This should come as no surprise, given that this definition was chosen specifically to distinguish *genuine* self-fulfillment from *illusory* self-confirmation, but it is important to be clear on this point. Let us briefly consider an example.

Above, we considered a picture of *homo economicus* as describing a deep-seated, inflexible disposition to act in self-interested ways whenever possible, i.e. provided the information needed to effectively do so and situations allowing for such behaviors. Now, let us consider a minimal conception of *homo economicus* that makes no claims concerning the reasons people behave in self-interested ways, but rather merely states the fact that they do so under certain conditions.

Despite their employment of the term 'self-fulfillment,' above it was argued that Ferraro et al.'s account is very plausibly read as a critique of and theoretical rival to the universal, motivation-based account, which it confronts with a charge of being illusorily self-confirming. If we consider the more moderate, behavior-based account, however, then the evidence presented by Ferraro et al. speaks for its genuine self-fulfillment. Their claim is that the self-interested behavior induced by actions that are content-responsive to the universal, motivation-based account constitutes merely spurious evidence in its favor. However, they do not dispute the fact that self-interested behaviors were induced, but rather just what evidential inferences this fact licenses.

So, if it was in fact the more modest, behavior-based representation (or if we attribute this content in light of content contingency) that ultimately induced self-interested behaviors, then the representation seems to, through its own working, genuinely improve its own epistemic stature. Self-fulfillment appears as self-improvement. But can it really be this easy to 'win' at the game of science? Is there some more subtle 'specious' element to the validity of such representations?

Felin and Foss (2009a, 655) believe such cases

> threaten the fundamental definition of science and theory as an attempt to understand and predict objective reality [...]. Specifically, the self-fulfilling nature of even false theories makes deeply problematic such traditional scientific notions as explanation, prediction, description, understanding, and control.

However, it is unclear why they think *all* of these 'traditional scientific notions' are called into question by genuine self-fulfillment. In the postulated case, it seems the statement in fact correctly *describes* the situation that actually occurs. Neither the fact or awareness of the self-fulfillment effect diminishes the plain (descriptive) accuracy of the representation understood in the strict sense of fit between *just* the content of the representation and its target system.

Where such statements seem clearly to fall short, of course, is in the points of explanation and understanding. The postulated representation does not even attempt to provide an explanation for the existence of the behavior it describes, nor does it seem capable of providing us with any sort of understanding thereof. But are these things to be counted against the success of a representation that displays as much conformation – i.e. 'epistemological success of content' – as it can, given its specific content? In a word, yes!

As noted in the previous chapter, despite the pride of place often granted to empirical adequacy in our usual notions of epistemic evaluation, this theoretical virtue does not automatically trump all others, and representations that ensure high marks in empirical adequacy by sacrificing scope or explanatory depth are epistemically deficient (compared to some alternative). The same, apparently, goes for conformation. Some representation that maximizes its conformation with a target system simply by claiming very little about it might be technically correct, but simply being correct isn't usually enough to be a good theory or representation.

Of course, we've been discussing a very slim representation indeed, and it might be wondered if worries such as Felin and Foss' might be yet warranted concerning more robust representations that significantly increase their own conformation in this manner. However, it must be noted that whenever self-fulfillment is present, there is another, distinct representation of the same target system waiting to be, or perhaps already, discovered. This is the representation that is the result of incorporating insights gleaned from what we've been calling a meta-theory into the self-fulfilling first-order theory it seeks to describe and explain. In elucidating mechanisms by which the target system of the first-order theory can be affected in ways seemingly not captured by the first-order theory itself, these meta-theories not only suggest or prove the fact of self-fulfillment, but rather provide a valuable theoretical insight into the target system itself. The resulting, richer representation will almost undoubtedly possess both a higher degree of conformation and, more broadly, theoretic virtue than the first-order theory it replaces.

6.2.2 The return of self-correction

When considering the epistemic significance of self-fulfillment or illusory self-confirmation, we mustn't lose sight of the original goal that led us to consider such possibilities in the first place. The primary goal of inquiry is *not* to establish whether self-fulfillment has or has not occurred, or what content we must attribute to a specific representation in order to diagnose it, but rather to develop an epistemically successful representation of some target system in the world we seek to better understand or control through our increased understanding.

This shows, then, why we needn't be too concerned about genuine self-fulfillment in general. It may be the case that such representations in fact enhance their own epistemological success of content and thus, in some sense, epistemic success. However, epistemic success is relative, and the fact that self-fulfillment seemingly always entails the existence of a further (perhaps yet undiscovered) representation that incorporates first-order and meta-theories into an epistemically more satisfying whole means that we should get on with looking for these richer alternatives rather than despairing of the imminent demise of science on the basis of the marginal self-improvement of the first-order theories they might replace.

The lesson we should learn from discovering an impact of genuine self-fulfillment has, in fact, less to do with the fact that self-fulfillment has occurred and more to do with the fact that it *could* occur via the *mechanisms* that brought it about. It was noted in the case of illusory self-confirmation above that meta-theories should not be conceived of as hovering over the first-order theories they target, but as presenting alternative explanations for certain observed behaviors of the system targeted by the first-order theories. The same applies to accounts of genuine self-fulfillment. Kopec, at the end of his paper on reflexive prediction, also considers such a strategy:

> [M]uch more work will need to be done if we are to figure out how to react to the knowledge that a prediction that has been disseminated is weakly reflexive. Once we have figured out how we should change our evaluation of the evidential import of the observation, *we can make use of this knowledge in expanded models. Since the hypotheses, theories, or models at issue either ignore this relevant feature or take account of it incorrectly, they must be replaced with improved versions.* (Kopec 2011, 1258, emphasis added)

This is the correct kind of epistemic response to the realization that self-fulfillment has occurred. But we might also do with something less than an outright meta-theory. Kopec suggests we can improve the representations in question only once we have decided how we should change our evaluation of the evidential import of the observation. But this might be quite difficult to establish. As we have seen, it may be significantly easier to find mid-range theories that identify mechanisms that might or do typically exert causal impacts on the entities or situations in question. Furthermore, it seems quite plausible that these can be considered for incorporation into an improved model even when the exact nature of some specific previous effect remains unclear. Of course, in considering such strategies, we must be ever wary of the dangers outlined at the end of chapter four.

This discussion reinforces the idea that we should reject Callon's anti-critical stance toward the first-order theories investigated by performativity researchers. Recall again the would-be lessons to be drawn:

> [W]e have to abandon [...] the idea of critique of hard economists, which is intended to show them that there [sic] are wrong. [...] We recognize the right of economists to contribute to performing markets, but at the same time we claim our own right to do the same but

from a different perspective. [...] What is very important is to abandon the critical position, and to stop denouncing economists and capitalists and so on. (Callon et al. 2002, 301)

The anthropology characterizing [neo-classical] economics [...] which sees any individual as an autonomous subject capable of intentions and a free will, responsible for his or her acts, is becoming pervasive. The question is no longer 'Is this anthropology true or false?', but 'Is this anthropology able (Where? How? For how long and in which spaces?) to perform, to enact, a reality corresponding to what it says?' (Callon 2005, 10)

We saw in the previous chapter that there is nothing standing in the way of subjecting reality-altering scientific representations to epistemic evaluation in principle. But if we admit the possibility of continuing to evaluate the 'neo-classical anthropology' of self-interested *homo economicus* in epistemic terms, despite its purported ability to 'perform' or 'enact' a corresponding reality, then we must also recognize that microeconomic theory can and should be criticized *when it fails to incorporate the mechanisms that account for this ability into its (future) representations.*

Interestingly, the conclusion to be drawn from discovery of some self-fulfillment (or illusory self-confirmation) impact, whether actual or plausible, seems to be to return to the methods usually referred to in order to account for success in science, namely those constituting scientific self-correction. It seems quite unlikely that the resulting improved representations will also give rise to self-fulfillment, but if they do, the hope must be that they too will be discovered and incorporated into yet further improved theories and models. When considering the epistemological import of 'self-fulfillment,' it ultimately seems that most of the truly interesting issues for philosophers of science arise from the notion of illusory self-confirmation rather than self-fulfillment proper.

7 An engine, *and* a camera

7.1 Summary

This book has presented a framework for examining the phenomenon of scientific self-fulfillment (and its oft-neglected shadow, illusory self-confirmation) from the perspective of philosophy of science. We have made progress in, at least, more helpfully framing, if not always directly providing answers to, the questions of conceptualization, prevalence, and significance surrounding these issues. The novel characterization of scientific self-fulfillment as consisting in increased conformation brought about through content-responsive actions, as well as its explicit distinction from the phenomenon of illusory self-confirmation, helps clarify what precisely may be meant by those who argue for or against the 'self-fulfillment' of scientific theories. The suggested strategies for identifying or predicting self-fulfillment effects, as well as the (speculative) argument for the phenomenon's possibility in the natural sciences, suggest pathways for further empirical research. Finally, some of the more drastic claims concerning the epistemic significance of scientific self-fulfillment have been forcefully challenged, and, in their stead, the first steps taken toward a more nuanced consideration of the phenomenon's epistemic and epistemological import.

Given the long neglect of scientific self-fulfillment by philosophers of science, the framework developed here represents only a first step toward greater understanding. Many further issues of considerable interest could not be examined here. I have restricted my focus almost entirely to recent debates concerning the purported self-fulfillment of microeconomic theories of *homo economicus*. Given their prominence and influence, this restriction is justifiable, yet there are certainly other examples and debates worthy of consideration. Furthermore, I have considered only the possibility of scientific self-fulfillment via *causal* effects. Recent work from the perspective of Hacking's looping effects or naturalistic approaches to social construction more generally strongly suggest that an evaluation of scientific self-fulfillment in terms of *constitutive construction* could be highly illuminating. Finally, my consideration of questions of significance was limited almost entirely to epistemic issues. Some authors have suggested that the potential for self-fulfillment has serious implications for the broadly ethical or practical aspects of science as well, and I am certain this is correct. My hope is that the framework developed here may help spurn on and facilitate future research into these fascinating and important topics.

7.2 Multiple possible futures

To conclude, I would like to briefly consider once again MacKenzie's (2006a) suggestion that science is "an engine, *not* a camera." As we have seen, such statements could be read as suggesting that the potential for scientific representations to bring about the reality they envision renders our usual notions of epistemic success and evaluation inapplicable. Recall Callon's (2007, 321) suggestion that

> [o]ne of the main benefits of the notion of performativity is that it rids us of [...] the representational idiom, in terms of which the purpose of science is to create representations of reality.

I have argued that nothing stands in the way, at least in connection with scientific self-fulfillment, of continuing to work within the 'representational idiom' apparently repudiated by Callon. Indeed, the proper reaction to realizing the possibility of scientific self-fulfillment is not, I have claimed, to abort epistemic evaluation, but rather to consider the mechanisms through which it might come about as valuable explanatory factors to be incorporated into more accurate representations of the parts of the world they potentially affect.

But what of the suggestion that even if it is possible to continue in this fashion that it is somehow naïve or even immoral to do so? Callon intimates that we should "abandon the critical position" (Callon et al. 2002, 301) and that efficacy in transformation, rather than accuracy of representation, is the proper measure of success in science. This anti-critical stance is likely to strike many as cynical. Should we consider it a 'success' when some pessimistic description or outlook proves capable of bringing about the bleak reality it posits? How are we even to decide if the transformation in question has resulted in self-fulfillment or illusory self-confirmation if we swear off epistemic evaluation *tout court*? Surely, the difference must concern us.

Perhaps a more agreeable version of Callon's general proposal might result if we reintroduce the critical dimension. Even within the performativity perspective's own ranks, we encounter the suggestion that "performativity studies, despite dealing with a politically and ethically charged topic, have shied away from ethical engagement and political critique" and that recognizing the field's "emancipatory potential" represents the "real radicalism of the performativity thesis" (Roscoe 2016, 147). Ferraro et al. (2009) suggested that understanding and appreciating the mechanisms of self-fulfillment might show us the way to 'multiple possible futures' and imply a special moral responsibility for scientists to consider the consequences of what they teach and write.

Bergenholtz and Busch (2016, 38) see the "threat" of a special moral responsibility as easily dealt with by appeal to meta-theories:

> For self-fulfillment to imply a unique kind of ethical responsibility, the researcher must be in a position to know that the particular theory being suggested will activate changes to the (at the time of theory development) current state of the world. [...] In contrast, if the researcher is unable to predict what kind of impact his theory will have, any outcomes are unintentional, and it is difficult to ascribe moral value to the actions.

But this is too simple, as it ignores the possibility of *neglect*. We are not absolved of responsibility for our actions simply because we haven't considered them sufficiently. Meta-theories concerning particular first-order theories are in short order, but mid-range theories abound in many domains. Responsibility doesn't hinge upon the certainty that some consequence will follow but rather the reasonable anticipation that it could.

Felin and Foss (2009a, 655), on the other hand, worry that Ferraro et al.'s suggestions might "threaten the fundamental definition of science and theory as an attempt to understand and predict objective reality." As they see it, "if the content of our theories is arbitrary, then why not create the best of all possible worlds?" (2009b, 676). However, as we have seen, claims of scientific self-fulfillment neither entail nor imply that any arbitrary theory could create a corresponding reality. Taking the phenomenon seriously requires staking out both its possibilities and boundaries, and, hopefully, thereby enhancing our understanding of which 'worlds' are indeed 'possible' in the first place. Such a project in fact demands that we do not simply give up the 'fundamental definition of science.'

We needn't abandon the epistemic goals of science in order to appreciate that it may have legitimate non-epistemic goals as well. Indeed, this is the central message of recent work in philosophy of science concerning the proper role of values – both epistemic and non-epistemic – in science (cf. Elliott and McKaughan 2014). Scholars working in this tradition have shown intense concern for both of these dimensions and have made considerable progress in laying out the 'moral terrain of science' (cf. Douglas 2014) from a perspective that attempts to satisfy both to the greatest degree possible. Steel (2017, 58) eloquently expresses the conviction, widely shared within the field, that:

> while the aims of science are often bound up with broader social and ethical objectives (e.g., public health), science as an institution should promote those aims by advancing knowledge, and not by other means, such as fraud, propaganda, or marketing. [...] This entails limits on how science should go about its business. It should not operate in ways that are incompatible with basic criteria for advancing empirical knowledge.

Of course, situations arise in which epistemic and non-epistemic goals conflict; this is where the hard work of providing reasons and arguments for one's decision to come down on one side or the other begins. Scientists might be faced with such conundrums when forced to choose how to respond to the knowledge that their research could come to affect and alter its object of study. If the anticipated changes are for the (ethical) worse, so to speak, then the decision how to proceed resembles those faced by researchers working in fields that perform so-called *dual use research*.

However, given that science has both legitimate epistemic and non-epistemic aims, the prospect of self-fulfillment might be seen as suggesting a positive complement to these established notions. Ferraro et al. (2009, 673) optimistically claim that "we have the opportunity to both envision and create a different and maybe even better, more humane, and just world." This raises the question: if the anticipated possibility of negative ethical consequences gives us a reason to either halt or carefully curate research, might the anticipated possibility of positive consequences give us a reason to dedicate our resources to certain theoretical options over others?[67]

I do not have an answer for this. However, I believe that 'values and science' provides the best currently available framework for coming to terms both with questions such as these and the image that gives rise to them: science as an engine, *and* a camera.

---

[67] Kopec (2017) makes such a suggestion concerning the use of the game theoretic model of the 'tragedy of the commons' to predict and explain actions of stakeholders in international climate negotiations, which he posits as generating self-fulfilling predictions of noncooperation. Alternative models do not seem to entail the 'climate tragedy' predicted (and encouraged) by the 'tragedy of the commons' model, but enjoy less empirical support than this well-established rival. The question is: are we justified in diverting resources to exploring models with potentially more pleasing (non-epistemic) outcomes?

References

Asimov, Isaac. 1951. *Foundation*. New York: Gnome Press.
Austin, John L. 1975. *How To Do Things With Words*. 2nd ed. Cambridge, MA: Harvard University Press.
Bajpai, Vivek K., Madhu Kamle, Shruti Shukla, Dipendra Kumar Mahato, Pranjal Chandra, Seung Kyu Hwang, Pradeep Kumar, Yun Suk Huh, and Young-Kyu Han. 2018. "Prospects for Using Nanotechnology for Food Preservation, Safety, and Security." *Journal of Food and Drug Analysis* 26: 1201–1214.
Barnes, Barry. 1983. "Social Life as Bootstrapped Induction." *Sociology* 17 (4): 524–545.
Bartels, Andreas. 2006. "Defending the Structural Concept of Representation." *Theoria* 55: 7–19.
Bauman, Yoram, and Elaina Rose. 2011. "Selection or Indoctrination: Why Do Economics Students Donate Less than the Rest?" *Journal of Economic Behavior & Organization* 79: 318–27.
Bergenholtz, Carsten, and Jacob Busch. 2016. "Self-Fulfillment of Social Science Theories: Cooling the Fire." *Philosophy of the Social Sciences* 46 (1): 24–43.
Berger, Peter L. and Thomas Luckmann. 1966. *The Social Construction of Reality*. New York: Anchor Books.
Bhakthavatsalam, Sindhuja and Nancy Cartwright. 2017. "What's So Special About Empirical Adequacy?" *European Journal for Philosophy of Science* 7 (3): 445–475.
Biddle, Justin. 2013. "State of the Field: Transient Underdetermination and Values in Science." *Studies in History and Philosophy of Science* 44: 124–133.
Biggs, Michael. 2009. "Self-fulfilling Prophecies." In *The Oxford Handbook of Analytical Sociology*, edited by Peter Hedström and Peter Bearman, 294–314. Oxford: Oxford University Press.
Boghossian, Paul A. 2001. "What is Social Construction?" *Times Literary Supplement* 23: 6–8.
Bourdieu, Pierre. 1991. *Language & Symbolic Power*. Cambridge, UK: Polity Press.
Brissett, Nicolas. 2019. *Economics and Performativity: Exploring Limits, Theories and Cases*. Translated by Mila Webb. London: Routledge.
Brown, Donald E. 1991. *Human Universals*. New York: McGraw-Hill.
Buck, Roger C. 1963. "Reflexive Predictions." *Philosophy of Science* 30: 359–69.
Bull, Joseph W. and Martine Maron. 2016. "How Humans Drive Speciation As Well As Extinction." *Proceedings of the Royal Society B* 283: 20160600. http://dx.doi.org/10.1098/rspb.2016.0600
Buss, Allan R. 1978. "The Structure of Psychological Revolutions." *Journal of the History of the Behavioral Sciences* 14 (1): 57–64.
Callon, Michel. 1998. "Introduction: The Embeddedness of Economic Markets in Economics." In *The Laws of the Markets*, edited by Michel Callon, 1–57. Oxford: Blackwell Publishers.
Callon, Michel. 2005. "Why Virtualism Paves the Way to Political Impotence: Callon Replies to Miller." *Economic Sociology European Electronic Newsletter* 6 (2): 3–20.
Callon, Michel. 2007. "What Does It Mean to Say That Economics Is Performative?" In *Do Economists Make Markets?: On the Performativity of Economics*, edited by Donald MacKenzie, Fabian Muniesa, and Lucia Siu, 311–357. New Jersey: Princeton University Press.

Callon, Michel, Andrew Barry, and Don Slater. 2002. "Technology, Politics, and the Market: An Interview with Michel Callon." *Economy and Society* 31 (2): 285–306.

Caporael, Linnda R., Robyn M. Dawes, John M. Orbell, and Alphons J. C. van de Kragt. 1989. "Selfishness Examined: Cooperation in the Absence of Egoistic Incentives." *Behavioral and Brain Sciences* 12 (4): 683–739.

Carrier, Martin, and Alfred Nordmann. 2011. *Science in the Context of Application*. Dordrecht: Springer.

Carter, John R., and Michael D. Irons. 1991. "Are Economists Different, and If So, Why?" *The Journal of Economic Perspectives* 5 (2): 171–77.

Chakravartty, Anjan. 2007. *A Metaphysics for Scientific Realism*. Cambridge: Cambridge University Press.

Chomsky, Noam. 1957. *Syntactic Structures*. The Hague: Moutin.

Cipriani, Giam Pietro, Diego Lubian, and Algelo Zago. 2009. "Natural Born Economists?" *Journal of Economic Psychology* 30: 455–468.

Cofnas, Nathan. 2016. "Science is Not Always 'Self-Correcting': Fact-Value Conflation and the Study of Intelligence." *Foundations of Science* 21: 477–492.

Devitt, Michael. 2005. "Scientific Realism." In *Oxford Handbook of Contemporary Philosophy*, edited by Frank Jackson and Michael Smith, 767–791. Oxford: Oxford University Press.

Díaz-León, Esa. 2013. "What is Social Construction?" *European Journal of Philosophy* 23 (4): 1137–1152.

Díaz-León, Esa. 2018. "Kinds of Social Construction." In *The Bloomsbury Companion to Analytic Feminism*, edited by Pieranna Garavaso, 103–122. London: Bloomsbury Academic.

Dick, Philip K. 1956. "The Minority Report." *Fantastic Universe* 4 (6): 4–36.

Douglas, Heather E. 2009. *Science, Policy, and the Value-Free Ideal*. Pittsburgh, PA: University of Pittsburgh Press.

Douglas, Heather E. 2010. "Engagement for Progress: Applied Philosophy of Science in Context." *Synthese* 177: 317–35.

Douglas, Heather E. 2014. "The Moral Terrain of Science." *Erkenntnis* 79: 961–79.

Douglas, Heather E. 2016. "Values in Science." In *The Oxford Handbook of Philosophy of Science*, edited by Paul Humphreys, 609–630. New York: Oxford University Press.

Dumont, Louis. 1977. *From Mandeville to Marx: The genesis and triumph of economic ideology*. Chicago, IL: University of Chicago Press.

Edgeworth, Francis Y. 1881. *Mathematical Physics: An Essay of the Application of Mathematics to the Moral*. London: C. Keagan Paul & Co.

Elgin, Catherine Z. 2017. *True Enough*. Cambridge, MA: MIT Press.

Elliott, Kevin C. 2017. *A Tapestry of Values: An Introduction to Values in Science*. New York: Oxford University Press.

Elliott, Kevin C., and Daniel J. McKaughan. 2014. "Nonepistemic Values and the Multiple Goals of Science." *Philosophy of Science* 81: 1–21.

Felin, Teppo, and Nicolai J. Foss. 2009a. "Performativity of Theory, Arbitrary Conventions, and Possible Worlds: A Reality Check." *Organization Science* 20 (3): 676–78.

Felin, Teppo, and Nicolai J. Foss. 2009b. "Social Reality, the Boundaries of Self-Fulfilling Prophecy, and Economics." *Organization Science* 20 (3): 654–68.

Ferraro, Fabrizio, Jeffrey Pfeffer, and Robert I. Sutton. 2005. "Economics Language and Assumptions: How Theories Can Become Self-Fulfilling." *Academy of Management Review* 30 (1): 8–24.

Ferraro, Fabrizio, Jeffrey Pfeffer, and Robert I. Sutton. 2009. "How and Why Theories Matter: A Comment on Felin and Foss (2009)." *Organization Science* 20 (3): 669–75.

Frank, Björn, and Günther G. Schulze. 2000. "Does Economics Make Citizens Corrupt?" *Journal of Economic Behavior & Organization* 43: 101–113.

Frank, Robert H., Thomas Gilovich, and Dennis T. Regan. 1993. "Does Studying Economics Inhibit Cooperation?" *The Journal of Economic Perspectives* 7 (2): 159–71.

Frank, Robert H., Thomas Gilovich, and Dennis T. Regan. 1996. "Do Economists Make Bad Citizens?" *The Journal of Economic Perspectives* 10 (1): 187–92.

Frey, Bruno S. and Reto Jegen. 2001. "Motivation Crowding Theory." *Journal of Economic Surveys* 15 (5): 589–611.

Frey, Bruno S. and Stephan Meier. 2003. "Are Political Economists Selfish and Indoctrinated? Evidence From a Natural Experiment." *Economic Inquiry* 41 (3): 448–462.

Friedman, Milton. 1953. *Essays in Positive Economics*. Chicago, IL: University of Chicago Press.

Frigg, Roman and James Nguyen. 2016. "Scientific Representation." In *The Stanford Encyclopedia of Philosophy* (Winter 2016 Edition), edited by Edward N. Zalta. https://plato.stanford.edu/archives/win2018/entries/scientific-representation/, last accessed July 23, 2020.

Gergen, Kenneth J. 2015. *An Invitation to Social Construction*. 3rd ed. London: Sage.

Ghoshal, Sumantra. 2005. "Bad Management Theories Are Destroying Good Management Practice." *Academy of Management Learning & Education* 4 (1): 75–91.

Ghoshal, Sumantra and Peter Moran. 1996. "Bad For Practice: A Critique of the Transaction Cost Theory." *Academy of Management Review* 21 (1): 13–47.

Giere, Ronald N. 2004. "How Models Are Used to Represent Reality." *Philosophy of Science* 71 (5): 742–752.

Gilbert, Natasha. 2010. "African Elephants Are Two Distinct Species." *Nature*, December 21. http://www.nature.com/news/2010/101221/full/news.2010.691.html, last accessed July 23, 2020.

Goodman, Nelson. 1976. *Languages of Art*. Cambridge: Hackett.

Gordon, Ascelin, Joseph W. Bull, Chris Wilcox, and Martine Maron. 2015. "Perverse Incentives Risk Undermining Biodiversity Offset Policies." *Journal of Applied Ecology* 52 (2): 532–537.

Grünbaum, Adolf. 1956. "Historical Determinism, Social Activism, and Predictions in the Social Sciences." *British Journal for the Philosophy of Science* 7: 236–240.

Grunberg, Emile. 1986. "Predictability and Reflexivity." *The American Journal of Economics and Sociology* 45 (4): 475–488.

Guala, Francesco. 2016a. "Performativity Rationalized." In *Enacting Dismal Science: New Perspectives on the Performativity of Economics*, edited by Ivan Boldyrev and Ekaterina Svetlova, 29–52. New York: Palgrave Macmillan.

Guala, Francesco. 2016b. "Philosophy of the Social Sciences: Naturalism and Anti-Naturalism in the Philosophy of Social Science." In *The Oxford Handbook of Philosophy of Science*, edited by Paul Humphreys, 43–64. New York: Oxford University Press.

Guala, Francesco. 2016c. *Understanding Institutions: The Science and Philosophy of Living Together*. Princeton: Princeton University Press.

Hacking, Ian. 1986. "Making Up People." In *Reconstructing Individualism*, edited by Thomas Heller, Morton Sosna, and David Wellberry, 222–236. Stanford: Stanford University Press.

Hacking, Ian. 1995. "The Looping Effects of Human Kinds." In *Causal Cognition: A Multidisciplinary Debate*, edited by Dan Sperber, Davis Premack, and Ann James Premack, 351–83. Oxford: Oxford University Press.

Hacking, Ian. 1999. *The Social Construction of What?* Cambridge, MA: Harvard University Press.

Hacking, Ian. 2007. "Kinds of People: Moving Targets." *Proceedings of the British Academy* 151: 285–318.

Haslanger, Sally. 2012. *Resisting Reality: Social Construction and Social Critique*. New York: Oxford University Press.

Hedström, Peter and Peter Bearman. 2009. "What Is Analytical Sociology All About? An Introductory Essay." In *The Oxford Handbook of Analytical Sociology*, edited by Peter Hedström and Peter Bearman, 3–24. Oxford: Oxford University Press.

Hedström, Peter and Lars Udehn. 2009. "Analytical Sociology and Theories of the Middle Range." In *The Oxford Handbook of Analytical Sociology*, edited by Peter Hedström and Peter Bearman, 25–47. Oxford: Oxford University Press.

Henrich, Joseph, Robert Boyd, Samuel Bowles, Colin Camerer, Ernst Fehr, Herbert Gintis, Richard McElreath, et al. 2005. "'Economic Man' in Cross-Cultural Perspective: Behavioral Experiments in 15 Small-Scale Societies." *Behavioral and Brain Sciences* 28: 795–855.

Henshel, Richard L. 1978. "Self-Altering Predictions." In *Handbook of Futures Research*, edited by Jib Fowles, 99–123. Westport, CT: Greenwood Press.

Henshel, Richard L. 1982. "The Boundary of the Self-Fulfilling Prophecy and the Dilemma of Social Prediction." *The British Journal of Sociology* 33 (4): 511–528.

Hoyningen-Heune, Paul. 1987. "Context of Discovery and Context of Justification." *Studies in History and Philosophy of Science Part A* 18 (4): 501–515.

Humphreys, Paul, ed. 2016. *The Oxford Handbook of Philosophy of Science*. New York: Oxford University Press.

Ioannidis, John P. A. 2012. "Why Science Is Not Necessarily Self-Correcting." *Perspectives on Psychological Science* 7 (6): 645–654.

Jussim, Lee. 2012. *Social Perception and Social Reality: Why Accuracy Dominates Bias and Self-Fulfilling Prophecy*. Oxford: Oxford University Press.

Kay, Ira T. 1998. *CEO Pay and Shareholder Value*. Boca Raton, FL: St. Lucie Press.

Katzner, Donald W. 2001. "The Significance, Success, and Failure of Microeconomic Theory." *Journal of Post Keynesian Economics* 24 (1): 41–57.

Khalidi, Muhammad A. 2010. "Interactive Kinds." *The British Journal for the Philosophy of Science* 61 (2): 335–360.

Khalidi, Muhammad A. 2016. "Mind-Dependent Kinds." *Journal of Social Ontology* 2 (2): 223–246.

Kirchgässner, Gebhard. 2005. "(Why) Are Economists Different?" *European Journal of Political Economy* 21: 543–562.

Kitcher, Philip. 2001. *Science, Truth, and Democracy*. Oxford: Oxford University Press.

Kopec, Matthew. 2011. "A More Fulfilling (and Frustrating) Take on Reflexive Predictions." *Philosophy of Science* 78: 1249–59.
Kopec, Matthew. 2017. "Game Theory and the Self-Fulfilling Climate Tragedy." *Environmental Values* 26 (2): 203–221.
Krishna, Daya. 1971. "'The Self-Fulfilling Prophecy' and the Nature of Society." *American Sociological Review* 36 (6): 1104–1107.
Kuhn, Thomas. 1962. *The Structure of Scientific Revolutions*. Chicago, IL: University of Chicago Press.
Kuhn, Thomas. 1977. *The Essential Tension: Selected Studies in Scientific Tradition and Change*. Chicago, IL: University of Chicago Press.
Kukla, André. 1996. "Does Every Theory Have Empirically Equivalent Rivals?" *Erkenntnis* 44: 137–166.
Kukla, André. 2000. *Social Constructivism and the Philosophy of Science*. London: Routledge.
Kuorikoski, Jaakko, and Samuli Pöyhönen. 2012. "Looping Kinds and Social Mechanisms." *Sociological Theory* 30 (3): 187–205.
Laband, David N., and Richard O. Beil. 1999. "Are Economists More Selfish Than Other 'Social' Scientists?" *Public Choice* 100: 85–101.
Ladyman, James. 2016. "Structural Realism." In *The Stanford Encyclopedia of Philosophy* (Winter 2016 Edition), edited by Edward N. Zalta. https://plato.stanford.edu/archives/win2016/entries/structural-realism/, last accessed July 23, 2020.
Lakatos, Imre and Alan Musgrave, eds. 1970. *Criticism and the Growth of Knowledge*. Cambridge: Cambridge University Press.
Lakoff, George and Mark Johnson. 1980. *Metaphors We Live By*. Chicago, IL: University of Chicago Press.
Laudan, Larry. 1981. "A Confutation of Convergent Realism." *Philosophy of Science* 48 (1): 19–49.
Laudan, Larry. 1984. "Explaining the Success of Science: Beyond Epistemic Realism and Relativism." In *Science and Reality: Recent Work in the Philosophy of Science*, edited by J. T. Cushing, C. F. Delaney, and G. Gutting, 83–105. Notre Dame, IN: University of Notre Dame.
Laudan, Larry and Jarrett Leplin. 1991. "Empirical Equivalence and Underdetermination." *Journal of Philosophy* 88: 449–472.
Lepper, Mark R., David Greene, and Richard E. Nisbett. 1973. "Undermining Children's Intrinsic Interest with Extrinsic Reward: A Test of the 'Overjustification' Hypothesis." *Journal of Personality and Social Psychology* 28 (1): 129–137.
Liberman, Varda, Steven M. Samuels, and Lee Ross. 2004. "The Name of the Game: Predictive Power of Reputations Versus Situational Labels in Determining Prisoner's Dilemma Game Moves." *Personality and Social Psychology Bulletin* 30: 1175–1185.
Longino, Helen E. 2002. *The Fate of Knowledge*. Princeton, NJ: Princeton University Press.
Losee, John. 2004. *Theories of Scientific Progress: An Introduction*. New York: Routledge.
Lowe, Charles. 2018. "The Significance of Self-Fulfilling Science." *Philosophy of the Social Sciences* 48 (4): 343–363.
Machamer, Peter, Lindley Darden, and Carl F. Craver. 2000. "Thinking About Mechanisms." *Philosophy of Science* 67 (1): 1–25.
MacKenzie, Donald. 2006a. *An Engine, Not a Camera: How Financial Models Shape Markets*. Cambridge, MA: MIT Press.

MacKenzie, Donald. 2006b. "Is Economics Performative? Option Theory and the Construction of Derivatives Markets." *Journal of the History of Economic Thought* 28 (1): 29–55.

MacKenzie, Donald, and Yuval Millo. 2003. "Constructing a Market, Performing Theory: The Historical Sociology of a Financial Derivatives Exchange." *American Journal of Sociology* 109 (1): 107–145.

Mackinnon, Lauchlan A. K. 2006. "The Social Construction of Economic Man: The Genesis, Spread, Impact and Institutionalisation of Economic Ideas." PhD diss. University of Queensland.

Madsen, Ole J., Johannes Servan, and Simen A. Øyen. 2003. "'I Am a Philosopher of the Particular Case': An Interview With the 2009 Holberg Prizewinner Ian Hacking." *History of the Human Sciences* 26 (3): 32–51.

Mäki, Uskali. 2000. "Kinds of Assumptions and Their Truth: Shaking an Untwisted F-Twist." *Kyklos* 53: 317–336.

Mäki, Uskali. 2012. "Realism and Antirealism about Economics." In *Handbook of the Philosophy of Science, Volume 13: Philosophy of Economics*, edited by Uskali Mäki, 3–24. Amsterdam: Elsevier.

Mäki, Uskali. 2013. "Performativity: Saving Austin from MacKenzie." In *EPSA11 Perspectives and Foundational Problems in Philosophy of Science*, edited by Vassilios Karakostas and Dennis Dieks, 443–53. Cham: Springer.

Mallon, Ron. 2016. *The Construction of Human Kinds*. Oxford, UK: Oxford University Press.

Mallon, Ron. 2019. "Naturalistic Approaches to Social Construction." In *The Stanford Encyclopedia of Philosophy* (Spring 2019 Edition), edited by Edward N. Zalta. https://plato.stanford.edu/archives/spr2019/entries/social-construction-naturalistic/, last accessed July 23, 2020.

Marques, Teresa. 2017. "The Relevance of Causal Social Construction." *Journal of Social Ontology* 3 (1): 1–25.

Marti, Emilio and Jean-Pascal Gond. 2018. "When Do Theories Become Self-Fulfilling? Exploring the Boundary Conditions of Performativity." *Academy of Management Review* 43 (3): 487–508.

Marwell, Gerald, and Ruth E. Ames. 1981. "Economists Free Ride, Does Anyone Else?" *Journal of Public Economics* 15: 295–310.

Marx, Karl. 1844 [1988]. *Economic and Philosophic Manuscripts of 1844*. Translated by Martin Milligan. New York: Prometheus Books.

Mastilak, Christian M., Linda Matuszewski, Fabienne Miller, and Alexander Woods. 2018. "Self-Fulfilling Prophecy? An Examination of Exposure to Agency Theory and Unethical Behavior." *Research on Professional Responsibility and Ethics in Accounting* 21: 111–152.

McCloskey, Donald N. 1995. "Metaphors Economists Live By." *Social Research* 62: 215–237.

McMillan, John. 2003. "Market Design: The Policy Uses of Theory." *American Economic Review* 93: 139–144.

McMullin, Ernan. 1984. "The Goals of Natural Science." *Proceedings and Addresses of the American Philosophical Association* 58 (1): 37–64.

McMullin, Ernan. 1996. "Epistemic Virtue and Theory Appraisal." In *Realism in the Sciences*, edited by Igor Douven and Leon Horsten, 13–34. Leuven: University of Leuven Press.

Merton, Robert K. 1936. "The Unanticipated Consequences of Purposeful Social Action." *American Sociological Review* 1 (6): 894–904.

Merton, Robert K. 1948. "The Self-Fulfilling Prophecy." *Antioch Review* 8: 193–210.
Merton, Robert K. 1957. *Social Theory and Social Structure*, revised and enlarged ed. New York: The Free Press.
Merton, Robert K. 1967. *On Theoretical Sociology: Five Essays, Old and New*. New York: The Free Press.
Mill, John S. 1836 [2008]. "On the Definition and Method Political Economy." In *The Philosophy of Economics: An Anthology*, 3rd ed., edited by Daniel M. Hausman, 41–58. Cambridge: Cambridge University Press.
Miller, Cecil. 1961. "The Self-Fulfilling Prophecy: A Reprisal." *Ethics* 72 (1): 46–51.
Miller, Dale T. 1999. "The Norm of Self-Interest." *American Psychologist* 54 (12): 1053–1060.
Morgenstern, Oskar. 1972. "Descriptive, Predictive, and Normative Theory." *Kyklos* 25: 699–714.
Muniesa, Fabian and Michel Callon. 2009. "La Performativité des Sciences Économiques." In *Traité de Sociologie Économique*, edited by Philippe Steiner and François Vatin, 289–324. Princeton, NJ: Princeton University Press.
Musgrave, Alan. 1981. "'Unreal Assumptions' in Economic Theory: The F-Twist Untwisted." *Kyklos* 34: 377–387.
Nagel, Ernest. 1961. *The Structure of Science: Problems in the Logic of Scientific Explanation*. London: Routledge.
Newton-Smith, William H. 2000. "Underdetermination of Theory by Data." In *A Companion to the Philosophy of Science*, edited by William H. Newton-Smith, 532–536. Malden, MA: Blackwell.
Oreskes, Naomi. 2003. "From Continental Drift to Plate Tectonics." In *Plate Tectonics: An Insider's History of the Modern Theory of the Earth*, edited by Naomi Oreskes, 3–30. Boulder, CO: Westview Press.
Persky, Joseph. 1995. "The Ethology of *Homo Economicus*." *Journal of Economic Perspectives* 9 (2): 221–231.
Pettit, Philip. 1995. "The Virtual Reality of *Homo Economicus*." *The Monist* 78 (3): 308–329.
Pinker, Steven. 2002. *The Blank Slate: The Modern Denial of Human Nature*. New York: Penguin Books.
Polanyi, Karl. 1977. *The Livelihood of Man*, edited by Harry W. Pearson. New York: Academic Press.
Popper, Karl R. 1957. *The Poverty of Historicism*. London: Routledge.
Popper, Karl R. 1963. *Conjectures and Refutations: The Growth of Scientific Knowledge*. London: Routledge & Kegan Paul Limited.
Psillos, Stathis. 2016. "Having Science in View: General Philosophy of Science and Its Significance." In *The Oxford Handbook of Philosophy of Science*, edited by Paul Humphreys, 137–160. New York: Oxford University Press.
Reichenbach, Hans. 1938. *Experience and Prediction: An Analysis of the Foundations and the Structure of Knowledge*. Chicago, IL: University of Chicago Press.
Reiss, Julian and Jan Sprenger. 2017. "Scientific Objectivity." In *The Stanford Encyclopedia of Philosophy* (Winter 2017 Edition), edited by Edward N. Zalta. https://plato.stanford.edu/archives/win2017/entries/scientific-objectivity/, last accessed July 23, 2020.
Romanos, George D. 1973. "Reflexive Predictions." *Philosophy of Science* 40: 97–109.

Roscoe, Philip. 2016. "Performativity Matters: Economic Description as a Moral Problem." In *Enacting Dismal Science: New Perspectives on the Performativity of Economics*, edited by Ivan Boldyrev and Ekaterina Svetlova, 131–150. New York: Palgrave Macmillan.

Ross, Stephen A. 1987. "Finance." In *The New Palgrave Dictionary of Economics*, vol. 2, edited by John Eatwell, Murray Milgate, and Peter Newman, 332–336. London: Macmillan.

Roth, Alvin E. 2002. "The Economist as Engineer: Game Theory, Experimental Economics and Computation as Tools of Design Economics." *Econometrica* 70: 1341–1378.

Rubinstein, Ariel. 2009. "A Sceptic's Comment on the Study of Economics." *The Economic Journal* 116: C1-C9.

Salganik, Matthew J. and Duncan J. Watts. 2008. "Leading the Herd Astray: An Experimental Study of Self-Fulfilling Prophecies in an Artificial Cultural Market." *Social Psychological Quarterly* 71 (4): 338–355.

Santos, Ana C. and João Rodrigues. 2009. "Economics As Social Engineering? Questioning the Performativity Thesis." *Cambridge Journal of Economics* 33: 985–1000.

Searle, John R. 1995. *The Construction of Social Reality*. New York: The Free Press.

Searle, John R. 2010. *Making the Social World: The Structure of Human Civilization*. Oxford: Oxford University Press.

Sen, Amartya. 1977. "Rational Fools: A Critique of the Behavioral Foundations of Economic Theory." *Philosophy & Public Affairs* 6 (4): 317–344.

Simon, Herbert A. 1954. "Bandwagon and Underdog Effects and the Possibility of Election Predictions." *The Public Opinion Quarterly* 18 (3): 245–253.

Soros, George. 2013. "Fallibility, Reflexivity, and the Human Uncertainty Principle." *Journal of Economic Methodology* 20 (4): 309–329.

Stanford, P. Kyle. 2001. "Refusing the Devil's Bargain: What Kind of Underdetermination Should We Take Seriously?" *Philosophy of Science* 68: S1–S12.

Stanford, P. Kyle. 2017. "Underdetermination of Scientific Theory." In *The Stanford Encyclopedia of Philosophy* (Winter 2017 Edition), edited by Edward N. Zalta. https://plato.stanford.edu/archives/win2017/entries/scientific-underdetermination/, last accessed July 27, 2020.

Steel, Daniel. 2017. "Qualified Epistemic Priority: Comparing Two Approaches to Values in Science." *Current Controversies in Values and Science*, edited by Kevin C. Elliott and Daniel Steel, 49–63. New York: Routledge.

Stuart, Bryan L., Anders. G. J. Rhodin, L. Lee Grismer, and Troy Hansel. 2006. "Scientific Description Can Imperil Species." *Science* 312: 1137.

Suárez, Mauricio. 2016. "Representation in Science." In *The Oxford Handbook of Philosophy of Science*, edited by Paul Humphreys, 440–459. New York: Oxford University Press.

Swoyer, Chris. 1991. "Structural Representation and Surrogative Reasoning." *Synthese* 87: 449–508.

Tabuchi, Hiroko. 2016. "'Rolling Coal' in Diesel Trucks, to Rebel and Provoke." *The New York Times*, September 4, 2016. https://www.nytimes.com/2016/09/05/business/energy-environment/rolling-coal-in-diesel-trucks-to-rebel-and-provoke.html, last accessed July 27, 2020.

Thomas, Michael A., Gary W. Roemer, C. Josh Donlan, Brett G. Dickson, Marjorie Matocq, and Jason Malaney. 2013. "Ecology: Gene Tweaking for Conservation." *Nature* 501: 485–486.

Titmuss, Richard M. 1970. *The Gift Relationship: From Human Blood to Social Policy.* London: Allen & Unwin.

Tyson, Neil deGrasse. 2017. "Science in America." Video published April 2017 by Redglass Pictures. http://www.redglasspictures.com/science-in-america, last accessed March 3, 2021.

Ubbink, Johan B. 1960. "Model, Description, and Knowledge." *Synthese* 12: 302–319.

Van Fraassen, Bas. 1980. *The Scientific Image.* Oxford: Oxford University Press.

Venn, John. 1888. *The Logic of Chance.* London: Macmillan and Co.

Vetterling, Mary K. 1976. "More on Reflexive Predictions." *Philosophy of Science* 43: 278–82.

Waters, Colin N., Jan Zalasiewicz, Colin Summerhayes, Anthony D. Barnosky, Clément Poirier, Agnieszka Gałuszka, Alejandro Cearreta, et al. 2016. "The Anthropocene is Functionally and Stratigraphically Distinct From the Holocene." *Science* 351 (6269). https://doi.org/10.1126/science.aad2622.

Wilholt, Torsten. 2009. "Bias and Values in Scientific Research." *Studies in History and Philosophy of Science* 40: 92–101.

Winther, Rasmus G. 2016. "The Structure of Scientific Theories." In *The Stanford Encyclopedia of Philosophy* (Winter 2016 Edition), edited by Edward N. Zalta. https://plato.stanford.edu/archives/win2016/entries/structure-scientific-theories/, last accessed July 27, 2020.

Wolf, Diana E., Naoki Takabayashi, and Loren H. Rieseberg. 2001. "Predicting the Risk of Extinction through Hybridization." *Conservation Biology* 15 (4): 1039–1053.

Wood, Stephen. 1996. "High Commitment Management and Payment Systems." *Journal of Management Studies* 33: 53–77.

Woolston, Chris. 2016. "DNA Reveals That Giraffes Are Four Species – Not One." *Nature* 537: 290–291.

Yezer, Anthony M., Robert S. Goldfarb, and Paul J. Poppen. 1996. "Does Studying Economics Discourage Cooperation? Watch What We Do, Not What We Say or How We Play." *Journal of Economic Perspectives* 10 (1): 177–1.

Index of Names

Ames, Ruth   28–30, 33f., 64f., 93, 108
Asimov, Isaac   105
Austin, John   18, 21, 72–74, 140, 142–149

Bajpai, Vivek   132
Barnes, Barry   47
Bartels, Andreas   88
Bauman, Yoram   29
Bearman, Peter   111
Beil, Richard   29
Bergenholtz, Carsten   25, 42, 44, 49, 105f., 108f., 124, 128–130, 155, 160, 177
Berger, Peter   39
Bhaktavatsalam, Sindhuja   137, 142
Biddle, Justin   164, 168
Biggs, Michael   99, 107, 119
Black, Fischer   19, 21
Boghossian, Paul   12
Bourdieu, Pierre   148
Brissett, Nicolas   26, 147–150, 152
Brown, Donald   159
Buck, Roger   8, 57–61, 64, 66, 82–88, 99–101, 122f., 166–168
Bull, Joseph   116–118
Busch, Jacob   25, 42, 44, 49, 105f., 108f., 124, 128–130, 155, 160, 177
Buss, Allan   98

Callon, Michel   34, 43, 47, 138–142, 146–148, 152, 173f., 176
Caporael, Linnda   45, 160
Carrier, Martin   123
Carter, John   29f.
Cartwright, Nancy   137, 142
Chakravartty, Anjan   127
Chomsky, Noam   159
Cipriani, Giam   29
Cofnas, Nathan   4
Craver, Carl   111

Darden, Lindley   111
Devitt, Michael   126
Díaz-León, Esa   74

Dick, Philip K.   105
Douglas, Heather   123–126, 177
Dumont, Louis   40

Edgeworth, Francis   44f., 47, 68f., 159
Elgin, Catherine   136
Elliott, Kevin   124, 126, 177

Felin, Teppo   41, 44, 124–126, 128–130, 150, 152, 155, 157–160, 168f., 171f., 177
Ferraro, Fabrizio   34–36, 38f., 41–48, 56f., 64, 66–70, 72, 74–76, 81, 83f., 87f., 93, 99, 106, 112–114, 124–126, 128, 130, 154–161, 163, 165f., 168, 171, 176–178
Foss, Nicolai   41, 44, 124–126, 128–130, 150, 152, 155, 157–160, 168f., 171f., 177
Frank, Björn   29
Frank, Robert   29–34, 93, 107
Frey, Bruno   29, 36–38
Friedman, Milton   22, 69
Frigg, Roman   77–79, 88f.

Gergen, Kenneth   12
Ghoshal, Sumantra   42f., 46, 48f., 68, 93
Giere, Ronald   88
Gilbert, Natasha   115
Gilovich, Thomas   30, 34
Gond, Jean-Pascal   114f., 120, 150, 152
Goodman, Nelson   78
Gordon, Ascelin   118
Grünbaum, Adolf   8, 99f.
Grunberg, Emile   7
Guala, Francesco   57, 97, 124, 146f.

Hacking, Ian   9, 11, 13–18, 20–22, 34, 47, 73, 99, 102f., 109f., 112, 120, 175
Haslanger, Sally   73, 128
Hedström, Peter   111
Henrich, Joseph   45, 107, 160
Henshel, Richard   7, 96f.
Hoyningen-Heune, Paul   122
Humphreys, Paul   133

Ioannidis, John   4
Irons, Michael   29f.

Jegen, Reto   36–38
Johnson, Mark   39f.
Jussim, Lee   7, 118f.

Katzner, Donald   160
Kay, Ira   39
Khalidi, Muhammad   103, 127f.
Kirchgässner, Gebhard   28
Kitcher, Philip   2, 163f.
Kopec, Matthew   47, 57, 61–66, 81, 126, 173, 178
Krishna, Daya   58, 98, 101, 103
Kuhn, Thomas   4, 123, 136, 162f.
Kukla, André   12, 162
Kuorikoski, Jaakko   18, 34, 38, 43, 47, 110–112

Laband, David   29
Ladyman, James   135
Lakatos, Imre   4
Lakoff, George   39f.
Laudan, Larry   131f., 135, 162f.
Leplin, Jarrett   162f.
Lepper, Mark   36f.
Liberman, Varda   39f., 107
Longino, Helen   90f., 135
Losee, John   3f.
Lowe, Charles   128f.
Luckmann, Thomas   39

Machamer, Peter   111
MacKenzie, Donald   19–22, 34, 36, 47, 68, 70–72, 75f., 79, 81, 88, 95, 114, 140, 146, 148, 176
Mackinnon, Lauchlan   7, 18
Madsen, Ole   16
Mäki, Uskali   69, 72f., 124, 129, 145f.
Mallon, Ron   11f., 73, 120
Maron, Martine   116f.
Marques, Teresa   74
Marti, Emilio   114f., 120, 150, 152
Marwell, Gerald   28–30, 33f., 64f., 93, 108
Marx, Karl   26
Mastilak, Christian   27, 43

McCloskey, Donald   40f.
McKaughan, Daniel   126, 177
McMillan, John   36
McMullin, Ernan   79, 132
Meier, Stephan   29
Merton, Robert C.   19, 21
Merton, Robert K.   6, 7, 47–50, 52–55, 58, 70f., 75, 79f., 93, 97–102, 104, 110f., 123, 133, 155–157, 165
Mill, John Stuart   46
Miller, Cecil   58
Miller, Dale   35, 113
Millo, Yuval   19f., 68
Moran, Peter   42, 46, 48, 68, 93
Morgenstern, Oskar   98
Muniesa, Fabian   148
Musgrave, Alan   4, 69

Nagel, Ernest   8
Newton-Smith, William   162f.
Nguyen, James   77–79, 88f.
Nordmann, Alfred   123

Oreskes, Naomi   4

Pascal, Blaise   110
Persky, Joseph   26, 46
Pettit, Philip   46
Pfeffer, Jeffrey   34
Pinker, Steven   159
Polanyi, Karl   26f., 50, 93, 108, 165
Popper, Karl   4, 8, 47, 135
Pöyhönen, Samuli   18, 34, 38, 43, 47, 110–112
Psillos, Stathis   131

Regan, Dennis   30, 34
Reichenbach, Hans   122
Reiss, Julian   162
Rodrigues, João   43, 141
Romanos, George   8, 57, 59–64, 66, 82f., 86, 100f., 122f., 166f.
Roscoe, Philip   176
Rose, Elaina   29
Ross, Stephen   19
Roth, Alvin   36
Rubinstein, Ariel   20, 29

Salganik, Matthew 107
Santos, Ana 43, 141
Scholes, Myron 19, 21
Schulze, Günther 29
Searle, John 73 f.
Sen, Amartya 44 f.
Simon, Herbert 63
Soros, George 47
Sprenger, Jan 162
Stanford, Kyle 79, 161–164, 168
Steel, Daniel 177
Stuart, Bryan 117
Suárez, Mauricio 77
Sutton, Robert 34
Swoyer, Chris 78 f.

Tabuchi, Hiroko 86
Thomas, Michael 117

Titmuss, Richard 36 f.
Tyson, Neil deGrasse 2

Ubbink, Johan 88
Udehn, Lars 111

Van Fraassen, Bas 136
Venn, John 7
Vetterling, Mary 8, 60 f.

Waters, Colin 5
Watts, Duncan 107
Wilholt, Torsten 85, 124
Winther, Rasmus 77
Wolf, Diana 117
Wood, Stephen 39
Woolston, Chris 115

Yezer, Anthony 29, 33

Index of Subjects

anti-realism See *realism*

Black-Scholes-Merton model   19–22, 35 f., 68, 114, 143, 148
bootstrapped induction   47

causal vs. constitutive processes   21, 72–74, 129, 145–147, 152, 175
conformation   49, 82, 88, 90–92, 95, 101 f., 106, 109, 112–115, 117, 119, 135, 141, 152, 154, 170–172, 175
content contingency   21, 27, 55 f., 66, 69 f., 92–94, 106, 108 f., 116, 171
content-responsiveness   81, 85, 87, 91–93, 95, 101 f., 104, 106–108, 113–115, 151 f., 156 f., 165, 167, 170 f., 175
content-world relation   77 f., 84, 88, 95

economics
– assumptions   27, 35, 37 f., 47, 67 f., 158
– economic fallacy   26, 50, 93
– effects of economic training   28–35, 40 f., 68 f., 72, 106, 109, 113, 159–161
– self-interest as a fundamental assumption   44 f.
empirical adequacy   136–138, 141 f., 153, 170, 172
epistemic authority   2 f., 5, 12, 22
epistemic evaluation   24, 76–78, 133–137
epistemic success   6, 18, 78, 88–91, 130–138, 170–174

first-order theory See *meta-theory*
free-riding   38, 64

Hacking instability   120
homo economicus   10, 18, 21, 23, 25–27, 30, 34, 36, 41–44, 46 f., 49 f., 52, 55, 57, 64, 68 f., 74–76, 81, 92–96, 106, 108, 112, 114, 121, 124, 154, 156, 158–160, 165 f., 168–170, 174 f.
human kinds   16
human nature   158–160, 165 f., 168 f.

illusory self-confirmation   54–56, 92–94, 154–169, 173–174
– definition   92
inductively derived prophecy   119
interactive kinds   103

looping effects   9, 11, 13–18, 34, 43, 47, 57, 99, 102, 109–112, 120, 124, 175

mechanistic explanation   109–113
meta-theory   105–109, 115, 118, 129, 151, 160, 167, 172 f.
mind-independence   126–129
motivation crowding-out   36–39, 43, 45, 84, 93, 102, 112

natural kinds   16, 127
natural science   7, 11, 58, 96–100, 110, 112 f., 115, 117, 175

observer-independence   129
Oedipus effect   8, 47

performativity   9, 11, 18–22, 34, 43, 47 f., 51 f., 68, 70–75, 88, 121 f., 124, 126, 128–130, 138–141, 145–154, 173, 176
– Barnesian performativity   47, 71 f., 75 f., 88, 95, 114, 128
– performativity thesis   71, 176
Plate Tectonics   4 f., 7 f.

realism   12, 17, 74, 106, 121–130, 155
reflexive prediction   8 f., 51 f., 56–70, 99–101, 122–124, 173
– acting-on-beliefs account   57–59, 65, 82–88, 100
– formulation/dissemination style   60–62, 82, 166
– probabilistic account   61, 63, 66
– reflexivity   56 f.
– standard account   59, 61, 63, 65, 82
– strongly reflexive prediction   63
– weakly reflexive prediction   63 f., 70

Index of Subjects

relativism   12, 39
representations   6, 53, 76–81, 140–143
- differing standards of accuracy   78–80, 88–91, 94
- directionality   78, 88f.
- idealizations   69, 76f., 79, 90, 94
- misrepresentation   78, 88f.
- types of representation   76–81
- universalism about representations   89

science
- relevant notion of science   6
- science as a camera and/or an engine   1, 18, 21–23, 86, 109, 175f., 178
- science as self-correcting   See *self-correction*
- science as self-fulfilling   See *self-fulfilling science*
- scientific progress   3f.
- scientific success   22–24, 121, 130–133, 135, 138
self-correction   3–6, 8, 14f., 88, 121, 172, 174
self-fulfilling predictions vs. other types of self-fulfilling represetations   66f., 79–81
self-fulfilling prophecy   19, 23, 38, 42f., 47f., 50, 52, 54, 56, 58, 71, 76, 80, 97, 148, 155f., 169
- bank run example   53, 55, 58, 79, 94, 97, 102, 148, 155
- self-defeating prophecy   7, 12, 57f., 99
- union segregation example   53–55, 79f., 93, 156f.
self-fulfilling science   1, 6, 8, 10f., 14–16, 18, 23, 52, 64, 85, 121, 124–127, 143, 147
- boundaries of self-fulfilling science   96–104
- criterion of malleability   103f., 107, 112f., 116, 159f.

- definition   91
- mechanisms of self-fulfilling science   34–41, 113–120, 155–160, 172–174
- unique-to-human-affairs thesis   97–103
- unique-to-social-science thesis   101–104
- vs. illusory self-confirmation   See *illusory self-confirmation*
self-fulfillment   7, 47–55
self-interest   10, 29, 33, 35f., 43–47, 49f., 67–69, 72, 85, 113, 143, 158–160
- induced self-interest   28, 42, 57, 64, 66f., 71, 74–76, 128, 140, 145
- selection vs. treatment effects as explanations   29f., 32f., 159–161
- self-interested behavior   29, 35, 41, 46, 50, 68f., 74, 93f., 106, 159, 165, 171
- self-interested motivation   42, 46, 50, 93f., 113, 165
social construction   11–13, 18, 39, 73f., 110, 126–128, 175
social science   7f., 13, 16, 42–44, 46, 49, 57f., 61, 63, 96–100, 103, 105, 122, 124, 129, 141, 166
sociology   26, 57, 110f., 149, 162
- Analytical sociology   111
- sociology of economics   9, 18, 70

technology   20, 35, 81, 85, 98, 101, 103f., 107, 148
theoretic virtues   21, 28, 38, 53, 74, 88, 136–138, 160, 162, 169, 172
theory evaluation   24, 133, 162f., 170
truth and truth-aptness as conditions of self-fulfillment   48–50, 53–55, 64–69, 76–80

underdetermination   137, 154–170

values   19, 38, 58–61, 63, 68, 101, 110, 123, 126, 136f., 162, 164, 177f.

www.ingramcontent.com/pod-product-compliance
Lightning Source LLC
Chambersburg PA
CBHW031429150426
43191CB00006B/454